CRITICAL STUDIES

from

ELIZABETHAN

to

ROMANTIC POETRY

selected & edited by

Dr. Nilanko Mallik

M.A., Ph.D. (A.M.), TESOL (Arizona)

Published by Woven Words Publishers OPC Pvt. Ltd., 2017

Copyright© Nilanko Mallik, 2017

This book is sold to the condition that it shall not, by way of trade or otherwise, be lent, resold, hired out, or otherwise circulated without the publisher's prior consent in any form of binding or cover other than that in which it is published and without a similar condition, including this condition, being imposed on the subsequent purchaser.

ISBN-13: **978-81-934093-0-5**

ISBN-10: **8193409302**

Price: ₹350

This book is for educational and research purposes. The author/editor of the book has taken all reasonable care to ensure that the contents of the book do not violate any copyright or other intellectual property rights. In the event that the author/editor has not been able to track any source, and if any copyright has been inadvertently infringed, please notify the author/editor in writing, so that corrections can be carried out in future editions.

Woven Words Publishers OPC Pvt. Ltd.,
Vill: Raipur, P.O: Raipur Paschimbar, Dist: Purba Midnapore, Pin: 721401, West Bengal, India.
www.wovenwordspublishers.net

Printed by **Bhavish Graphics, Chennai**, India

CONTENTS

About the Book
Acknowledgements
I. Elizabethan and Jacobean Poetry
   1. Introduction to Elizabethan and Jacobean Poetry
      13
   2. Edmund Spenser   20
      a. About the Poet   20
      b. *One Day I Wrote Her Name*   *21*
   3. Sir Philip Sidney   24
      a. About the Poet   24
      b. *Loving in Truth*   *25*
   4. William Shakespeare   32
      a. About the Poet   32
      b. Overview of the Folio and Quarto Editions-33
      c. Overview about the Sonnets   34
      d. *Sonnet 18: Shall I Compare Thee To A Summer's Day*   *36*
      e. *Sonnet 73: That Time of the Year Thou May'st in Me Behold*   *43*
      f. *Sonnet 87: Farewell, Thou Art Too Dear for My Possessing*   *48*
      g. *Sonnet 130: My Mistress' Eyes Are Nothing Like the Sun*   *57*
   5. John Donne   64
      a. About the Poet   64
      b. *The Good Morrow*   *65*
      c. *Donne's 'The Good Morrow'* - Eleanor Tate   70
   6. Andrew Marvell   78
      a. About the Poet   78
      b. *To His Coy Mistress*   *78*
II. The English Epic and the English Mock-Epic
   7. Introduction to the Epic   87
   8. John Milton   89
      a. *Paradise Lost* – Background Information and Reading   89

                i. Genesis 2: The Creation of Man and Woman and the Garden of Eden
                ii. Genesis 3: The Temptation and the Fall of Man
                iii. Celestial Order, as Believed at the Time
          b. *Paradise Lost: Book 1*   *93*
     9. Alexander Pope   145
         a. Introduction to the Mock-Heroic   145
         b. *The Rape of the Lock – Canto 1*   *148*
         c. *The Rape of the Lock – Canto 2*   *157*
         d. *The Rape of the Lock – Canto 3*   *164*
         e. *The Rape of the Lock – Canto 4 (unannotated)*   *185*
         f. *The Rape of the Lock – Canto 5 (unannotated)*   *190*
         g. *A Key to the Lock*   *195*

III.   Pre-Romantic and Romantic Poetry
     10. Introduction to Pre-Romantic Poetry   217
     11. William Blake   218
         a. About the Poet   218
         b. *The Lamb*   *221*
         c. *The Tyger*   *226*
     12. Introduction to Romantic Poetry   235
     13. William Wordsworth   238
         a. About the Poet   238
         b. *Tintern Abbey*   *240*
     14. Samuel Taylor Coleridge   263
         a. About the Poet   263
         b. *Kubla Khan*   *264*
     15. Percy Bysshe Shelley   278
         a. About the Poet   278
         b. *Ode to the West Wind*   *279*
         c. *To a Skylark*   *293*
     16. John Keats   308
         a. About the Poet   308
         b. *Ode to Autumn*   *309*
         c. *Ode to a Nightingale*   *314*

References-   325

This book is dedicated

to

all those who, at some point of time

during studies

have wished the poems were never written!

ABOUT THE BOOK

Critical Studies from Elizabethan to Romantic Poetry is the expanded work from the former work *Critical Studies in Poetry: From Elizabethan to Romantic Age* (Notion Press, 2016).

The book has been written keeping the needs of the Indian universities, particularly those in West Bengal.

This book is different from the others in several ways. The annotations of the book are on the pages where the lines are found, so students do not have to turn pages to find an explanatory list. The annotations aim not just in explaining the lines, but also provide critical insight into the text, and sometimes, point out other texts which can be studied for comparative purposes.

Each poem is preceded by a brief introduction about the poet, and each section starts with an introduction on the characteristic features of the poetry in each age. Students would find a lot of relevant matter in them. After the poem, important topics are discussed.

Hope that the students will find the book useful.

Nilanko Mallik

Kolkata 2017

ACKNOWLEDGEMENTS

I would like to thank

New Asia College for giving me the permission to reproduce the article by Eleanor Tate on *The Good-Morrow*.

Naeem Educational Organisation for giving their kind permission to use the article entitled, 'Satan's Speeches in "Paradise Lost" Book-I'.

e-notes support for giving the permission to use the article, which over here, has been entitled, 'Satan's Speeches and Character – Was Milton of 'the Devil's party'?'

In writing this book, I was helped a lot by **Amarnath Ghosh, Sandipan Mondal and Sourabh Nath** (names appear alphabetically), three of my former students, who patiently checked all the lines of the poems that are there in this book, to correct all mistakes in words and punctuations. If there are mistakes in the lines of the poems, they are my fault.

I would like to thank **Sagnik Bagchi**, one of my present students, who took out valuable time to note the typing errors and other mistakes in the earlier work.

I would like to thank my **former professors and friends** who have shown their support in my writing career.

SECTION 1

ELIZABETHAN AND JACOBEAN POETRY

1. Introduction to Elizabethan and Jacobean Poetry

The Ages

As the name suggests, Elizabethan poetry is the poetry written during the reign of Queen Elizabeth I. However, this does not go to say that it began on the day she ascended the throne and ended on the day she died. Elizabethan age is so named after the most famous monarch of that time, but it refers to the age which was there a while before her coming to the throne, and it certainly continued to be there even after she had died. Students should bear in mind that an age cannot start and end from a date and on a date. The demarcations that are made are purely for giving an idea of the time, but in reality, all these ages came to be so gradually. So, in general, when the term Elizabethan Age, or Elizabethan period is stated, it refers to the age *around* which Queen Elizabeth I reigned; it can be before her coming to the throne, it can be during her reign, or it can be after her death. The next question that would arise in the minds of the readers is that, if that is so, how can the end be known? One might make a mistake of placing a poet of another age to be in the Elizabethan age, thinking that as the age continues even after her death, one can safely do that. Such mistakes are bound to happen, if the other aspect is not kept in mind: an age continues, till there is a remarkable shift in the things, so that one can say it has become different. Then, a new age will dawn. So, five years after the death of Queen Elizabeth the first might be referred to as the Elizabethan age in general, but a time which is a hundred years from that will certainly not belong to that age, for there will have come remarkable changes to make it fall into another age.

The other question that should come to the reader's mind is what the Jacobean age is. Jacobean age is named after King James I of

England,[1] who came to the throne after the death of Queen Elizabeth I. Jacob is the Hebrew name, from which the name James is derived, and so, the adjective becomes Jacobean.[2] It should be told here that Elizabethan age in general also encompasses the Jacobean age. In other words, if someone refers to the period of the Elizabethan age in general, without naming any particular year, he would refer to the reign of Queen Elizabeth I as well as King James I of England. The next question that should come to the reader is that if that is the case, why Jacobean age is referred at all. This is because while Elizabethan age continues its influence even in what is actually the Jacobean age, a poet belonging to the Jacobean age cannot be identified properly, if he is said to be in the Elizabethan age. In other words, if a poet or a poem needs to be identified by a specific year, then it would be important to note if it was in the Elizabethan age or the Jacobean age. For example, Shakespeare lived predominantly during the reign of Queen Elizabeth I, and a little bit during the reign of King James I. In general, one might say that Shakespeare lived during the Elizabethan age. However, the play *Macbeth* was written during the reign of King James I, and so, if one wishes to date the play, he would have to say that it belongs to the Jacobean age.

---

[1] I say James I of England because he is was first king by the name of James in England. However, he came from Scotland, and there, he was preceded by other James's. So, in Scotland, he is known as King James VI! In this book, King James I would refer to James I of England, even if I do not state the "of England" all the time.

[2] The name does not come directly from Hebrew to English. The Bible was first compiled in Greek and then in Latin. The Greek name for Jacob is Iakobos and in Latin, it becomes Jacobus. The spelling undergoes a change with the passage of centuries, and in Modern Latin, the spelling becomes Jacobæus. In Modern English, the 'æ' is shortened to 'e' and the suffix '-an' is added to it, making it Jacobean.

The Poets and the Poetry

So much for the ages. Now, let us come to the poets. The greatest name in the Elizabethan age belongs to the same person who is perhaps the greatest name in all the ages of English Literature, and that is Shakespeare. With 154 sonnets and five narrative poems, his contribution to poetry is not little. Though there were others in the same age who wrote larger volumes of sonnets like Sidney and Spenser, Shakespeare's sonnets abound with the borrowed originality that is common in his plays too. What I mean is that the reason why Shakespeare's plays are acclaimed over the other plays of other playwrights is the same as to why his sonnets are acclaimed.

The plays that used to be written in those days were dominated by **blank verse**, but in that, Shakespeare showed his originality by introducing some other rhythms, and maintaining the reasons for introducing those changes, so that they do not seem haphazard.[3] The poems that were popular in those days were the sonnets. The Elizabethan age was the time when the impact of the Renaissance came to be felt in England. Classical texts were revived during the Renaissance, and a lot of interest was shown in the European literature, especially, Latin and Greek, and the contemporary language of Italy, Italian. Therefore, a lot of the plays in this age abound in Latin, Greek or Italian words, and if not the words directly from the language, then in translations. This is especially seen in the writings of the University Wits.

The English sonnet was influenced by the **Petrarchan sonnets**,[4] which was in turn influenced by older Italian poems. **The Italian**

---

[3] Students who are more interested in this should refer to the chapter on blank verse in, *Compact English Prosody and Figures of Speech* (Macmillan, 2009).

[4] Scholars now make a distinction between Petrarch's sonnets and Petrarchan sonnets. The former refers to the sonnets following the system developed by Petrarch, while the latter refers to sonnets written by Petrarch. Needless to say, all Petrarch's sonnets are Petrarchan, but not all Petrarchan sonnets are Petrarch's (as

sonnet was actually created by Giacomo (a.k.a. Jacopo) da Lentini (C. 1201-1249).[5] The Petrarchan sonnet is named after the poet Francesco Petrarca (1304-1374), better known as Petrarch, who wrote love sonnets addressed to Laura, whose identity remains debatable. The Petrarchan Sonnets follow the pattern of having an octate/octet and a sestate/sestet. The octet would be the first eight lines, and would present the issue of the sonnet, and the sestet would be the last six lines, presenting the solution to the issue. The ninth line, thus, creates the turn. This is called *volta*. The rhyme scheme of the octet would be *abbaabba*. The sestet could have various possibilities, but generally, the convention was to make it *cdedce* or *cdccdc*. Other combinations were used later on, such as *cdcdcd*. **The English Sonnet** was introduced in England by Sir Thomas Wyatt (1503-1542), and because of the Elizabethan age, it is also known as the **Elizabethan sonnet**.[6] With the passage of time, this form began to change, and the Elizabethan sonnet, the origin of the Sonnet in English, became different from other forms of sonnets that began to be written in other ages.

With Philip Sidney's *Astrophel and Stella*, the art of writing sonnets in a collective continuation started, and this is called the *Elizabethan Sonnet Sequences*. They generally follow the Petrarchan tradition, both in the division of lines into octets and sestets and in the rhyme scheme.

The Spenserian sonnet differs from this tradition. The rhyme scheme of the Spenserian sonnet, named after Spenser, is *abab bcbc cdcd ee*. There is no octet-sestet division. There are three tercets, and a couplet.

The Shakespearean sonnet is another variation. The rhyme scheme of a Shakespearean sonnet happens to be *abab cdcd efef*

Wordsworth has written Petrarchan sonnets, but not Petrarch's sonnets).

[5] In the same way, it can be stated that not all Italian sonnets are Petrarchan, although Petrarchan sonnets are Italian.

[6] Although Wyatt brought the sonnet form in Enlish Literature, the English Sonnet better known as Shakespearean Sonnet, due to the historical favour on the Bard with the passage of the centuries.

gg. Sometimes, there is the division of lines into octets and sestets, but the rhyme scheme is always the same. At other places, where there are no octet-sestet divisions in the theme, the sonnets are one woven piece, and present one idea. The couplet rounds off the matter of the sonnet.

Shakespeare did not publish his plays during his lifetime, and they were published post humously. However, the sonnets were published by him, and they had been circulating among some people even before they were published. There is a personal touch in his sonnets, and Wordsworth wrote a sonnet in praise of the sonnet form, where he said, "with this key/Shakespeare unlocked his heart" ('Scorn not the Sonnet'). This is, of course, the Romantic poet who is underpinning the personal touch in the poems. Browning, the Victorian, who is more interested in the creation of drama in poems, responds to this with negative reaction:

> ...'With this same key
> Shakespeare unlocked his heart,' once more"
> Did Shakespeare? If so, the less Shakespeare he!
> ('House')

Critics are always divided (as they always are) as to whether the sonnets of Shakespeare reveal his personal mind and are autobiographical, or just exercises of dramatic conversation. G. Blakemore Evans writes in this regard, "To some extent, of course, all significant art is autobiographical" (Evans 1997). The best solution to the sonnet sequences being autobiographical, semi-autobiographical or fictional, is provided by Matthew Arnold, who wrote in his poem, *Shakespeare*, "We ask and ask. Thou smilest, and art still". This is true for the poems as well as the plays.

Proceeding on to Jacobean poetry, it needs to be told that it is also labelled as **Metaphysical Poetry.** This term was not really applied by the poets themselves, but was first used by Samuel Johnson on one occasion when he referred to them. *Meta* in Greek means both "change" and "beyond". Metaphysical uses both the meanings. There is both a change in the physical state of being, as well as going beyond the physical limits of a being. Metaphysical poetry tried to imbibe the Platonic concept of *de anima*, that is, the soul, while talking about love. Previously, the Elizabethan sonnets (especially those by Wyatt, Spenser, Sidney)[7] emphasised the physical beauty of the beloveds, and the lovers, that is, the poets, used to look upon themselves as knights who would be going through hardships to win the heart of the beloved. Nothing of this sort is to be found in the Metaphysical poets, for they disliked talking of love in this way, and felt it was too shallow and superficial. It lacked the real passionate fire of love.

Instead, Metaphysical poetry tries to present the carnal aspects of love in actions, and bring feelings which would be of the soul. In other words, the actions would be very carnal, but the feelings would not be animal-like, but sublime. To achieve this kind of an effect, Metaphysical poetry constantly shifts the focus; there would be a variety of images found in the poems – all of them extremely physical in nature. The image of the globe and the sphere is very common in the poems of John Donne. There are unusual similes evoked through these images, as we shall see in the poems. Ideas are often used from Geography and its sub-discipline, cartography. The effect of these images is to arouse physical images, and these images result into what has previously been stated as change of physical state of being. To associate the being with these images would also mean to extend the physical capabilities of the being.

Another important aspect of Metaphysical poetry is the total silence of the beloved.[8] The lover is the one who speaks and seems to understand the problems of the beloved and present solutions, and decide what to do. He is the sole speaker of their love; the beloved remains mute. This is not so in the Elizabethan sonnets. In Sidney and Spenser's poems, the beloved does address the lover, and it is the beloved who presents the solution to the lover.

The *carpe diem* theme is very important in Metaphysical poetry. *Carpe diem* means to "pick up the day", or "seize the day".[9] *Carpe*

---

[7] It needs to be clarified here that Shakespeare did not write sonnets of this kind, and after a close analysis of his sonnets and the metaphysical poems, students would notice a striking similarity between the two.

[8] This is good ground for feminist criticism.

[9] This comes from a phrase used by Horace in one of his poems. It is part of the line *Carpe diem quam minime credula postero.*

diem, therefore, means to utilise the day. In Metaphysical poetry, there is a lot of activity expressed by the lover, suggesting the utilization of each and every minute. Andrew Marvell's *To His Coy Mistress* is a very good example of this. T.S. Eliot was very fascinated by Metaphysical poetry, and delivered quite a lot of lectures on it, and also wrote essays on it. He expresses his fascination for the images used by them, particularly, Donne, and he mentions them in some of his poems.[10]

(Utilise the day, that is, the present time, with minimum faith in placing things in future).
[10] *Whispers of Immortality* is one such poem.

2. Edmund Spenser

(1552-1599)

About the Poet

Edmund Spenser was born of humble origins, to a father (John Spenser) who made clothes to earn his living. Little is known about her mother, Elizabeth. It is not known for sure when Edmund was born, as the records were not well-maintained in the times, and his records, even if they existed, were destroyed in the Great Fire of 1666. From records of his attending Merchant Taylor's School, and from allusions to his sonnet sequence, *Amoretti*, 1552 is speculated to be the year of his birth. In the poem *Prothalamion*, Spenser writes that he belived himself to have descended from "An house of auncient fame," i.e., the DeSpensers. While in school, he was under the able guidance of Richard Mulcaster, who had lots of connections with universities. After completing school, he attended Cambridge University, but records show he was already composing poetry before that time. He completed his BA degree in 1573 and MA in 1576, and although he was not hailed as a scholar, he had gratitude towards his "mother Cambridge" as he wrote in *The Faerie Queene* (IV.xi.34).

In 1580 he became private secretary to Arthur Grey, the new Lord Deputy of Ireland. It is believed that he married before he set out for Ireland, and that his wife, Machabyas Chylde, bore him two children, Sylvanus and Katherine. He married Elizabeth Boyle afterwards. He lived about twenty years in Ireland, and embarked upon *The Faerie Queene*, whose first three books were published in 1590, and republished with three new books in 1596. Queen Elizabeth granted him a royal pension. He returned in 1591, and by 1595, had published *Amoretti* and *Epithalamion*. His last work was published posthumously in 1609, named *Mutabilitie Cantos*. Spenser fled with his family to Cork in 1598, when rebels attacked and burned Kilcolman Castle. In December, he returned to England

CRITICAL STUDIES FROM ELIZABETHAN TO ROMANTIC POETRY

to deliver a report on the Irish crisis, but died a few weeks later, on 13 January, 1599. He is buried in the Poet's Corner, Westminster Abbey.

Background information on the *Amoretti* Sonnets

The *Amoretti* sonnets are a group of 89 sonnets (the collection also has a few other poems) which are arranged in the order of the progress of time. The sonnets depict the poet's courtship and eventual marriage of Elizabeth Boyle. The word *Amoretti* means verses of love. In the first two sonnets, the poet writes of his power of words to ultimately attain his goal. Sonnets 3 to 62 present the wooing of the poet, and the beloved's apparent disdain for his suit. The poet presents a lot of contrasting metaphors to depict the love-relationship: predator and prey, fire and ice, victor and prisoner, to name a few. From Sonnet 63, the theme changes, as the lady accepts the proposal. The poet expresses exuberance, and till Sonnet 85, depicts the beauty of the beloved. The last four sonnets present a separation, due to some reports which the beloved hears and believes about the poet. *Amoretti* ends in a note of hope of future union. The collection then lists a few stanzas on Cupid, called *Anacreontics*, at the end of which the poet places himself in the ways of Cupid's arrows, even if it means to suffer endlessly in unrequited love. The collection then moves on to *Epithalamion*, which celebrates the marriage.

One Day I Wrote Her Name[11]

One day I wrote her name upon the strand,[12]
But came the waves and washed it away:
Again I wrote it with a second hand,[13]

---

[11] This sonnet is in the second group, after the beloved has accepted the proposal, and is numbered 75.

[12] *strand* – beach

[13] *second hand* – a second time

> But came the tide, and made my pains his prey.[14]
> "Vain man,"[15] said she, "that dost in vain assay,[16]
> A mortal thing so to immortalize;[17]
> For I myself shall like to this decay,[18]
> And eke[19] my name be wiped out likewise."[20]
> "Not so," (quod[21] I) "let baser things devise[22]
> To die in dust, but you shall live by fame:[23]

---

[14] *But came...his prey* – The waves of the tides came and once more, the name written on the sands was erased.

[15] *Vain man* – this is a transferred epithet. The man is not vain, but the efforts. However, one might take it to mean that the man suffers from vanity.

[16] *assay* – attempt to do something.

[17] *A mortal...to immortalise* – i.e., to attempt to turn something perishable (*mortal thing*) to something which will never be destroyed (*immortalise*). Notice the similarity in theme with Shakespeare's Sonnet 18, where the poet attempts to immortalise the fair youth. However, unlike the poet here, Shakespeare understood right from the start the futility of nature, and came up with the solution to immortalise through verses.

[18] *For I...this decay* – the beloved says that she too, will die. Just like the name has been erased by the waves of the water, so will she be erased from the face of the earth with the waves of time.

[19] *eke* – This is an obsolete word. It had more than one meaning. Here, it means 'also'.

[20] *And eke...out likewise* – It must be noticed that the beloved does not refer to the wiping out of the name from the sands. In this line, she refers to her name being forgotten from memory.

[21] *quod* – quote = spoke

[22] *devise* – plan (how to)

My verse your vertues[24] rare shall eternize,
And in the heavens write your glorious name:[25]
Where whenas[26] death shall all the world subdue,
Our love shall live, and later life renew."[27]

---

[23] *But you...by fame* – Perhaps it dawns on the poet (from the previous words of the beloved about being forgotten from memory) that the way to immortalise the beloved is to keep the flame of fame (reputation) alive. Compare this with Cassio's line in *Othello* about reputation being the immortal part of a person. "I have lost my reputation! I have lost the immortal part of myself, and what remains is bestial." (II.3.)

[24] *vertues* – virtues, i.e., good qualities.

[25] *And...name* – Perhaps a Biblical allusion to the names being written in the Book of Life in Heaven, which will ensure eternity of the soul in paradise?

[26] *whenas* – when

[27] *Our love...renew* – The end of the poem becomes almost metaphysical in thought. When all else will die, their love, i.e., the story of their love, will remain, and will give hope to others in future.

3. Sir Philip Sidney

(1554-1586)

About the Poet

As suggested by the title 'Sir', Philip Sidney was born to an aristocratic family. His father was Sir Hendy Sidney and his mother was Lady Mary Dudley. When Elizabeth I came to power, Henry Sidney was made lord president of Wales. Philip's uncle was the earl of Leicester. At the age of ten, Shrewsbury School, and then went to Christ Church, Oxford. He travelled widely across Europe, acquiring knowledge of French, Latin and Italian. He was sent on diplomatic missions to Germany, although it did not yield much fruitful results. Philip Sidney was knighted in 1583, and later that year, he married Frances, who was the daughter of Sir Francis Waslingham. Their daughter was named Elizabeth. In 1579, he wrote to the queen, asking her not to marry the Duke of Anjou, heir to the French throne.

Sidney was one of the few who had active interest in the newly discovered Americas, then known as "The New World", and desired to go on an expedition to accompany Sir Francis Drake against the Spaniards. He was interested in a wide range of subjects, from Art to Chemistry (then branded as Alchemy). Some of Philip Sidney's famous works of literature include the sonnet sequence *Astrophel and Stella* (composed in 1582 and published in 1591), *The Defence of Poesie* (Poetry) (composed in 1592 and published in 1595). A collected edition of his works was published in 1598. He died in 1586 from wounds received while attacking the Spaniards from sending supplies to Zutphen. He was buried at St. Paul's Cathedral on February 16, 1587.

Astrophel[28] *and Stella*: **Background Information**

This is a sequence of 108 sonnets and 11 songs, and is a milestone work of the English Renaissance. Etymologically, *Astrophel* means loving the star. *Stella* also means *star*, but it is also a female name. If one conceives of "loving the star" as one person, then "star" becomes the other person. So, *Astrophel* is the lover and *Stella* is the beloved. It is claimed that the sonnets are autobiographical, and relates to the unrequited love of Sidney for Penelope Devereux. Sidney's father had hoped that she would marry his son, but she married to lord Robert Rich, the first Earl of Warwick, after which it is believed that Sidney expressed his love for her through these sonnets. In the sonnets, Astrophel at first woos Stella and later comes to know that she is married. He is agonized, but continues to woo her, in the hopes that she would love him. Stella eventually falls in love with Astrophel, and Astrophel once kisses her while she is sleeping, but when she comes to know of it, she refuses to be physically intimate with him and remains true to her marriage vows, even though she is unhappy in her marriage. She decides to end the relationship.

Loving in Truth[29]

Loving in truth,[30] and fain[31] in verse my love to show,[32]

---

[28] Alternatively spelled *Astrophil*.

[29] This is from the sonnet sequence *Astrophel and Stella* (alternatively spelled *Astrophil and Stella*), and is the first sonnet of the 108 sonnets in the collection.

[30] *Loving...truth* – Readers should not right from the start the vehemence on part of the poet to claim his love as true. The poet does not wish to accuse himself of loving others falsely (and the beloved here truly), but there is a strong undercurrent that the others who profess love might not love truly. This is something

> That she, dear she,[33] might take some pleasure of my pain,—[34]

---

which Shakespeare also hints at in Sonnet 130, in the closing couplet.

[31] *Fain* – this is an archaic usage. It meant 'satisfied' or 'inclined'.

[32] *And fain...to show* – although the poet states that he is satisfied to show his love in verse, the very statement contains the hidden tone that it is not enough, and that it is foolishness on part of the poet to be satisfied in thinking that love can be shown merely through verses.

We can see what the poet is doing – he is taking the conventional route of writing love sonnet sequences, and at the same time, very carefully criticizing it to fall short of the actual action of loving someone in reality. If a person were to actually love someone "truly", he would not be satisfied to show his love through the sonnets only.

[33] *She...she* – notice the emphasis. Although used as a sign of dearness, it seems almost forceful on part of the poet to call her "dear", as it is clearly an afterthought to add the adjective in the second time, after the careless omission of the first time.

[34] *Pleasure...pain* – This should force the readers to ask why the beloved appears so sadistic, and why does the poet laud her for such a trait? Indeed, it is cruel if the beloved takes pleasure of the poet's pain. The poet is no doubt sarcastic, and it is obvious he does not wish to take pain, whether or not the lady enjoys it. It, therefore, seems plausible to state that the poet perhaps mocks the system which existed earlier, in the Arthurian romances, where the knights had to undertake a lot of hard tasks to rescue the damsels in distress. He is, at the same time, criticizing the ladies of the age, who liked to relate themselves to damsels in distress, to be wooed by their lovers.

There is another meaning of pleasure, which is provided in the annotation of the next line.

> Pleasure might cause her read, reading might make her know,
> Knowledge might pity win, and pity grace obtain,— [35]
> I sought fit words to paint the blackest face of woe;[36]

---

[35] *Pleasure might...grace obtain* – As can be studied, there are four parts in these two lines, and they follow sequentially. Such an arrangement is called *syllogism*, where ideas are logically arranged to prove something, or come to a conclusion.

Let us look at the parts in detail now.

Pleasure...read – Reading is to be contrasted with studying. Studying is for academic purpose, but reading is for pleasure. So, when a book is read, it is for pleasure, when a book is studied, it is a more serious purpose.

reading...know – Even though reading is for pleasure, one can still gain knowledge. So, studying is not the only way to get knowledge. What would the lady know? The poet means that she would be aware of his pains. So, it becomes quite clear from this that the beloved is in such a state where she is not even aware of the pains of the lover, and the lover has to make her aware of that through writing. Once she reads them (for pleasure), she would get to know the pains of the lover.

Knowledge...win – Although the first part leads to the second, there is no direct link between the second and this one, the third. Even if she knows, she may not take pity. But here, the poet depicts the lady to be ignorant, to save her from the accusation of being unkind, and hopes that once she gets to know his pain, she will definitely be moved to pity. Nevertheless, the thought remains that she is not aware of the poet's painful actions (whatever they are) and needs to read them like a sensational matter for pleasure to be roused up to fill pity.

and...obtain – The fourth part would follow if the third were to be obtained, making her take pity on the poet's pains.

Studying inventions fine[37] her wits to entertain,
Oft turning others' leaves,[38] to see if thence would flow
Some fresh and fruitful showers upon my sunburn'd brain.[39]
But words came halting forth, wanting invention's stay;
Invention, Nature's child, fled step-dame Study's blows;[40]

---

[36] *I sought...of woe* – The poet had a hard time finding the right words to being out the intensity of his pain. It should be noticed by the reader that the word "pains" now changes to "woe". The poet now lets us understand that by pains, he meant "grief". What causes his grief is not hard to understand. The ignorance of the beloved that he loves her truly causes the grief. He wants to write a love poem to her, expressing his love for her and making her aware of the same. He expects the lady will be moved to pity to love him.

[37] *Studying...fine* – i.e., studying fine (good) ways of writing (*inventions*). Notice the difference between the beloved's anticipated action of "reading" for pleasure, and the poet's more serious action of "studying" the art of composition.

[38] *Oft...leaves* – leaves means pages. The poet means he looked at words of previous poets to borrow from them suitable words and lines. He intentionally presents himself in this belittling state, so that the readers elevate him for the humbleness and for the artful manner of composition.

[39] *fresh...brain* – The words of other poets have been referred as the fresh and fruitful showers, which would cool his heat-oppressed brain. He has thought a lot, but has not been able to come up with solutions (*sunburn'd brain*).

[40] *Invention...blows* – The image is extremely playful. Invention results in new forms, and so, it is creative. What is creative is natural, as things are created in nature. So, the poet says that "invention" (which is creativity), is the child of "Nature". In other words, it cannot be forced out – it has to come out naturally. However, the child Invention is afraid of Study, which is presented as a harsh step-mother, who hits out creativity, as it seeks to bring it in a proper shape and form. It is clear that the poet is lashing out against the conventions of writing of the times, which were studied

And others' feet still seem'd but strangers in my way.[41]
Thus great with child to speak and helpless in my throes,[42]
Biting my truant pen,[43] beating myself for spite,[44]
"Fool," said my Muse to me, "look in thy heart, and write."[45]

Critical Summary of *Loving in Truth*

In the opening sonnet of the sequence *Astrophel and Stella*, Sidney introduces the anthology and prepares the readers for his art. It is clear from the start that in the sonnets, Astrophel will seek to get Stella, and the efforts have to be genuine in order to him to get her. Although the poet creates the persona of Astrophel, it is doubted

---

during the Renaissance. He feels one should write naturally, and not by mimicking others.

[41] *And others'...my way* – i.e., the paths laid out my other poets (at whose lines he had been looking) seemed strange for him to take up. He did not feel any familiarity with the words and style.

[42] *Thus...throes* – The metaphor is that of a pregnant lady in labour pain. Throes mean pangs and spasms, or great struggle. The poem which he wants to write is the great child, which needs to be born out of him.

[43] *truant pen* – This is an example of a transferred epithet. The pen is not truant; the poet's thoughts are, which keep fleeing from him.

[44] *spite* - Here, it means both "spite" (he hates himself for his incapability) and "respite" (he beats himself to perhaps let the words flow which would bring him respite).

[45] The poet does not explain who the Muse is. It is clearly not the beloved. The poet perhaps hints at his conscience. Readers should notice the difference between mind and heart. In the Renaissance, it was customary to treat the heart as the seat of emotions and mind (brain) as the seat of logic.

that he poet betrays his own desire towards Penelope, and acknowledges that his love for her is real.

In the opening poem, Astrophel hopes that by writing of his love (of which the beloved is ignorant at present), he will make her take pity on his love and accept him. In this regard, it can be seen as a continuation of the medieval theme, where the knights in shining armour would undertake a lot of hard tasks to rescue the damsels in distress. Although Astrophel is clearly not undertaking hard tasks, the Renaissance poets often bestowed on themselves the armour of knights, who sought to please the ladies by undertaking hard tasks in their poems. Here, the "pains" which Astrophel wants Stella to know is his feelings of love, which make him suffer.

Astrophel decides to take the help of other writers' words in writing the love sonnets. He realizes that the words of others cannot help him, and regards them as strange paths. It is ironical that he professes true love, yet seeks superficiality to present his love. This superficial art is labelled as "Invention" and there is a beautiful family drama which the poet has created inside the limited lines of the sonnet. "Invention" should be born out of mind, and so, it is "Nature's child". By saying this, he means that composition should be written naturally, and not in an affected style. It is here that the learning of the wits pose a problem. "Study" is the personification of the learned art, as taught in schools and universities. It has been presented as a step-mother, who has no fondness for the child and rebukes and chastises the child, forcing "Invention" to follow set paths and patterns.

Sidney continues the image of the child and mother by placing on himself the role of mother, rather, on his mind the role of mother. His thoughts – the sonnets – would be the child. He compares himself to that of a mother in labour pain, and declares his helplessness (till the child is born). He is ultimately helped by the Muse (not named), who advises him to look into his heart and write. During the time of the Renaissance, body parts were supposed to be the seats of different traits. The mind (brain) was the seat of logic and heart was the seat of emotions. Liver was thought to be the seat of courage, as we find in *Macbeth* "Thou lily livered boy" hinting at the lack of courage. Other than emotions, heart is also associated with truth. The words of the Bible "and the thoughts of all hearts shall be releaved" and "I am He Who searches the minds and hearts" refer to heart in that sense. So, the Muse does not only advise to write from passion (emotions) but also write truthfully.

Perhaps this is a subtle criticism on part of Sidney towards others of the age, whose writings show affected praise. This criticism is also made by Shakespeare, particularly in the couplet of Sonnet 130

> And yet, by heaven, I think my love as rare
> As any she belied with false compare.

Through this, Sidney actually asserts his stand as a poet. This is his declaration to the readers of the age that he will not follow the steps of others, but create his own art of composition. True to that, the poems are not written in iambic pentameter, but iambic hexameter, also known as Alexandrine.

ELIZABETHAN AND JACOBEAN POETRY

4. WILLIAM SHAKESPEARE

(1564-1616)

About the Poet

Shakespeare needs no introduction to the students of Literature, and, I dare say, to other students too.[46] Even though such is the case, it is really ironical that not much is known about the early life of Shakespeare. I would be more accurate if I say that not much *was* known about the early life of Shakespeare. Scholars have, in the last few decades, been unraveling the unknown facts about Shakespeare's life. Students who are interested in this aspect would do well to go through the book *Shakespeare's Professional Career*.

There have been lots of claims about the identity of the Bard, and some have raised doubt on the very existence of the Bard. This is, I feel, way too beyond rational judgement, or the result of conclusions drawn from not looking at the necessary things. Claiming that Shakespeare did not live at all would bring into serious doubt the *facts* that there is his baptism registration; that the house where he was born is still there for the public to view; that he had a wife and children; that his name is mentioned in the *Stationer's Register*; that he had got the position of a "Gent" by the virtue of his skills in his career; that he moved to another house when his fortunes were high; that other University Wits were jealous about him, and wrote spiteful comments, naming him;[47] that his fellow actors decided to publish his plays, and they were

---

[46] Nevertheless, I have got some curious answers from some students, who were under the impression that Shakespeare lived in Rome!

[47] I am alluding to the letter of Greene, where he calls Shakespeare an "upstart crow".

part of their team;[48] and that there is a historic document, which is his will.[49]

Nevertheless, even if doubts are cleared that there was a person named Shakespeare, there are doubts as to who has written his plays.[50] There is no doubt about the fact that the plays are borrowed from other sources, but they are not just mere copies; they are renditions; they are adaptations. The originality of the artist is revealed in the excellent way in which he has crafted the plays after taking them from their sources.

An Overview of the Folio and Quarto Editions

The one disadvantage about his plays (which becomes an advantage for the critics) is that they were not published during his lifetime. After his death, John Heming and Henry Condell, his fellow actors, published his plays collectively, and that was known as the Folio edition of 1623.[51] However, there were quite a few typing errors, and the Folio edition had to undergo subsequent revision. But even before the publication of the Folio edition, fourteen of his plays were already in circulation. They were in Quarto booklets. However, the Quarto editions were not held to be authentic, and so, the Folio edition was taken out. It must be told here that several of his plays were privately published, and they are called Pirated. *Hamlet*, one of his greatest plays, was pirated in 1603. Because of so many haphazard publications, the lines of

---

[48] His group of actors, called Chamberlain's Men, were later called The King's Men.

[49] The will of Shakespeare has also been a subject of dispute, as it is not written in Shakespeare's hand, but in the hand of a scribe. However, the will bears his signature (although Shakespeare is known to have used more than one type of signature).

[50] The film *Anonymous* deals with this subject matter. However, the film is not always true to history.

[51] The Sonnets were not published in this edition.

some plays vary a lot, though basically, the matter remains the same.

An Overview of the Sonnets

This is not the case with the Sonnets. In 1599, in the anthology called *The Passionate Pilgrim*, Sonnets 138 and 144 were published by William Jaggard. In 1609, Shakespeare's Sonnets properly appeared in a volume published by Thomas Thorpe.[52] There is a dedication in these sonnets, and that is to a mysterious man, by the initials of 'W.H.'. It has been suggested that *W.H.* are the reversed initials of the Earl of Southampton, Henry Wriothesley, or that they are the initials of the Earl of Pembroke, William Herbert. Historic letters have revealed that marriage prospects of William Herbert with Bridget Vere, a daughter of the Earl of Oxford were prematurely stopped. Rolfe (1891) writes that Shakespeare may have written the first few sonnets at the request of William Herbert's mother to urge the son to marry.

As Shakespeare dedicated some of his earlier poems to the Southampton, it is also believed that Southampton might have been the person. Added to this is the fact that there were talks of his marrying (like Herbert) another daughter of the Earl of Oxford – Elizabeth Vere, although he did not accept the proposal.

Some feel that *W.H.* is simply Shakespeare's wordplay, and he means William Himself (as he is the only rightful begetter of the sonnets!).

In 2015, Geoffrey Caveney, an American researcher, stated that the initials belong to William Holme (not Holmes, as the latter was another person), who had personal and professional connection to Thorpe. His claim is that Pembroke and Southampton, being aristocrats, would not have been addressed as "Mr.", as that would have been insulting. That is why, it is more favourable for William Holme to have been the person in the dedication. There has been

---

[52] It is believed that this volume was not authorised by Shakespeare.

great debate as to the arrangement of the Sonnets, but so far, the numbering remains unchanged.

Structurally, the Sonnets can be divided into three groups, and thematically, into four groups. Let us come to the Structural division first. It is believed, from an analysis of the Sonnets, that from 1 to 126, they are addressed to a young man, and from 127 to 152, they are addressed to a woman.[53] Sonnets 153 and 154 are addressed to Cupid. The division into three groups can be broadened out to make two divisions, for the last two Sonnets also speak about a woman, and so, even if they are addressed to Cupid, they are part of the Sonnets which deal with a dark woman. This woman is identified as the "Dark Lady" of the Sonnets. There are lines which suggest that she is totally dark, yet beautiful in her own way.[54]

Thematically, there can be four divisions of the Sonnets, even though this division is also based on the numbering of the Sonnets in their proper order. Sonnets 1 to 14 deal with the theme of procreation; Sonnets 18 to 126 deal with love-relationship with a friend of the poet;[55] Sonnets 15 to 17 can be treated as transition Sonnets; and Sonnets 127 to 154 deal with the theme of black beauty.

In this love-relationship with the poet's friend, there are several complexities. Sometimes, the poems are about the beauty of the person; sometimes, they are about a fading love-relationship (which is more of a fear in the poet than a reality); sometimes, they

---

[53] This has raised issues of Shakespeare being a bi-sexual.

[54] Some scholars suggest the Dark Lady to be Mistress Mary Fitton, who was associated with the Chamberlain's Men. She was Elizabeth's maid of honour, and bore a child to Herbert in 1601 (Rolfe, 1891).

[55] Readers should note that I am avoiding the word "beloved", which would give a feminine identity, and "beautiful youth", which would tend to give the identity of a beautiful young man.

are about a rival poet, who seems to be taking away the poet's love, and the poet feels jealous, but cannot do anything, for he feels the rival poet is superior. If the view is accepted that the young person is male, the natural conclusion that comes up is that the rival poet must also be bi-sexual, if not homosexual.[56] The only way to overcome this obstacle of a proposition and to maintain the claims of bi-sexuality on the poet, would be to state that the poems are not in a proper order. So, it can be that the rival poet does not make love to the young man, but to the "Dark Lady". However, as no change in numbering has been done so far, that does not hold water. Therefore, some tend to look at the Sonnets as simply exercises of the mind; in other words, they see the Sonnets as the creative work of the great dramatist, who tried to make a drama out of Sonnet sequences, taking drama and sonnet writing to new heights.[57] Whether they are personal or fictional or semi-fictional, there is no doubt about the fact that they retain the singular appeal that his plays have, and these Sonnets are all about love.

SONNET 18

Shall I compare thee to a summer's day?[58]
Thou art more lovely and more temperate:[59]
Rough winds do shake the darling buds of May,[60]

---

[56] Somehow, critics and editors and other commentators avoid this aspect.

[57] *Astrophel and Stella* and *The Faerie Queene* are compositions that are somewhat of this type.

[58] *summer's day* – synecdoche for summer season, which is glorious. In summer, the sun shines in its full strength and so, the poet asks if his friend would like him to be compared with the glorious summer.

[59] *Thou...temperate* – summer might be gloriously beautiful, but the friend is more lovely to behold and feel, and is without the defect of summer (scorching sun), and is temperate.

And summer's lease hath all too short a date;[61]
Sometime too hot the eye of heaven[62] shines,
And often is his gold complexion dimmed;[63]

---

[60] *Rough...May* – The winds and the buds are all personified. The darling buds are feminine and delicate, and winds are roughly blowing upon them and they stand in danger of falling out. Just as a girl might be harassed by a ruffian, the "darling buds" are being harassed by the rough winds. The birds represent beautiful growth that characterises spring and summer. Shakespeare tells that the beautiful things that grow in summer are threatened to fall out soon. The beauty is, in other words, short-lived, even though one might call the season beautiful.

[61] *And...date* – Summer is personified in this line. Summer seems to be a feudal lord, who has leased out something (that is, given something on a rental basis for some duration only), and the duration of that lease is very short. Summer has leased out beauty for a very short time after which it takes the beauty away. The other meaning is that Summer, a beautiful time, is itself present as a lease, and its time is running out. In other words, the beautiful time lasts for a short while only, and even while it lasts, it is subject to harshness.

Shakespeare thus, begins by stating the glorious summer season, but goes on to state that it is not so glorious after all.

[62] *the...heaven* – This was a common metaphor used to refer to the sun. Here, it also represents Fate, or Fortuna.

The sun is not always uniformly bright; sometimes, it is too scorching. Fortune is not always glorious; sometime, it is hard.

[63] *And...dimm'd* – The sun might not shine gloriously at all; it is often clouded. The image of the glorious summer becomes a myth, as Shakespeare shows that in reality, it is not so glorious.

gold complexion – The golden colour of the sun, symbolizing brightness and glory.

> And every fair from fair sometime declines,[64]
> By chance or nature's changing course untrimmed:[65]
> But thy eternal summer shall not fade,[66]

In connection to Fortune, the line would read that often, Fortune does not give adequately.

Other than the metaphor of Sun and Fortune, the lines are also a critique against the practice of putting make-up. Some days, the make-up is put on just a little too much, while on other days, it may not be to the adequate amount. The ranting against make-up is seen in some of Shakespeare's dramas also, like *TN* and *Ham.* (refer to topics after Sonnet 130).

[64] *And...declines* – Every fair person falls from fairness. Every beautiful person falls from beauty at some point of time. This brings in the image of Fortune and Fortuna's wheel, where there is a cyclical movement in one's fortune – at one point, a person is down; at another point, the person is up.

The beautiful people are at the height of the wheel; as the wheel rolls on, they will fall.

[65] *By chance* – by fortune; readers can draw the reference to Fortuna's wheel.

nature's...untrimm'd – The juxtaposition of something which is changing and is untrimmed is to be noted. The oxymoronic words tell us that nature is always changing, and that the change is inevitable.

The use of the word 'untrimm'd' also brings in the image of the wheels growing in the path, which are not cut. The growing words represent the fading beauty.

[66] *But...fade* – Shakespeare turns the wheel around with the stroke of his pen. The movement of Fortuna's wheel is arrested by the use of the word 'But' and there is a reversal of situation. The images of fading beauty, created in the octave, brought about by the destructing power of Time, Fortune and Nature, fade away before the stronger power of the poet, who asserts his friend's beauty to

Nor lose possession of that fair thou ow'st,[67]
Nor shall Death brag thou wand'rest in his shade,[68]
When in eternal lines to time thou grow'st.[69]

So long as men can breathe or eyes can see,

---

be an 'eternal summer'. It must be noted here that in this eternal summer, the defects which were presented in the octave are not to be found.

[67] *Nor...ows't* – This is to e taken in contrast with 'summer's lease', where the beauty was given as a lease for a short time. Here, Shakespeare tells that his friend would not lose the possession of fairness; his friend would forever hold on to it, for it is not a lease, but an ownership.

fair – fairness

ows't – own.

[68] *Nor...shade* – Death has been personified. Death shall not be able to boast that the friend has come to him. Here, Death has been presented as a beguiler, who seems to offer shade (this shade is to be contrasted with the heat of summer) to the persons, and thus, make them his. The image of the glorious summer has already been cast out, and so, shade would seem a welcoming resort from the threats of summer. Death cunningly offers his shade so that the others take recluse there. Death shall not have the advantage of doing that with the poet's friend, for the poet will give shelter.

[69] *When...grows't* – Not only is the fading beauty cast out by the "eternal summer", but the beauty also grows. Time, which had given the beauty for some duration, is defeated, for the beauty will not only remain undiminished; it will grow with Time, totally reversing the effects of Time. The poet shall be able to do this by his writing ('eternal lines'). There is no doubt a proud assertion of the poet in making such a statement, and confidently stating that his lines will be 'eternal', that is, they will always remain and will be read.

So long lives this, and this gives life to thee.[70]

Conflict Between Art and Nature in Sonnet 18

The Renaissance was an age where Art swelled in various and varied productions. Shakespeare lived during the English Renaissance, and the sonnets of the age depicted man's desire to beauty creation with his own art. Spenser and Sidney had their sonnet sequences, which are wonderful works of art in themselves, and also bring out man's bent towards the artistic world, in the presence and surrounding of the natural.

Shakespeare's sonnets deal with the theme of love, and there is debate whether or not the sonnets are personal. The debate over the autobiographical authenticity will never end, but it does not diminish the beauty of the sonnet for its themes. A mere reading of Shakespeare's sonnets will reveal the poet's preoccupation against the ravages of time, with an emphasis on natural beauty. Sonnet 18 explores how everything dies with time in the natural world

>By chance, or nature's changing course, untrimmed

And how the poet's artistic genius can immortalise the fair youth.

>When in eternal lines, to time thou growst

The poem, thus presents a view of nature which is quite contradictory to normal notions, even to poets of other ages. For Wordsworth, Nature is a healer, and he might dance with the daffodils when he sees them swaying in the gentle breeze. For Shakespeare, that is not so. The world of Nature is rather

---

[70] *So...thee* – Shakespeare seals the eternity of the beauty of the friend by his charming couplet, which almost seems like an incantation. The poet invests eternity upon his friend through his writing, and states that as long as people will live on the earth and will be able to see and read, his poem will also be read, and as long as his poem will be read, his friend will be read, and will live through the poem.

Darwinian – it is in a state of constant conflict, where things are temporary and death is only a matter of time. He does not look upon the flowers swaying in the breeze, for he realizes that for the delicate flowers, it must be "rough winds", and they do not sway, but "shake".

> Rough winds do shake the darling buds of May

The bitter truth rings out loud, and the poet goes on to deglorify nature during its height in Summer.

> Summer's lease hath all too short a date.

The Sun itself is not constant - it can be too bright or clouded. The most important confirmation is perhaps when the poet says that everything will invariably fall at some point of time.

> And every fair from fair sometime declines.

In contrast, it is art which comes to the rescue. Art, which gives us the word artificial, is the savior from the ravages of time. But before going further, one must understand that Shakespeare makes a distinction between art and superficiality. Although not apparent in Sonnet 18, the later Sonnets, particularly those addressed to the Dark Lady, talk in favour of one's natural beauty, but is totally against making oneself fairer by applying make-up. In *Hamlet*, in the famous Nunnery Scene, Shakespeare makes Hamlet utter lines against the use of make-up.[71] Indeed, there is a hint towards the same in Sonnet 18, in the lines about the Sun:

> Sometime too hot the eye of heaven shines
>
> And often is his gold complexion dimmed

This might be a reference to the practice of make-up. Too much make up can have the same adverse effect as a too little make-up.

---

[71] See 'Theme of True and Unflattering Love and the Theme of Natural Beauty' in for Sonnet130.

Therefore, although Shakespeare clearly refers to art as the giver of immortality, it is not superficial art, which is made of tangible objects (therefore, made from the base nature itself) which can grant immortality. Art is created in the mind, and even if papers and ink fall to the ravages of time, the created art will not. This is not true for all types of art, certainly not of sculpture. If a sculpture is razed, it is turned to oblivion, for it is made out of the things which exist in nature. One might refer to Shelley's *Ozymandias* to get a better view of this, where only two "trunkless" legs of a great statue remain.

That is not the situation for a poem. It can live in the minds of the people forever, and so, pass from generation to generation.

So long lives this, and this gives life to thee.

Sonnet 18 is Structurally Petrarchan, but Thematically Shakespearean

Sonnet 18 falls under the group of transitory sonnets (numbers 15-18), which talk of immortalising the beloved's beauty through verse. Sonnets 1-14 are related to the theme of progeny through procreation. It is believed that the sonnets in this group are addressed to a young man, although there have been debates over the issue.[72]

The sonnet form originated in Italy through the hands of Lentini, and Petrarch, who lived a century after Lentini, added features to the existing Italian Sonnet, so much so that scholars have labelled sonnets modeled after his style as Petrarchan Sonnets. The Petrarchan Sonnets are structurally divided into octet and sestet, and in addition, there is a thematic division as well. The octet deals with the issue of the sonnet, the problem that is faced by the poet. The sestet offers a solution. The change in theme is marked at the start of the sestet by what is called **volta**, which brings a halt to the problems and gradually offers a solution. The rhyme scheme of a

---

[72] See About the Poet for details.

Petrarchan Sonnet is *abbaabba* (for the octet) and *cdecde* or *cdcdcd* (for the sestet).

If we examine Sonnet 18 from these angles, we will see that it fits some of the labels for Petrarchan sonnet. The first eight lines quite clearly present the problem of the sonnet – the theme of decay and death in nature with time. The last six lines offer a solution – although the corporeal self will die, the fair youth will remain forever evergreen in the verse created by the poem. The ninth line (the opening of the sestet) marks the change by the use of "But", which quite clearly signifies the *volta*.

However, there are several aspects in which the poem cannot be called Petrarchan, and that is in the structure. The rhyme scheme is not Petrarchan, but Shakespeare's own – *abab cdcd efef gg*. There is no structural division of octet and sestet. Instead, the octet is broken into two quatrains, and the sestet has been broken into another quatrain and a couplet. So, in total, there are three quatrains and a couplet. So, structurally, it can be seen that the sonnet follows the typical Shakespearean sonnet pattern.

It is indeed Shakespeare's brilliant craftsmanship that he uses his own structure, but draws inspiration from the Petrarchan sonnets, as revealed in the thematic division.

SONNET 73

That time of year[73] thou may'st in me behold[74]
When yellow leaves, or none, or few, do hang

---

[73] The time of late Autumn or early Winter. As will be studied in *Ode to the West Wind*, Autumn, when used symbolically, stands for decay and old age, as the leaves begin to turn yellow and fall.

[74] The line should be read as: "When you see in me that time of the year", i.e., the time of old age and decay, and not "That time of the year when you see (something) in me".

> Upon those boughs which shake against the cold[75],
> Bare ruin'd choirs,[76] where late[77] the sweet birds sang.
> In me thou see'st the twilight of such day,[78]
> As after sunset fadeth in the west,[79]
> Which by-and-by[80] black night doth take away,
> Death's second self,[81] that seals up all in rest.[82]

It must be clarified at the start that the poet has not actually turned old, and talks of a possibility in distant future, when he would, and the fair youth would see him as such.

[75] *Upon...cold* – It is not just the leaves which are shaking with cold, but the branches themselves.

[76] *Bare...choirs* – The branches have been alluded to in this manner. In Spring and Summer, the birds would sing on the branches (and so, would form the choir). Now, it is empty (*bare*) and the place is ruined, as the branches are devoid of their leafy foliage.

[77] *late* – previously

[78] This is the start of the second quatrain, and the metaphor now changes. The poet now uses the metaphor of the day instead of the season. Twilight comes before evening and night, and this is the apt time to relate to old age.

[79] *As...west* – Notice that the poet remarks that it is not the beginning of twilight, but almost the end of it, as the sun has set and the light (which forms twilight) is fading.

The second quatrain hastens the image of impending doom. In the first quatrain, it was in future, but in the second one, it seems as if the time has come at present, for the poet remarks, "thou see'st" and "fadeth" which are in present tense.

[80] *by-and-by* – gradually

[81] *Death's...self* – This is a recurrent metaphor in Shakespeare, to relate night and sleep to a temporary death. Such metaphors abound in *Macbeth* and *Hamlet*.

> In me thou see'st[83] the glowing of such fire
> That on the ashes of his youth doth lie,[84]
> As the death-bed whereon it must expire[85]

---

[82] *that...rest* – The word "seal" relates to sealing the coffin. "Rest" refers to the eternal sleep of death. Death seals up everything in eternal rest, and night covers up (so seals in a layer) everything in darkness, and that is the time for them to rest from the day's work.

[83] The third quatrain continues the time being set to present. The purpose is not to say that the person has aged miraculously with the recitation or reading of the sonnet, but to bring out the intensity of emotions in the addressee by visualizing such a sight of the senile lover.

[84] *The glowing...doth lie* – The poet does not allude to a great fire, but a smouldering fire, which is near the last phase of burning, before it dies out.

The third quatrain becomes even more intense as the poet adds the loss of vigour in addition to the image of age. In other words, not only as the lover aged, the lover has also lost energy, and is now weak.

There is also the possibility that the fire refers to the passion of love inside him, which is fast dying out. Placing this sonnet in the group with other sonnets, it will be noticed that after a few more sonnets, we enter the group of Rival Poet sonnets. So, perhaps the poet's love is fading on that account, which he mentions in this sonnet, and braces us for the theme of the rival poet in the sonnets which follow soon.

[85] As the third quatrain draws to a close, the image gets most intense with the mention of "death-bed". The poet refers to the going out of the fire, which is in its death-bed, i.e., in its last phase, and also relates to the energy of his life, which is about to expire.

The lover is of course, not on a death-bed. The purpose is to provoke feelings by visualizing the possibility of such a state.

> Consum'd with that which it was nourish'd by.[86]
> This thou perceivest,[87] which makes thy love more strong,
> To love that well which thou must leave ere long.[88]

---

[86] *Consumed…by* – Fire burns itself up (*consumes*) by feeding on something, which was its nourishment. Unable to get nourishment – as it has burned it up – it dies.

The meaning related to love also continues in this line, as that is the only proper explanation of the figurative meaning of the line. The lover was consumed by the fire of love, and the addressee's betrayal (of which we learn in the later sonnets) has resulted in the death of his feelings. So, his love (the person) has resulted in the death of the passion of love.

[87] *This…perceivest* – The addressee seems to understand this. But indeed, what does the fair youth understand? The strong images, or the hint contained in them, that the passion of love has died in the speaker?

[88] *To love…ere long* – The fair youth, realizing the frailty of the poet, begins to love him with more intensity, as the poet will stay for a brief time in the world. That is the meaning which comes up if we look at the lines literally. However, as our analysis has revealed, the poet does not only provoke striking images, but talks of the death of his feelings of love. If that is so, it would appear that the couplet seems to negate it. However, on closer reading, it would be clear that the speaker perhaps means that the addressee decides to love the speaker for the little while that remains, before leaving him and going for the rival. The poet does not say "which must leave thee ere long" but "which *thou* must leave ere long". The meaning is clear. The accusation is more towards the addressee, who the poet knows, will leave in near future. It is perhaps an attempt on part of the poet to evoke the striking images as a last resort to make the fair youth stay? Perhaps. But if one were to take the rest of the sonnets into view, it would appear that although it seemed to have worked for a while, the fair youth leaves the poet.

Imagery in Sonnet 73

Sonnet 73 falls in the second group of Shakespeare's Sonnets, starting from Sonnet 19, which talk of the poet in a love-relationship with the addressee, an apparently fair youth. In this sonnet, the speaker attempts to bring out the feelings of love in the addressee for him. The poet paints senile images of himself, in the hope that the images would evoke the desire in the fair youth to hold on to the poet dearly. The three quatrains present three distinct images, each rising in intensity.

The first quatrain presents the image of late autumn, when the leaves turn yellow. The physical self of the speaker is compared with the bare branches of the tree. The image evokes a picture of desolation, with no birds singing joyfully. There is the undertone of abandonment, a tone which has been reinforced in the last line "which thou must leave ere long". The image of the branches as "bare" take away the spirit of liveliness. Scholars have pointed at the historic relevance of the image with the destruction of monasteries at the time of Henry VIII. But the poem is more than some allusion to historic events. It is a poem of personal love and loss, and the loneliness created in the first quatrain lends the soft melancholic mood to the poem.

The second quatrain shifts from the image of a devoid of foliage tree to the image of twilight. Both the images – that of late autumn and that of twilight – come before the ultimate, that is, winter and night (symbolizing death). The light is fading and the sun has set, and the sense of impending "black Night" creates a sense of foreboding.

The second quatrain is important not just in intensifying the mood from melancholy to foreboding, but also for brining closer the sense of impending doom. The first quatrain had presented the image of the bare branches of the tree as a state in which the addressee would behold the speaker sometime in future, but in the second quatrain, the image is presented in present tense.

> In me thou see'st"

and

> As after sunset fadeth in the west

clearly present the change in time. This does not go to say that time has passed from the first stanza to the second, but that the thoughts of death are more intense, so much so that the present tense is used to make the addressee visualize them with more sensitivity.

The third quatrain intensifies the images even more, in mentioning a fire. It is not a fire which burns in the darkness of the night, but a fire which is dying out. It is a smouldering fire. The fire represents the vigour of life and also represents the feelings of love which the lover feels is about to die.[89] Ironically, this fire is

> Consum'd with that which it was nourish'd by.

It feeds on its life source and is about to die once the material which has given scope for burning, is consumed.

The couplet presents the passion of the speaker, who seems to be roused to love the poet for the remaining time.[90]

SONNET 87

> Farewell, thou[91] art too dear[92] for my possessing,[93]
> And like enough[94] thou know'st thy estimate:[95]

---

[89] Refer to the annotations for the lines to get more details about this interpretation.

[90] Refer to the annotations for the lines to get more details about another interpretation.

[91] *thou* – See 'Overview of the Sonnets'. It has been told that this sonnet falls into the first group of Sonnets, as per the structural

division. It is supposedly addressed to a fair and youthful man. See the section on 'Overview of the Sonnets' to read about the complexities that would arise from this speculation. For the sake of avoidance of confusion, I shall refer to the addressee as "friend". In the same way, I shall refer to the writer of the lines as "poet", so as to avoid the identity confusion, that whether or not they are autobiographical. When talking about the style of the lines, I shall of course, mention Shakespeare.

[92] *too dear* – Too good (in the sense of love). Please note the irony of situation. The friend happens to be "dear" to the poet, but instead of that bringing them closer, the poet says he has to go away. This "too dear" therefore, is not really "too dear" to the poet, that is the meaning of the irony. The poet feels that there is someone else who can do justice to loving such a person.

[93] *possessing* – Laying claim on. Here, this has not been used in a derogatory sense, to objectify the friend, but to simply state the poet's claim on the physical self of the person. The poet cannot claim physical love from that person, for he feels he is too inferior for that. This is obviously not said by the poet's realisation, but by the poet's bitter feelings, that the friend finds someone else better to make love to. However, if the friend is willing to sell the self for better money (to the person who will pay the "too dear" amount to possess), there is the theme of prostitution. It appears that the friend had not loved the poet (while the poet had loved the friend) and the friend is now giving himself to another person by making his own esteem much high – higher than the poet's reach. It appears that out of bitterness, the poet pens words which can make the friend be interpreted like a prostitute.

[94] *And...enough* – i.e., In a similar manner ("like enough").

[95] *thou...estimate* – The friend is aware of the worth. So the poet says that just as he knows that the friend is a lot more in worth than can be recognised through him, the friend is also aware of that. In other words, the friend knows his merit and worth, and is aware

> The charter of thy worth[96] gives thee releasing;[97]
> My bonds[98] in thee are all determinate.[99]

---

that the poet falls below that, and so, the poet is not in a position to offer his love. Notice that the hidden theme of prostitution continues in the poem.

[96] *The...worth* – This is the second of the legal terms that are used in this poem, (the first one being "possessing") reducing the tone of love to something that is mechanically weighed. Perhaps the poet hints at the heartlessness of the friend to have gone for another person, or the way in which another person has statistically showed to the friend that the poet falls short before this second person, and so, this second person is the one to get the friend? There is no answer to that, but the hint that is given through the use of the legal terms does convey a very heart-broken poet, and if not a heart-broken poet, at least, a poet who feels bitter that the friend is weighing his worth, and thereby finding that the poet is not for him.

[97] *releasing* – Freedom from the poet. In other words, it frees the friend from loving the poet and being with the poet, and allows the friend to seek love elsewhere. However, it appears that the friend has prepared a list of the qualities, and has presented it to the poet, thereby claiming his release, and the poet sadly has to accept it.

[98] *bonds* – Legal bonds, that is documents, stating a contract. There is also the pun on "bonds" in the sense of ties, that is, the mutual ties they had.

[99] *determinate* – Till a certain date, after which they will be terminated. Here, the sense is that they are already terminated. Compare this with "Summer's lease hath all too short a date" in Sonnet 18. Once more, there is a hint at prostitution – that the poet has enjoyed the physical intimacy with the friend for a limited time, as stated out clearly in terms of agreement, and now that the time is up, he has to let the friend go.

For how do I hold thee but by thy granting,[100]
And for that riches where is my deserving?[101]
The cause of this fair gift in me is wanting,[102]
And so my patent[103] back again is swerving.

---

[100] *For…granting* – A rhetoric question, whose answer is "no way", that is, there is no way that the poet can hold the friend without the friend permitting him to do that. The poet cannot hold the friend without permission. Such a line brings out a distance in the relationship.

[101] *And…deserving* – Another rhetoric question, whose answer is once more in the negation. The poet says that the poet does not deserve the richness that he gets by holding the friend. While there is the overt tone of the poet humbling himself, a closer look at the line will bring out the deep sarcasm. The poet feels that he does not really deserve the rich moments of holding the friend, but he has just stated that he can only hold the friend by the friend's permission. Therefore, if looked upon from this point of view, the line would bring out the hidden meaning, that how can the poet feel his part in holding him, when it is by the friend's permission? Therefore, the poet sees no part of him in holding the friend, for it is by the friend's condescension.

[102] *The…wanting* – This line can also be similarly interpreted in two ways. One meaning is that the poet does not consider himself to have any reason (any potential) for the gift of the friend in touching him. The poet feels he has no known merit in him why he would get such a rich gift from the friend. The other meaning is on the sarcastic line. The poet finds that he plays no part in the friend's decision to touch him, and so, he says this rather bitterly, and in a hidden way. As it is purely the decision of the friend, the poet does not find himself to be any cause of the touch, and so, he says that he has no claim on the touch. Therefore, the lines bring out the rather coldness of the person in treating the poet so. The unrequited love of the poet makes him say these lines.

[103] *patent* – The exclusive right of someone to something. Here, the poet refers to his previous situation as the friend's lover as the

Thyself thou gav'st, thy own worth then not knowing,[104]
Or me, to whom thou gav'st it,[105] else mistaking;[106]
So thy great gift, upon misprison[107] growing,
Comes home again,[108] on better judgement making.[109]

Thus have I had thee as a dream doth flatter,[110]
In sleep a king, but waking no such matter.[111]

"patent". Now, the friend has decided to go for someone else, and so, the patent is returning empty to him.

[104] *Thyself...knowing* – Previously, the friend had been willing to submit to the poet's love. The poet says that that must have been in ignorance, when the friend was not aware of the true value.

[105] *Or...it* – The poet now offers another reason as to why the friend might have fallen for the poet's love. Here, the poet says that perhaps the friend had overestimated the merits of the poet, and had consented because of that, and now takes away the consent by knowing that the poet is not worth it.

[106] *else mistaking* – This is the third reason the poet gives. Here, the poet says that maybe the friend just made a mistake in previously choosing the poet, and now repents of that, and seeks the company of another.

[107] *misprison* – Wrong impression, more accurately, bound (prison) by wrong (mis-) impression. For another usage of the word, see *Twelfth Night*, where Feste exclaims, "Misprison in the highest degree!" when at first, Olivia comes with her guards to "take away the fool".

[108] *Comes...again* – i.e., Returns to the person.

[109] *on...making* – The poet says that the friend has later had "better judgement", that is, formed better opinions about falling in for the love of the poet, and has decided to withdraw it.

[110] *Thus...flatter* – The brief time that the poet has had the physical company of the friend has been like a dream to him. Just as, in a

Theme of Rival Poet

This Sonnet belongs to one of the Sonnets of the Rival Poet group (78-80, 82-87). Some would like to end the group of Rival Poet Sonnets on 86, but this Sonnet too, carries on the theme. Though it deals more with the addressee than the rival poet, this Sonnet explores the theme of rivalry through the addressee.

The poet seems to have surrendered to the fact that he no longer has the privilege of being loved in return, for his lover seems to have bestowed it on someone else, who, the poet confesses, is much better in his skills. The poet says that it was a mistake by which the lover had previously been faithful to the poet, and now, realising the mistake, wants to take it back and not love him anymore. The lover, in other words, realises that the poet is not worthy of such a great person.

> So thy great gift, upon misprison growing,
> Comes home again, on better judgement making.

---

dream, one can get something, and be happy with the delusion (flatter) that he has got the thing, so has the poet had been under the delusion so far that he had the love of the friend. Now that the friend goes in for another, the poet feels it has been a dream for him.

[111] *In...matter* – So, being in the dream, and dreaming that he has the friend, he was a king, to have got possession of the physical self of the friend. Waking up, he finds that has not been so. In other words, when the poet had the friend for him, he was as happy as a ruler who has possession of something. Now that the friend is going for the love of someone else, he feels that he has not no such feeling. Note the word play on "matter". In one sense, it means "case", that is, it was not really the situation of a king for him. Another meaning "substance", that is, the poet finds no substance (no physical matter), as the friend has left him for another person.

The poet acknowledges that he had held the friend only because the friend had permitted him to do so, in other words, he had not done it by his deserving, and in fact, he does not possess that deserving:

> For how do I hold thee but by thy granting,
> And for that riches where is my deserving?
> The cause of this fair gift in me is wanting,
> And so my patent back again is swerving.

The tone of the poet is, over here, that of someone who wants to rouse emotions in the other person by talking negatively about himself. Perhaps he hopes to spark up the little affection that remains in the friend by stating that the friend does not value him anymore? Of course, all of this is conjectural, for no one knows if this is autobiographical, and might be dramatic exercises for that matter, or a composition similar to the love sequences that were being written in the form of sonnets in those days. Nevertheless, the fact remains that this Sonnet brings out the theme of another poet who has made the friend go over to him, and the poet sadly acknowledges that by talking about the theme of unrequited love.

The Use of Legal Imagery

This Sonnet is especially noted for its use of legal terms. These terms abound throughout the poem, and goes so far that had they gone further, they might have ruined the quality of the poem. However, the bard knows the just amount, and the legal terms, though they are a lot, are not too much.

Right from the very first line, the legal imagery is created, though it becomes prominent only from the third line. The use of the word "possessing" in the first line brings in the image of owning a piece of land. However, at this stage, the legal allusions to ownership are not clear, till the reader reads the third line. In reading the first line, the reader would take it to mean "getting", as in getting love from the friend. In the third line, the word "charter" would make the reader think about the possibility of the legal meanings, and the use of the other legal words in the other lines would confirm it. The third line would read that the statement which lists the merits of the friend does not permit the poet to hold the friend – he is bound to set the friend free, and the fourth line would mean that the legal statements ("bonds") which had given the right to access the friend in terms of love, are terminated ("determinate"). The first line would, at this point, read that the poet is stating that the friend is too costly for him to buy and keep.[112]

In the fifth line, the use of the word "granting" does not merely mean to be willing towards something, but to sanction the use of something. The poet was sanctioned to make love to the body of the friend by the friend only, and the poet did not own that right. The poet, therefore, considers it his privilege to have been let to do so, for he has had access to "riches" in the body of the friend, and feels that by himself, he did not deserve it. Such a view of things would actually create the impression that there was no love in the mind and heart of the friend for the poet, and therefore, the readers would side with the poet.

In the ninth line, the use of the word "patent" is another instance of the legal imagery. Here, it conveys the idea that the poet did not own the exclusive right to make love to the friend, or that even if he did have that right, that is no longer valid, and so, what was once exclusive to the poet is not only non-exclusive, but also non-permissible. In other words, previously the poet used to be the only lover of the friend, but now, there seems to be another one who loves the friend, to whom the friend also seems to have bestowed love. Therefore, the "patent" of the poet with regard to the friend, that only he can love the friend, is no longer valid. However, this does not mean that the poet and the other person are both enjoying

---

[112] To all feminist readers, I would request not to bring in feminist criticism by keeping in mind that this might be a man about whom the poet is referring!

the love of the friend, for the friend seems to have bestowed it to the other poet. Therefore, the poet has not only lost the exclusiveness, but also lost the right to make love to the friend. The tone of surrender with which the poet speaks these lines brings out pity from the readers, and makes them sympathise with the poet, and feel negatively about the friend in treating the poet thus, who was faithful in loving the friend.

The question would then arise as to why the friend had once bestowed the right upon the poet in the first place. The answer is provided in the next line, with the use of the word "worth". The poet says that at that time, the friend had given to the love of the poet because the friend was not aware of the real value of his self, or else, mistook the poet's value to be more than what it actually is. The use of the words of price is certainly unpleasant to read in a love poem. However, this brings out clearly the perception from which the friend looked at the love, and now looks upon it.[113]

In the eleventh line, the use of the word "misprison" in the legal sense would mean neglect of duty. As the poet seems to have neglected his duty[114], the friend has made another judgement, which is better for him, but bad for the poet.

The couplet does not contain a legal image, but tells about the desire of the poet to have got the friend to be a dream.

Therefore, it can be seen that the use of legal terms in the poem goes very well to create a mood of lovelessness on part of the friend, which in turn goes to create a mood of sympathy for the poet on part of the readers, thereby making the poem successful to convey its thoughts to them.

---

[113] Now that the friend has got someone who is of more value, the friend seems to have gone for him totally, forgetting the faithful love of the poet.

[114] Which the readers would be bound to doubt.

SONNET 130

My mistress' eyes[115] are nothing like the sun;[116]
Coral is far more red than her lips' red;[117]
If snow be white, why then her breasts are dun;[118]
If hairs be wires, black wires grow on her head.[119]
I have seen roses damasked,[120] red and white,

---

[115] *My...eyes* – This is one of the "Dark Lady Sonnets". See 'Overview of the Sonnets' to note the number of poems that are addressed to the Dark Lady.

[116] *My...sun* – Readers should not fail to notice the similarity with Sonnet 18, which beings, "Shall I compare thee to a summer's day?" Over there, the poet compares the friend to the summer's day, only to state that the beauty of the person is better than the glorious sun. here, the poet refuses to compare the beauty with the sun at all, stating right at first that the lady is not at all fair in her appearance. This does not go to say that she is ugly; she has her own beauty, and that is what the poet tries to bring out.

[117] *Coral...red* – The reddishness that is there (which is not much), is also much redder than the reddishness that is there on her lips. In other words, even the lips are dark. They lack any sort of red colour.

[118] *If...sun* – i.e., just as snow is white in colour, her breasts are black ("dun") in colour.

[119] *If...head* – The image that is presented here might be a bit shocking. However, readers must not imagine hair absolutely straight and erect on the lady's head, sticking out in all directions. The poet simply means that the hair on the lady's head is as crudely black as black wire, and is rough and perhaps uncombed.

[120] *roses damasked* – Damask was a type of silk cloth, used as covering. Ingram and Redpath suggest that this refers to the softness of the silk cloth. Evans suggests that it is a mingling of the red and green roses. In Sonnet 99. Shakespeare refers to the youth as having "damasked" cheeks which leads us to think they were

But no such roses see I in her cheeks,[121]
And in some perfumes is there more delight
Than in the breath that from my mistress reeks.[122]
I love to hear her speak, yet well I know
That music hath a far more pleasing sound;[123]
I grant I never saw a goddess go –
My mistress when she walks treads on the ground.[124]

---

rather soft. So, perhaps he alludes to the fact that he has seen both the varieties of roses, red and white, in their softness. It might also mean that the poet has seen the red and white roses covered by a soft clothing – making them damasked.

[121] *But...cheeks* – There is no blush which appears on her cheeks, they are so dark.

[122] *And...reeks* – The breath of the lady is not at all good; there is no fragrance about it. In other words, the lady does not care for one bit of delicacy, but retains what has been given by God to her.

[123] *I...sound* – The sound of the lady's words have no sweetness in them – there is no melody in her words. The charm that should be there in a lady is totally missing from her. however, it is here that the poet asserts that he does not scorn her at all, and that this poem is not a poem to lock the lady's ugliness, but to discover the beauty that lies within the surface. The poet says, "I love to hear her speak", though he is well aware that the words have no graceful tone.

[124] *I...ground* – The poet confesses that he has never seen the walking of a goddess, but from the walking of this lady, he has no doubt that she, at least, is not a goddess, for she steps on the ground firmly with her steps when she walks. Shakespeare is over here referring to the practice of elevating beautiful ladies to the stature of goddesses by the praise of their lovers. In fact, many sonnets by contemporaries treat the ladies in such a manner. Shakespeare is scorning that tradition, and stating that he has not seen a goddess walk (meaning that neither have the other

And yet, by heaven, I think my love as rare[125]
As any she belied with false compare. [126]

Theme of True and Unflattering Love and the Theme of Natural Beauty

sonneteers who write about the ladies as goddesses, and that the other ladies who are praised as goddesses are falsely praised, and they are not goddesses at all).

[125] *And...rare* – The poet swears to it that his love is rare. This is again said in mockery of the conventional poems, where all the lovers would state that their love is rare, and all other lovers' loves common to their love. However, other than the satirical note of this line, the line also reveals the poet's intention towards the lady to be that of someone who loves her.

[126] *As...compare* – The poet tells that his love is no less than that of those other lovers who talk mightily of the beauty of the beloveds. The poet states that though he does not indulge in such majestic praises, which he calls "false compare", that is false praise, his love is by no means less worthy. He is very honest in his love and his praise.

However, the two lines open up another possibility, which has not really been explored. I would advise the students to be very cautions before writing this second observation. This second observation is actually the very opposite meaning of the first one. If the poet says that his love is as rare as that of all other poets who falsely praise their beloveds, how rare is that love? The answer is certainly not in the affirmative. The love, in that case, cannot be rare, and so, is not sincere at all, for the other poets who describe the love in a false manners cannot be called to be sincerely in love. Therefore, this observation throws light on the poem in an entirely new way, and so, I advise that students who are merely reading this for writing answers should not use this second observation. Those who are looking into it critically can certainly use this, provided that the criticism is for a research type of paper.

This sonnet belongs to those which are addressed to "The Dark Lady". As the name suggests, the complexion of the Lady is dark, as found in the descriptions in the poems. Moreover, the lady is absolutely plain, in fact, one might even call her coarse. However, she is the object of the poet's love, and the poet does not dislike her for her plain and even coarse nature, but rather, blows the trumpet about those aspects, and loves her in spite of them.

The poem is filled with the descriptions of "The Dark Lady" being unattractive in every sense of the conventional idea of beauty. Her hair is rough; her lips are plain; her walking is rather lacking in grace, and her complexion is also dark. But to the poet, these things do not lessen his love for her, and he holds her to be rare, and his love for her to be rare also. There are several places where the poet sarcastically comments on the tradition to elevate the beloved's beauty more than what it actually is. At the end, the poet tells that his love for her is by no means less than those who flatter their beloveds.

> And yet, by heaven, I think my love as rare
> As any she belied with false compare.

Through this, he also tells that the other persons who indulge in flattery are liars, and they are feeding their beloveds with lies. In this way, he sets his love out as true. He is not going to be like one of those people who lie to their beloveds to win their love – he is going to tell her the truth, and she is to find in him a truthful lover.

So, he comments sarcastically,

> I grant I never saw a goddess go –

"The Dark Lady" should not feel sorry that her lover is glorifying her in his poems, like the other contemporary sonneteers, for he states that his love is no lesser than theirs. Moreover, it has the advantage of being truthful.

The theme of natural beauty, as comes up in this poem, is something which is there in the plays of Shakespeare as well. Here, I will cite two instances which I consider to contain the poet's standpoint upon this.

The first instance is found in *Twelfth Night*, where Viola, disguised as Sebastian, comes to Olivia, and sees her beauty.

> OLIVIA: Look you, sir, such a one I was this present. Is't not well done?
>
> VIOLA: Excellently done, if God did all.
>
> OLIVIA: 'Tis in grain sir; 'twill endure wind and weather.

[*TN*. I:5:191-194]

The second instance is found in *Hamlet*, where Hamlet makes one derogatory remark after another to Ophelia, referring to the female gender in general.

> HAMLET: I have heard of your paintings too, well enough. God hath given you one face and you make yourselves another.

[*HAM*. III:1: 137-138]

So, as can be seen through these lines from his plays, artificial decoration was something that is strongly resented. The poet wants to love the beloved for the coarse lady that she is, because he knows that his love is true.

The Theme of Fidelity as Found in the Shakespearean Sonnets

It must be told at the start that two or three Sonnets are not enough to come to a comprehensive understanding of the Sonnets of Shakespeare. However, for the purpose of the selections which are there in the book, I shall restrict myself to these few Sonnets only.

Sonnet 87 treats the subject of fidelity of love through its negation. In other words, the poet utters his grief about the fact that the friend no longer has any love for him, and that the friend feels it to be a mistake that he had previously given himself to the poet's love. Now, upon realising his mistake, he seems to have bestowed the right to love him upon someone else, and that grieves the poet all the more. The poet, in this poem, accepts his being rejected with resignation. In other words, the poet states that there is nothing that he can do about it, as it was the person's wish to have loved him previously, and his wish still not to love him anymore. Moreover, he says that he is unworthy to love him.

Though *Sonnet 130* does not continue with the theme of *Sonnet 87*, and though it does not address the supposed male friend of the poet, but rather, "The Dark Lady", this sonnet seems to be an answer to the previous sonnet. In this sonnet, we see the poet asserting his love for "The Dark Lady" even though she is rough, and has got no least trace of what would be conventionally called beauty. In this poem, the poet is in a better place, and "The Dark Lady" seems to be a totally unworthy person to get the poet's love. So, it can be said that she is in a similar position in which the poet was previously, that is, in *Sonnet 87*. However, even though she is in a similar position, she does not seem to get the similar treatment as the poet had got. While the poet had been rejected by the friend when someone better came for him, or when the friend realised that the poet was not that worthy to love him, the poet does not do the same for "The Dark Lady". In fact, he tells in the poem all the things which would make it absolutely clear that she is, physically, inferior to the other ladies, and so, is not worthy to get the poet's love. However, the poet loves her in spite of that, or rather, the poet loves her because she is so true in her appearance. She might be rough in appearance, but the poet loves her with his heart, and so, does not bother about the fact that the appearance is not that good.

So, the second poem brings out the fidelity of love by the poet's decision to love her even though she is not conventionally beautiful. That is the desired action to take when someone loves someone, which is lacking in *Sonnet 87*.

Therefore, as seen through this analysis, both the sonnets present the theme of fidelity of love, but while one states it through its negation, the other states it through its assertion.

5. John Donne

(1572-1631)

About the Poet

John Donne was born in London. At the age of 11 he went to Oxford University where he stayed for three years. Some say that he went to the University of Cambridge after that, but he did not take a degree from any of the Universities. He began studying law at Lincoln's Inn in 1592 and it seemed that he would make a career in that field. He was appointed the private secretary to Sir Thomas Egerton in 1598. He married Anne More in 1601. She was the niece of Egerton. As a result of this marriage, he was dismissed from the service and was imprisoned for a short while. After that, for a few years, he lived on a meagre income as a lawyer. During this period, Donne wrote the *Divine poems* (1607). In 1615, he became a priest of the Anglican Church, and later became the Royal Chaplain. In 1621, he became the Dean of St Paul's Cathedral. He got famous as a preacher, and delivered sermons which are very brilliant and eloquent.

Donne's poetry is on secular as well as religious subjects. He also wrote poems about inconstancy and true love. His poems reveal the characteristics which were common in the metaphysical poets: play upon words, often sexually; use of paradoxes; syllogistic arguments; use of unusual metaphors taken from law, physiology, scholastic philosophy, and mathematics.

Donne also excelled in prose, which also have metaphysical elements in them. His Sermons, about 160, are specially known for their decisions of Biblical passages and explorations on the theme of love which is divine and decay and resurrection of the body. Donne also preached a sermon which he called his funeral sermon "Death's Duel". This was done just a few weeks before he died on March 31, 1631.

The Good-Morrow[127]

I wonder, by my troth,[128] what thou and I
Did, till we lov'd? were we not wean'd[129] till then?
But suck'd on country pleasures, childishly?[130]
Or snorted we in the Seven Sleepers' den?[131]

---

[127] *The Good-Morrow* – This means "The Good Morning". Here, it refers to both the wish that is made in the early morning, and also the fact that the morning is good.

[128] *troth* – Truth. The poet swears by truth.

[129] *wean'd* – Weaning is the feeding of milk to the baby by the mother from her breasts. In other words, breast-feeding. Here, the poet means that before the time that they loved each other, they must have been in the infantile state of sucking milk, and were extremely naïve. In other words, before loving each other, all of their previous times were childishly spent. Meeting each other and falling in love, they have become grown-ups.

Although it appears that the poet and the beloved were in an ignorant state before meeting each other, there is also another meaning, which suggests that they were enjoying sexual pleasure with others without the mature understanding that they now have.

[130] *But...childishly* – As has been told above, the poet means that previously, they would derive pleasure like children. Here, the poet tells what those pleasures would be. They would take delight in the simple sights of country (country means village). Here, by metaphysical comparison, the poet metaphorically calls that to be "sucking". Just as a child would take delight in sucking the milk from the mother's breast, and his food would be that only, the poet and the beloved used to take total delight in the sights of the country. There is also a pun on "country pleasures" as Dr. Gupta points out. One meaning has been stated, and the other meaning is that they had rather brutal, animal-like raw sexuality with others, before meeting each other.

'Twas so;[132] but this, all pleasures fancies be:[133]
If ever any beauty I did see,
Which I desir'd, and got, 'twas but a dream of thee.[134]

---

[131] *Or...den* – This is an allusion to the legendary tale of seven Christian youths who hid inside a cave outside the city of Ephesus (west of present Turkey), to escape being persecuted by the emperor Decius. This is before the time when Christianity became the state religion of Rome. Decius ordered the cave to be blocked from the outside. But, instead of being starved to death, the seven men fell into a sleep that miraculously lasted for 187 years. After waking up, they found that Christianity had become the state religion of Rome.

What the poet means is that the time that they spent before knowing each other was like the time when they were sleeping, and now, being in each other's company, they are fully awake, and they are looking at things from a new and true perspective.

[132] *'Twas so* – Though this is a confirmation by the poet, some would like to state that the poet hesitates. However, the note of confirmation rings clearly through these words. The poet confirms to what he has been saying previously. In other words, he accepts that the time spent with others was indeed like being "wean'd" on "country pleasures" and sleeping "in the Seven Sleepers' den".

[133] *but...be* – i.e., In comparison to this, all other pleasures were mere imagination; they did not give that pleasure in reality. In this relationship, they actually feel the pleasure. So, the physical aspect of love is brought out through this expression.

[134] *If...thee* – The poet acknowledges the superior beauty of the beloved over all others. The poet says that all the ladies whom he had thought to be beautiful have turned out to be illusions ("dream") of her. So, the poem should not be read as a poem which proclaims the naivety of the poet regarding sexual intercourse. In fact, the poet says that he has been in other relationships ("see" "desir'd" and "got"), but they were nothing compared to this relationship. They were like dreams; she is the reality.

> And now good-morrow to our waking souls,[135]
> Which watch not one another out of fear;[136]
> For love, all love of other sights controls,[137]
> And makes one little room, an everywhere.[138]
> Let sea-discoverers to new worlds have gone,[139]
> Let maps to others, worlds on worlds have shown,[140]

It should be noted that in these few lines, the poet has been arousing images of waking from sleep. In the next line, he addresses the wakeful selves. This makes the poem *au bade*.

[135] *And…souls* – It should be noted that the "good-morrow" is to the souls, not the bodies. The images aroused in the previous stanza were about the physical selves; they lead on to the images of the soul. So, as has been said, there is both physical and the spiritual in metaphysical poetry; the spirit is sought to be got by physical actions.

[136] *fear* – Insecurity. The poet states that there is no insecurity in their love.

[137] *For…controls* – i.e. Their love for each other dominates over their desire for other things ("other loves").

[138] *And…everywhere* – It is from here that the poet begins the characteristic metaphysical geographical comparisons. They are so satisfied with their love that a little room does not seem to them a tiny space; it becomes the world for them. It is their world of love-making. However, readers should note the hyperbolic metaphor.

[139] *Let…gone* – This is a reference to the voyages of discovery and the many explorations that were undertaken during the Renaissance. The Americas were called the "new world" initially.

[140] *Let…shown* – The sea explorations led to the discovery of the American Continents, and also detailed on previously known places. So, the maps were undergoing a lot of changes during that time. Maps using grid lines were first invented during this age.

Let us possess one world, each hath one, and is one.[141]

My face in thine eye, thine in mine appears,[142]
And true plain hearts do in the faces rest;[143]
Where can we find two better hemispheres,[144]
Without sharp North, without declining West?[145]

---

[141] *Let...one* – The poet says that let the sea explorers discover new lands, and let map-makers make new maps and draw new lands upon existing lands ("worlds on worlds"), and then tells that let them in their own way, have their one world. The next part, however, creates confusion. If they have one world, how will each have one? The poet clarifies later that he means "one hemisphere" to be in possession of each.

[142] *My...appears* – Here, the poet leaves the image of the "world" for a few lines, and moves on to another image. The readers understand that "each hath one, and is one" means that as they see each other's faces, they can each have their faces, and yet the two would be one, for they reflect each other.

[143] *And...rest* – The true love that they have for each other is revealed by the expression of their faces. However, does this not take the readers away from the sexual image presented in the first stanza? It does. But now, the poem blends the physical with the spirit.

[144] *Where...hemispheres* – Now the poet talks about the world to mean "hemispheres". By saying world, he had referred to their faces being the world for them. So, each person would make up one half of the total, therefore, is the world is spherical, each would form a sphere.

[145] *Without...West* – In the real world, the North is at the top, and is pointed in that sense. Think of the needle of a compass, which always points to "sharp North". In fact, "sharp North" has become an expression in the English Language.

Similarly, the West falls along to meet the South, so the West is said to be declining.

Here, Donne talks about the limitations of the real world. He says that in the real world, North would be sharp, and West would be

What ever dies,[146] was not mix'd equally;[147]
If our two loves be one, or, thou and I
Love so alike,[148] that none do slacken,[149] none can die.[150]

---

falling. So, there is not evenness in the surface. This is not the case for the two lovers, whose faces make up their world. So, there is no "sharp North" and "declining West".

[146] *dies* – I have given the modern spelling here, but the old spelling brings out the pun. *Dyes* has been used in both the senses of dying a death, and dying a cloth.

[147] *What...equally* – If the first meaning of *dyes* is taken the line would refer to the theory of humours, that was in practice in those days. It was thought that the world is made up of four principal elements – earth (soil), fire, air and water. This concept is Greek in origin. During the Renaissance, the theory of humours came up, which applied this Greek concept into medicine. As per that, a human body, being made up of these four elements, will function properly when these elements are in proportion to each other. if not, it would result into diseases. A human personality was thought to have developed as per the mixing of these elements. So, here, Donne refers to that and says that what ever dies in nature did not have proper mixture of the elements. However, this is not the case for their love; it has been mixed properly, and so, their love will never die.

The second meaning of the line is once more a characteristic feature of metaphysical metaphor. The metaphor is that of dying clothes. Donne says that a particular colour is able to form on the cloth (*dyes*) because that colour has been added to it out of proportion to its ordinary colours. In other words, this colour is extra, and it creates lack of proportion among the colours that are there on the cloth, and so, because of the dominance of this colour, this colour forms on the clothes, what he means over here is that for them, there will not be any one aspect which will be stronger than the others. All of their love will be in proportion.

DONNE'S "THE GOOD-MORROW"
ELEANOR TATE[151]

Brief Commentary

"The good-morrow," as the title suggests, is really an *aubade,* or morning song usually "sung" by a lover to his mistress after a night of love. Donne takes this conventional form and gives it his own unusual treatment. Clay Hunt comments that, although at first sight the short poem appears simple and lucid, yet it is "actually the densest and most tightly organized of Donne's major love poems."[1]

The poem opens dramatically and rather explosively with a series of short exclamatory questions, the first containing an oath, which the lover addresses to the woman beside him. The broken lines, Hunt suggests, contain the "rhythms of impassioned speech."[2] The first four lines convey the speaker's amazed surprise at his new discovery of love and his scorn for his former, unbelievably naive ignorance. To achieve sincerity of feeling, then, Donne abandons the conventional complimentary love-song opening and startles us, rather, with energetic, colloquial, and realistic language. True, he uses hyperbole to contrast their states before and after their discovery of love, but the exaggeration is

---

[148] *Love...alike* – Love so similarly, that both the loves are of the same magnitude and intensity.

[149] *slacken* – Slow down. The poet says that for them, no one's love will slow down. Both will always love each other equally.

[150] *none...die* – No one's love will die, for they will always remain constant in love.

[151] I have not changed nay of the words of the document. They are given as written by the author, and I have only added the sub-headings for matters of clarifications for students. The article was originally published by New Asia College of Chinese University, Hong Kong, in the Academic annual, vol. 1966, no. 8 (Sept 1966).

earthy and entirely outside the usual courtly love vocabulary, having here something even of a comic effect, as Hunt notes.[3]

Imagery with Words

The terms *wean'd, suck'd, countrey pleasures,* and *childishly* all suggest that in this new love they have suddenly come to maturity in their knowledge and experience. Line four, "Or snorted we in the seaven sleepers den?", alludes to the legend of the seven Christian youths of Ephesus who hid in a cave during the persecutions of Decius and slept there for more than two hundred years, awaking, amazed, in the fifth century to find Christianity triumphant. *Snorted,* in Donne's time meant, for one thing, "to sleep heavily or sluggishly," or it could mean "to convert (oneself) *into* something [else] by idleness."[4] Both meanings are perhaps relevant here. The lovers, their souls just awakened, realise that all of life until this time has been as a drugged sleep, their world a den, shut oil from all reality. The second meaning seems to apply, too. Because of their former idle or foolish activities (What did we "till we lov'd?"), they had not realized their own true being; until now they had not been themselves.

There is an alternate reading to these lines, apparently an earlier version:

But suck'd on childish pleasures seelily?
Or slumbred we in the seven sleepers den?

Donne has gained greater concreteness and emphasis on his contrasting states by eliminating *seelily* and adding **countrey.** And *snorted* is far more forceful— scornfully so—than **slumbred,** along with **countrey** suggesting the vulgarity of all earlier experience.

As Hunt notes, the "dramatized excitement" "ends with the exclamatory
"T' was so."[5] And the remainder of stanza one forms a transition between the vigorous opening lines and the smoother, more harmonious last two stanzas. Except for this love ("But this"), the speaker declares, all pleasures are only illusions.

The last two lines, however, do contain a shock. The lover confesses to his beloved that he had desired other beauty before her, and had got it. *Got,* placed in the middle of the line, with the caesura following it, receives great weight of emphasis. Then he hastens to add that all these earlier experiences of beauty, and the strong implication is that they were former loves, were but a dream of her. Hunt feels that the word *got* gives sudden new meaning to the first four lines, implying that the childish, country pleasures he now scorned were other sensual loves.[6] The first stanza, then, is not only a statement of his surprised discovery of a new type of love, but it is also a sort of confession (the lover shifts into the first personal pronoun in the last two lines) and at the same time a renunciation of all other loves, which he now realizes had been merely on the level of lust and thus not love at all. ***Dreame*** of the last line gives the whole stanza Platonic overtones, the woman becoming the very archetype of beauty. The speaker's earlier affairs arc to this new love as the cave shadows *(den,* 1. 4) of experience are to ultimate reality, or the ideal.

The Theme of the New Birth: The Theme of Progression

The second stanza opens with the lovely line, serene and peaceful, "And now good morrow to our waking soules." The past is behind them; their souls have just been touched into life. New-created, they awake to all the wonder of their love, which, being of the soul is eternal. The second line reminds one of the Scriptural statement, "There is no fear in love; but perfect love casteth out fear" (I John 4: 18). In the speaker's mind, this love is perfect, altogether beyond the realm of distrust, for it has reached the height of spiritual love. And it will now control all other lesser loves or desires. The word *controule* seems especially well chosen. From the fourteenth century on it meant to check or verify; in the sixteenth century it also meant "to take to task, call to account, rebuke, reprove (a person)," or "to challenge, find fault with, censure, reprehend, object to (a thing)." Further, during this same period it could mean "to overpower, overmaster" or in legal terms "to overrule." Then, of course, it also held our modern meaning, "to hold sway over, exercise power or authority over; to dominate, command."[7] All these meanings seem applicable and all at the same time. The lovers have come into a new wisdom, the speaker says, through which they see all things clearly in their true light. In fact, indirectly he calls this love sight by his use of the phrase "other sights." One could perhaps paraphrase line 10, "For this sight, or insight, all love of other sights controls." It will reprove for a wrong desire or censure it; it is a love which will overpower all false loves, being to the lover his one authoritative, motivating principle.

Lines 8, 9, and 11 remind us of the actual situation of the poem—the two lovers lying in bed, contemplating each other. Their "little roome" is in direct contrast to the den of line four. While it is true that both shut off from the world, yet the den was a confining prison, whereas the "little roome" becomes an expanding world of its own. Hunt suggests that it symbolizes the entire contentment of a love that enables them to renounce not only other loves but also all of the normal activities of life in the world....The transforming power of their love.... has converted "one little room" into the entire world ("an every where").[8]

Metaphysical Images: Topical References to the Voyages of Discovery and the Great Explorations

In the last three lines of the stanza Donne considers the great discovery voyages of his age, the new worlds discovered, including probably celestial worlds, and writes them off as inconsequential in comparison to his new world of love. The world which he considers well lost for love "is not a drab affair of getting and spending; it is a magnificent world of romantic adventure and heroic enterprise."[9] There is greatness in his very casualness in casting it off. Each of these lines begins with *Let,* but in the last line the meaning shifts. In lines 11 and 12 it means "What if." By the time he gets to the last line the term has gathered force for his use of it in the imperative sense.

This line is really the only persuasive one in the poem, and we have no feeling that the suggestion is in any way opposed by the woman addressed. "The good-morrow," then, is not one of Donne's logically arranged arguments; rather, the poem is a wondering statement of discovery and revelation.

Robert L. Sharp has made some interesting comments on the map reference in line 13. He believes that Donne had in mind a cordiform or heart-shaped map, a type produced in the sixteenth contury. The best of these maps, he writes, "show 360° of the earth's surface in either a single projection or twin hemispherical projections, one northern and one southern. The heart shape is due to the upward and outward curve of the meridians from a depressed pole." In contrast to the multiplicity of worlds revealed by map is the singleness of the lovers' world, "because they constitute it, all else being excluded. At the same time, paradoxically, each has a world (having the other) and is a world (for the other to discover and have)." And in the last stanza, where each is reflected in the other's eyes, as in the double cordiform maps, "each heart is a hemisphere: the two hearts together make one world."[10]

The Theme of Spiritual Love and Physical Lust

In an effort to establish the contrast between lustful and spiritual love as the main organizing principle of the poem ("it functions as the organizing concept for the thought and imagery of the entire poem"),[11] Hunt would give the sea discoveries and the map reading of stanza two sexual connotations. I feel that by doing so he unjustifiably narrows the meaning of the poem. Unger seems closer to what Donne has achieved in his outer and private world contrast when he comments that "each world represents an attitude—the worldly attitude and the lover's attitude . . . . He dismisses the geographical world and affirms the world of love."[12]

Stanza three opens with the literal description of the lovers gazing into each other's eyes. Donne continues his geographical imagery. The hearts and hemispheres of lines 16 and 17 are apparently related to the maps of line 13, as discussed above. The world the lovers represent is without coldness ("sharpe North") and alteration ("declining West"), infinitely superior to the geographical world. The word *plaine* is an interesting choice. Hunt suggests that it means "frank and without guile."[13] No doubt it does mean this, but other possible meanings fit the context and greatly enlarge the meaning of the phrase "plaine hearts." One obsolete meaning, current in Donne's day, was "full, plenary, entire, perfect."[14] With this one simple word, the lover describes the very nature of this new love. The two of them have been brought to perfection or maturity through their experience. Thus stanza three has been linked by theme to stanza one. And another curious meaning of the period was "of simple composition or preparation; not compounded of many ingredients; not elaborate."[15]

This idea connects the phrase with the last three lines of the poem, the medieval concept that death is the result of an inharmonious combination of elements, as, say, the conjunction of soul and body, or matter and spirit, in man. Grierson paraphrases and interprets these last difficult lines:

> If our two loves arc *one,* dissolution is impossible; and the same is true if, though *two,* they are always alike. What is simple—as God or the soul—cannot be dissolved; nor compounds, e. g. the Heavenly bodies, between whose elements there is no contrariety.

And he quotes Thomas Aquinas:

> Impossibile autem est quod forma separetur a se ipsa,

concluding,

> The body, being composed of conrrary elements, has not this essential immortality.[16]

But they could achieve it in their perfect, equal love, which had made of their two souls one harmonious whole.

Unity in the Poem

In considering the unity of the poem as a whole, one notes that there is no single continuous line of imagery, nor extended metaphor, probably, for one reason, because the poem is not in the form of a tight, logical argument. Rather, it is a growing revelation, and the speaker moves from figure to figure as his understanding expands. There is, however, a relationship between the various images and a strong sense of progression in the poem.

Unger comments on the fact that the childhood images of stanza one are not used again, noting that Donne introduces a series of new figures throughout the poem which are "reiterative" rather than related or dependent on each other.[17] But, while it is true that the conceits do not grow out of each other, it seems to me that they arc definitely related, cither by contrast or sense of progression. As already noted, the speaker moves from a state of childish ignorance to one of mature knowledge and wisdom through his new experience in love. The idea of perfection, inherent in which is the concept of maturity, is suggested both in stanza two (their perfect love free of all fear) and in stanza three (their "true plaine hearts" and their one eternal love which cannot die). The "sleepers den" of the first stanza is in contrast to the "little roome" of the second, which expands into the world of stanzas two and three, an eternal world, which is itself set against the Elizabethan world or age and, more than that, against the geographical world and even the celestial universe. The fancies and dreams of stanza one give way to the newly discovered eternal values that will not slacken or die. Their mutual rest in each other's love in line 16 is a great advance over the snorting sleep of line 4.

Then, too, the awakening and discovery figures really comprise one theme, in fact the main theme of the poem. The souls of the lovers have just awakened; and the poem is the statement of their growing discovery of the nature of their love. In stanza one the lover takes a backward look; in stanza two he considers their relationship and his own attitudes and feelings "now"; in stanza three his thought pushes forward into eternity. The title, too, carries this forward thrust.

Another means by which Donne achieves this sense of progression and growth in the poem, I feel, is through his handling of tone. The colloquial, realistic tone of stanza one seems to balance the extravagant language of stanzas two and three. The contrast serves to establish the speaker's sincerity. There is a masculine vigor in the first stanza which precludes by its very realism any notion that this lover is merely praising in conventional hyperbole some mistress of the moment. He moves from the amazed surprise of stanza one to the awed wonder of stanza three, and it is this sense of wonder at his new discovery of love that motivates the language of verses two and three.

Surely Gosse was misreading the poem when he slated that "'The Good Morrow' is the perfectly contented and serene record of an illicit, and doubtless of an ephemeral, adventure."[8] Rather, in its themes of the growth and eternity of love, the union of souls, and their completeness in each other, it reminds of other serious poems, such as "Lovers infiniteness"; or "The Anniversarie; or "A Valediction: of weeping," this last also embodying the concept of a new creation through love, or "A Valediction: forbidding mourning," with its circle image of perfection and eternity. The last poem we believe on Walton's authority Donne wrote to his wife, and it seems highly possible, as Hunt and Leishmam suggest, that

"The good-morrow" was also written to Anne More, for whom Donne had, in a real sense, given up a world. [12] It celebrates the revelation of a wholly satisfying love, one combining both body and spirit, *a* love which by its creative power had touched its participants into a wondrous new awareness of their own being.

1 Clay Hunt, *Donne's Poetry: Essays in Literary Analysis* (New Haven, 1954), p. 53.
2 *Ibid.,* p. 54.
3 *Ibid.,*
4 *NED,* IX, 328.
5 *Op. tit.,* p. 55.
6 *Ibid.*
7 *NED,* 11, 927.
8 *Op. tit.,* p. 59-
9 Ibid., p. 60.
10 "'Good-Morrow' and Cordiform Maps." *MLN,* LXIX (1954), 493-5-
11 *Op. tit.,* p. 58.
12 Leonard linger, *Donne's Poetry and Modern Criticism* (Chicago, 1950), p. 25.
13 *Op. tit.,* p. 63.
14 *NED,* VII, 937.
15 *ibid.,* 936.
16 Herbert J. C. Grierson, *The Poems of John Donne* (Oxford, 1912), II, 11.
17 *Op. tit.,* pp. 22-3.
18 Edmund Gosse, *The Life and Letters of John Donne* (New York, 1899), I, 65-
19 Hunt, pp. 68-9; J. B. Leishman, *The Monarch of Wit* (London, 1951), p.175.

6. Andrew Marvell (1621-1678)

About the Poet

Andrew Marvell was born in Winestead in Yorkshire. He was employed as a tutor to Oliver Cromwell's ward and later became an assistant to John Milton in 1657. He studied at Trinity College Cambridge and received his bachelor of arts degree in 1639. He remained there still 1641. He could not complete his Master of arts degree. He held a seat in the parliament from 1659. He is famous as a metaphysical poet. His work shows a lot of influence by John Donne. However there is also formality and elegance and smoothness, which shows influence from "the tribe of Ben". The "tribe of Ben" refers to the poets who were influenced by Ben Jonson and formed the Cavelier school.

To his Coy[152] Mistress

Had we but world enough, and time,
This coyness lady were no crime.[153]
We would sit down, and think which way

---

[152] *Coy* – Shy.

[153] *Had...crime* – Right from the start of the poem, there is the suggestion of hurry, of not staying idle. The poet tells the beloved that if the two of them had lots and lots of time, the shyness of the lady would have been appreciated. But there is not much time, and the poet asks the lady not to be timid and idle, but active. The *carpe diem* theme sets in right from the start of the poem. The lines that follow are about the poet telling what would they have done if they had so much of time.

> To walk, and pass our long Love's Day.[154]
> Thou by the *Indian Ganges'* side
> Should'st Rubies find: I by the Tide
> Of *Humber* would complain.[155] I would
> Love you ten years before the Flood:[156]
> And you should if you please[157] refuse
> Till the Conversion of the *Jews*.[158]

---

[154] *We...Day* – If the two of them had got all the time in the world, they would have sat down and thought on and on as to which direction to take for walking.

[155] *Thou...complain* – These lines have evoked a lot of criticism. The poet says that the beloved will be by the side of The Ganges, finding rubies, and the poet would lament the fact the beloved is not with her, sitting by the side of the river Humber. This is written in mockery of those poems which used to talk about the beloved happily picking up flowers in the garden, while the lover would be far away, in some hard task. This is also an allusion to the trade and commerce that had started flourishing during the Renaissance, due to the voyages of discovery. The traders had already started coming to India during the time of Queen Elizabeth I, and there was a lot of speculation about India to be a country which was rich in jewels. Though rubies by the side of Ganges is really hyperbolic, Indians should be aware that precious stones used to be found on the sea shores, and there were some people who used to collect them, or dive down the sea to pick them up, and sell them to the others. Perhaps, because of this, some foreigners believed that they are found along all water bodies in India.

[156] *I...flood* – The previous lines were hyperbolic in terms of physical aspects. Here, and in the lines following, the hyperboles are about time. The Flood over here refers to the flood mentioned in the Bible, when God destroyed the population of the world, and saved Noah and his family.

[157] *And...please* – i.e., And you can, if you want to.

[158] *Till...Jews* – This is an allusion to the dominance of Christianity over the Jews. The Jews, at first, resented "The New Faith", because of which it had to separate, and the followers were first called Christians by the Greeks. But the Jews kept on stirring the

> My vegetable Love should grow
> Vaster than Empires,[159] and more slow.[160]
> An hundred years should go to praise
> Thine Eyes, and on thy Forehead Gaze.
> Two hundred to adore each Breast:
> But thirty thousand to the rest.
> An Age at least to every part,
> And the last Age should show your heart.[161]
> For Lady you deserve this State;

---

people against this New Doctrine, and the Christians were persecuted by the Romans for a few centuries, till it was adopted as the state religion by Constantinople. The Jews then faced the persecution, and a lot of them had to convert to Christianity.

The poet says that he might begin proposing to the beloved ten years before the beginning of The Flood, and she might keep on refusing till the time of the conversion of the Jews. The poet obviously does not actually mean these two events, but the time span between them. In other words, he means that if they had nothing to worry about time, they would have spent a great amount of time wooing.

[159] *My...Empires* – This line is another one which has aroused a lot of interpretations. The words "vegetable Love" compares love with a vegetable that grows. Just as a crop would grow in the field, his love would grow. The territory of that love becoming vaster than empires is, of course, hyperbolic. But the comparison of vegetable love with empires brings images of agriculture opposing with industry. The Industrial revolution had, of course, not taken place yet, and by "industry", I mean trade and commerce, on which the Empires were becoming more and more interested. The simple, agrarian love is better than the material wealth, that is the suggestion. The comparison of the two things "vegetable" and "Empires" is an example of the metaphysical conceit.

[160] *slow* – Slow in the sense that there will not be any hurry. But it also means steady.

[161] *And...heart* – This is an allusion to the Bible, which says that at the end of the age, at the Second Coming of Christ, "the thoughts of every heart will be revealed".

Nor would I love at lower rate.[162]
　　But at my back I alwaies[163] hear
Time's winged Chariot hurrying near:
And yonder all before us lie
Deserts of vast Eternity.[164]
Thy Beauty shall no more be found;[165]
Nor, in thy marble Vault,[166] shall sound
My echoing Song: then Worms shall try
That long preserv'd Virginity:[167]
And your quaint Honour turn to dust;
And into ashes all my Lust.[168]
The Grave's a fine and private place,

---

[162] *For...rate* – The physical and the material aspects are joined together. The poet says that if he had the time, he would have done all this, that is, given so much of time for praising each part of her body, for she deserves it, and his magnitude of love also makes him love in such a high rate. Look at the pun on "State". On the one hand, it means "condition", and on the other hand, it means "territory". The second meaning brings back the comparison with "Empires".

[163] *alwaies* – i.e., always.

[164] *Deserts...Eternity* – Eternity is not now, but later. In life, they are always hurried by Time. The word "deserts" might not be to suggest not only the vastness, but also barrenness and hopelessness.

[165] *Thy...found* – After life, she will not have any body which the poet will praise in all eternity.

[166] *marble vault* – i.e., Her tomb.

[167] *Then...Virginity* – The Worms will get to enjoy her body after her death, and the poet mockingly says that as she is shy not to have sexual intercourse with him in life, Worms will have the pleasure of doing that. All this is to urge her to have sexual intercourse with him.

[168] *And...Lust* – All his lust for her would be burned up.

But none I think do there embrace.[169]

Now therefore, while the youthful hue[170]
Sits on thy skin like morning dew,[171]
And while thy willing Soul[172] transpires
At every pore with instant Fires,
Now let us sport us while we may;[173]
And now, like am'rous birds[174] of prey,
Rather at once our Time devour,[175]
Than languish in his slow-chapt pow'r.[176]

---

[169] *And...embrace* – Human beings cannot love each other in the graves. The poet, by this, says that this is the life to make love. This might be an allusion to the words of Jesus, when he tells the scribes that in Heaven, "nor do they marry, nor are given in marriage".

[170] *youthful hue* – that is, the colour of youth, in other words, while the body is till young.

[171] *Sits...dew* – The colour of youth is as soft and gentle as dew drops.

[172] *willing Soul* – The Spirit is willing to make love to the poet, even though she may be coy in the actions. This is an allusion to the Bible, where Jesus tells his disciples, "the spirit indeed is willing, but the flesh is weak", when they fall asleep when Jesus asks them "to watch and pray".

[173] *Now...may* – i.e., let them make love now that they have the time.

[174] *am'rous birds* – Birds of love. Here, however, they do not refer to doves. They refer to birds of prey, like the vulture or the eagle. Their condition is like these birds of prey when they are making love. The need to associate love with these birds is perhaps to bring out the passion in them, which would not have come out in the image of doves making loves.

[175] *Rather...devour* – As the birds of prey devour dead bodies, the poet says that the two of them should devour Time. The theme of *carpe diem* once more comes out from this line.

[176] *Than...pow'r* – i.e., instead of wasting time and crying over the waste of time, they should utilise this time in making love.

Let us roll all our Strength, and all
Our sweetness, up into one Ball:[177]
And tear our Pleasures with rough strife,
Thorough the Iron gates of Life.[178]
Thus, though we cannot make our Sun
Stand still, yet we will make him run.[179]

Carpe-diem theme in *To His Coy Mistress*

The theme of carpe-diem, that is, seize the day, is very beautifully found in this poem. Right from the start of the poem, the poet urges the beloved to rouse up, be excited and passionate, and make love, for they do not have an eternity on this earth. The poet tells the beloved to utilize each and every moment to the fullest.

This sense is achieved in two ways in the poem. In the first place, the poet conveys the lack of time by exaggerating things. He says, if they had all the time in the world, he would have spent a lot of years just to adore some parts of her body.

"An hundred years should go to praise
Thine Eyes, and on thy Forehead Gaze.
Two hundred to adore each Breast:
But thirty thousand to the rest.
An Age at least to every part,
And the last Age should show your heart."

---

[177] *Let...ball* – Notice the similar image of the sphere or spherical objects. However, the sexual innuendo should not be missed.

[178] *Through...Life* – The image that is presented in these lines is that of a hard life, which rules out all softness, and embraces the need to be always working passionately.

[179] *Thus...run* – The poet says that though they cannot make the Sun stand still (notice the contrast with *The Good-Morrow*), they will make sure that it runs hard after them all the time, for they will be ahead of it, and the Sun will have a hard time catching up.

The purpose of this exaggeration is to tell starkly that the situation is rather the opposite. They do not have such an amount of time to spare, in fact, they will never have this time in their lives. The effect that is intended is to make the beloved get out of her coyness, and passionately make love.

The second way by which the poet achieves this is by telling openly that there is no time. In other words, the poet tells her directly to make love, for the time is short.

> And now, like am'rous birds of prey,
> Rather at once our Time devour,
> Than languish in his slow-chapt pow'r.

The beloved, who has realised the fact that her coyness is only making them love their valuable time, which they can otherwise spend in making love, will now agree to the direct proposal of making love. In fact, the poet, in some lines, also tells her that her youth is now, and the time of making love is the present. If she does not do so in her life, worms will get possession of her body, and so, she will have wasted her opportunity in making love to him.

> then Worms shall try
> That long preserv'd Virginity:
> And your quaint Honour turn to dust;
> And into ashes all my Lust.

The poet, after these lines, asks her to directly make love to him. As is the aspect found in the metaphysical poems, we do not get to see the beloved's point of view. We only hear the part of the lover. However, readers would of course hope (even feminist readers, I should hope) that the beloved makes love to her, so that they can be happy in their relationship.

SECTION 2

THE ENGLISH EPIC

AND

THE ENGLISH

MOCK-EPIC

(Restoration and Neo-classical Poetry)

THE ENGLISH EPIC AND THE ENGLISH MOCK-EPIC

7. Introduction to The Epic

Epic

In simple words, epic is a composition which is a long narrative poem, whose subject matter is serious, which is narrated in the formal and elevated style, which centres around a hero or a figure who is above the ordinary human beings, on whose action depends the fate of a nation or a race. Epics fall into two types: the primary (the traditional) and the secondary (literary). The primary epics were originally oral. Secondary epics were written down.

The literary epics follow some conventions. The first convention is that the hero is a great figure. He is above the ordinary and the tale revolves around him. The second feature is that the epic encompasses a large geographical area. It can extend beyond the Earth into the heavens and also the underworld. Another feature of an epic is that the actions involve not just human beings but **duex-ex-machine** (machinery of the gods coming from outside). This means that the epic would not only feature human beings, but also supernatural beings. These supernatural beings would take an active and interesting part in the plot of the narrative. The other important aspect about the epic is that it is meant for ceremonial performance and so the style in which it is written is highly elevated. In other words, a lot of lofty words is used to give it a grand aspect.

Epic formulae

The beginning of an epic is with an argument. This tells the matter of the epic. The epic is divided into various books and the argument is to be found at the start of each book. Yet it begins with an invocation of the Muse, who is the inspiring agent for the poet. In the address to the muse, the poet questions him/her, and the answer marks the start of the narration.

The narrative begins in *medias res* (from the middle; at a critical point). The narration goes backwards and forwards in plot after opening in medias res.

There is a list of main characters introduced very formerly; some of them generally give speeches and the character traits are revealed through these.

FA Levers summarises the epic mode of narration by saying "unity of action, rapidity, the art of beginning in the middle, the use of the supernatural, the ornamental simile recurrent epithets and above all, the nobility which is truthfull, unrestrained and incomparable".

The style of the primary Epic

As the primary epics were oral, there was a lot of repetition. The lines were structured so that listeners could follow the lines. Pauses were avoided for they would make readers lose track. The language in which it was uttered needed to be familiar but not commonplace. This resulted in the elevated style of the epic. This gave it the feeling of a ritual.

The style of the secondary epic

The secondary epics were comfortably more intimate. Effects of the grand narrative could be achieved by the elevated grammatical and verse structure of the poem. Milton brings his grand style by the use of slightly unfamiliar words. A lot of proper names are used for enhancing the vision of the reader. Most of the names are sonorous, so as to add to the grand effect. Unlike the primary Epic, the secondary epic has the habit of sweeping the readers along the narrative. As it is written, the readers would not have difficulty in following.

8. John Milton

(1608-1674)

Paradise Lost – Background Information

Genesis, Chapter 2: The Creation of Man and Woman and the Garden of Eden[180]

7: And the LORD God formed man of the dust of the ground, and breathed into his nostrils the breath of life; and man became a living soul. 8: And the LORD God planted a garden eastward in Eden; and there he put the man whom he had formed. 9: And out of the ground made the LORD God to grow every tree that is pleasant to the sight, and good for food; the tree of life also in the midst of the garden, and the tree of knowledge of good and evil.... 15: And the LORD God took the man, and put him into the garden of Eden to dress it and to keep it. 16: And the LORD God commanded the man, saying, Of every tree of the garden thou mayest freely eat: 17: But of the tree of the knowledge of good and evil, thou shalt not eat of it: for in the day that thou eatest thereof thou shalt surely die. 18: And the LORD God said, It is not good that the man should be alone; I will make him an help meet for him. 19: And out of the ground the LORD God formed every beast of the field, and every fowl of the air; and brought them unto Adam to see what he would call them: and whatsoever Adam called every living creature, that was the name thereof. 20: And Adam gave names to all cattle, and to the fowl of the air, and to every beast of the field; but for Adam there was not found an help meet for him. 21: And the LORD God caused a deep sleep to fall upon Adam and he slept: and he took one of his ribs, and closed up

---

[180] The two chapters of the Bible are taken from King James Version, which is in the public domain. The numbers before the sentences indicate the verses.

the flesh instead thereof; 22: And the rib, which the LORD God had taken from man, made he a woman, and brought her unto the man. 23: And Adam said, This is now bone of my bones, and flesh of my flesh: she shall be called Woman, because she was taken out of Man. 24: Therefore shall a man leave his father and his mother, and shall cleave unto his wife: and they shall be one flesh. 25: And they were both naked, the man and his wife, and were not ashamed.

Genesis, Chapter 3: The Temptation and Fall of Man

1: Now the serpent was more subtil than any beast of the field which the LORD God had made. And he said unto the woman, Yea, hath God said, Ye shall not eat of every tree of the garden? 2: And the woman said unto the serpent, We may eat of the fruit of the trees of the garden: 3: But of the fruit of the tree which is in the midst of the garden, God hath said, Ye shall not eat of it, neither shall ye touch it, lest ye die. 4: And the serpent said unto the woman, Ye shall not surely die: 5: For God doth know that in the day ye eat thereof, then your eyes shall be opened, and ye shall be as gods, knowing good and evil. 6: And when the woman saw that the tree was good for food, and that it was pleasant to the eyes, and a tree to be desired to make one wise, she took of the fruit thereof, and did eat, and gave also unto her husband with her; and he did eat. 7: And the eyes of them both were opened, and they knew that they were naked; and they sewed fig leaves together, and made themselves aprons. 8: And they heard the voice of the LORD God walking in the garden in the cool of the day: and Adam and his wife hid themselves from the presence of the LORD God amongst the trees of the garden. 9: And the LORD God called unto Adam, and said unto him, Where art thou? 10: And he said, I heard thy voice in the garden, and I was afraid, because I was naked; and I hid myself. 11: And he said, Who told thee that thou wast naked? Hast thou eaten of the tree, whereof I commanded thee that thou shouldest not eat? 12: And the man said, The woman whom thou gavest to be with me, she gave me of the tree, and I did eat. 13:

And the LORD God said unto the woman, What is this that thou hast done? And the woman said, The serpent beguiled me, and I did eat. 14: And the LORD God said unto the serpent, Because thou hast done this, thou art cursed above all cattle, and above every beast of the field; upon thy belly shalt thou go, and dust shalt thou eat all the days of thy life: 15: And I will put enmity between thee and the woman, and between thy seed and her seed; it shall bruise thy head, and thou shalt bruise his heel. 16: Unto the woman he said, I will greatly multiply thy sorrow and thy conception; in sorrow thou shalt bring forth children; and thy desire shall be to thy husband, and he shall rule over thee. 17: And unto Adam he said, Because thou hast hearkened unto the voice of thy wife, and hast eaten of the tree, of which I commanded thee, saying, Thou shalt not eat of it: cursed is the ground for thy sake; in sorrow shalt thou eat of it all the days of thy life; 18: Thorns also and thistles shall it bring forth to thee; and thou shalt eat the herb of the field; 19: In the sweat of thy face shalt thou eat bread, till thou return unto the ground; for out of it wast thou taken: for dust thou art, and unto dust shalt thou return. 20: And Adam called his wife's name Eve; because she was the mother of all living. 21: Unto Adam also and to his wife did the LORD God make coats of skins, and clothed them. 22: And the LORD God said, Behold, the man is become as one of us, to know good and evil: and now, lest he put forth his hand, and take also of the tree of life, and eat, and live for ever: 23: Therefore the LORD God sent him forth from the garden of Eden, to till the ground from whence he was taken. 24: So he drove out the man; and he placed at the east of the garden of Eden Cherubims, and a flaming sword which turned every way, to keep the way of the tree of life.

Celestial Order, as believed at that Time

The following diagram explains the various layers in which the universe was thought to exist at that time. Each level was called a "Sphere". The *Prima mobile* was beyond these spheres and this sphere moved first, making the other spheres move under it. The movement of the spheres produced music, and this music was unheard by the human ears, and this music maintained harmony in the universe.

This belief was the Ptolemaic concept, which came down a little before the Renaissance. It was the Pre-Copernican concept.

Fig. 1: The Ptolamaic System of Universe

<https://upload.wikimedia.org/wikipedia/commons/2/28/Planisphaerium_Ptolemaicum_siue_machina_orbium_mundi_ex_hypothesi_Ptolemaica_in_plano_disposita_%282709983277%29.jpg>[181]

The central position is that of the Earth. The first sphere over it is that of the Moon, then, Mercury, Venus, Sun, Mars, Jupiter, Saturn, then, the sphere of the stars and zodiac signs, then, the *Prima mobile*. Beyond that lay the heavens. The sphere of the stars

---

[181] Licensed to reproduce under Creative Commons Attribution 2.0 Generic License.

and that of the moon produced high and low music, respectively, and the other spheres produced music that rose in pitch as per their number. In other words, from the sphere of the moon to the sphere of the stars, there was a rise in music from low to high.[182]

The Text

Book 1

THE ARGUMENT

This first Book proposes, first in brief, the whole Subject, Mans disobedience, and the loss thereupon of Paradise wherein he was plac't: Then touches the prime cause of his fall, the Serpent, or rather Satan in the Serpent; who revolting from God, and drawing to his side many Legions of Angels, was by the command of God driven out of Heaven with all his Crew into the great Deep. Which action past over, the Poem hasts into the midst of things, presenting Satan with his Angels now fallen into Hell, describ'd here, not in the Center (for Heaven and Earth may be suppos'd as yet not made, certainly not yet accurst) but in a place of utter darkness, fitliest call'd Chaos: Here Satan with his Angels lying on the burning Lake, thunder-struck and astonisht, after a certain space recovers, as from confusion, calls up him who next in Order and Dignity lay by him; they confer of thir miserable fall. Satan awakens all his Legions, who lay till then in the same manner confounded; They rise, thir Numbers, array of Battel, thir chief Leaders nam'd, according to the Idols known afterwards in Canaan and the Countries adjoyning. To these Satan directs his Speech, comforts them with hope yet of regaining Heaven, but tells them lastly of a

---

[182] Interesting to note would be the fact that together, there would be eight such notes of music, and it is this which comprises the octave in music: do, re, me, fa, so, la, ti and do respectively, with the first do and the last do being low and high respectively. The concept of the octave comes from this concept of eight spheres.

new World and new kind of Creature to be created, according to an ancient Prophesie or report in Heaven; for that Angels were long before this visible Creation, was the opinion of many ancient Fathers. To find out the truth of this Prophesie, and what to determin thereon he refers to a full Councel. What his Associates thence attempt. Pandemonium the Palace of Satan rises, suddenly built out of the Deep: The infernal Peers there sit in Councel.

> OF Mans[183] First Disobedience,[184] and the Fruit
> Of that Forbidden Tree, whose mortal tast
> Brought Death into the World, and all our woe[185],
> With loss of Eden, till one greater Man[186]
> Restore us, and regain the blissful Seat,[187] [5]

---

[183] I have not given the apostrophe, as it was not originally there in the poem. The use of apostrophe for forming possessives is a later development.

[184] It is the custom of the epic poets to state the subject matter right at the start of the poem. Homer begins *The Iliad* by stating "Achilles baneful wrath" (Chapman's translation). It is very important to note the subject matter of *Paradise Lost*, for a lot of people think it is to regard Satan as a hero. Milton states clearly that his subject matter is "Of man's first disobedience", and refers to Satan as the "infernal serpent" who caused the disobedience.

[185] It is stated in *The Bible* that God tells Adam and Eve that if they eat of the fruit of the forbidden tree, they would die. So, it is taken to mean that had they not eaten, man would have lived eternally.

[186] This is a reference to Christ, who came as the Saviour to redeem man from his sins.

[187] A place in heaven.

> Sing Heav'nly Muse[188], that on the secret top
> Of Oreb[189], or of Sinai[190], didst inspire
> That Shepherd[191], who first taught the chosen Seed[192],
> In the Beginning how the Heav'ns and Earth
> Rose out of Chaos:[193] Or if Sion Hill[194] [10]

---

[188] Epic poets addressed their poems to a "muse". A muse was one of the nine classical deities who had their expertise in various fields of learning. Although Milton does not mention the name of the Muse in the first book, he later calls the Muse to be "Urania", who was the muse of Astronomy. However, as that would be heretic, Milton tells that he only takes the name, and does not refer to the classical muse Urania. He wants to refer to the Holy Spirit, which is akin to Christian theology.

[189] Mount Horeb, where Moses received the law from God.

[190] Mount Sinai, where Moses received the Ten Commandments.

[191] Moses is referred as "That Shepherd" for he had fled from the palace of the Pharaoh and was living as a shepherd when God instructed him through the burning bush.

[192] The "chosen Seed" refers to "Israel" who were held as captives in Egypt. Moses led them out of Egypt and gave them the laws which he received from God.

[193] It is believed that Moses was the one who wrote the first five books of *The Old Testament*. However, Milton fuses Christian theology with Greek theology. Christianity states that everything was a formless mass at the start, and the "Spirit of God moved over the face of the waters" and was creating vapour. Then "God said, 'Let there be light' and there was light". The theory of chaos is found in ancient Greek theosophy and is not Christian.

[194] Mount Sion or Zion. Christianity states that at the Second Coming of Christ, the believers will be gathered on Mount Zion. Jerusalem was built on Mount Zion and Mount Moriah (Prince, 1962).

> Delight thee more, and Siloa's Brook[195] that flow'd
> Fast by the Oracle of God; I thence
> Invoke thy aid to my adventrous Song[196],
> That with no middle flight intends to soar
> Above th' Aonian Mount[197], while it pursues [15]
> Things unattempted yet in Prose or Rhime.[198]
> And chiefly Thou O Spirit, that dost prefer
> Before all Temples th' upright heart and pure,[199]

---

[195] Shiloah "was both a pool situated on the south-west side of Temple Mount...and a spring on the eastern side of the Mount connected by the channel with the pool" (Daiches). Milton wants o draw a parallel with the river which flowed down Mount Helicon, where the classical muses resided. The name of the classical spring was Apanippe.

[196] The primitive epic was "sung" by the poet, and not written down. Although this is a secondary epic, Milton gives it attributes of a primary epic.

[197] Mount Helicon, where the nine Muses resided. Milton hopes to soar higher than the reaches of the classical muses.

[198] Milton might claim that no one has done what he is about to do, that is, write an epic, but that is obviously not true. What he means is that he is the first English poet to write an epic.

[199] This refers to the Holy Spirit, which comes inside those who truly believe in Christ. The lines also express a puritan sentiment. The puritans renounced the customary modes of worship and wanted to worship from the heart and soul. However, they were not really followers of what they preached. Shakespeare presents a puritan who is a hypocrite in *Twelfth Night*. However, Credit must be given to them for trying to reform the Anglican Church of its un-Christian-like behaviour. In *The Bible*, Christ tells that people will go neither on the mountain, not in the temple, to worship God, but the true worshippers will worship the Father "in spirit and in truth" for God "is Spirit, and is seeking such to worship Him".

Instruct me, for Thou know'st; Thou from the first
Wast present,[200] and with mighty wings outspread [20]
Dove-like satst brooding on the vast Abyss
And mad'st it pregnant:[201] What in me is dark
Illumine,[202] what is low raise and support;
That to the highth of this great Argument
I may assert Eternal Providence,[203] [25]
And justify the ways of God to men.

Say first, for Heav'n hides nothing from thy view
Nor the deep Tract of Hell, say first what cause
Mov'd our Grand Parents[204] in that happy State,
Favour'd of Heav'n so highly, to fall off [30]
From their Creator, and transgress his Will

---

[200] This asserts the omnipresence of God.

[201] The image is that of a dove which is sitting and brooding. The image of the dove coming and sitting with outstretched wings is an allusion to the Bible, where, after the baptism of Jesus, the Holy Spirit alights upon him in the form of a dove, and remains upon him.

The image of brooding is an ancient concept, where doves were considered to be both male as well as female and so, the image of one dove brooding without the need of another "to make it pregnant" is used in that sense.

[202] This should be taken literally as well as figuratively. Figuratively, Milton wants to state that the Holy Spirit should make him know the things which he does not know ("dark"). Literally, it is an allusion to the fact that Milton was blind.

[203] Providence = Deliverance

[204] This does not mean grandparents, but parents who are grand. Milton uses the Latin syntax quite a lot of times to express in this manner. The reference over here is to Adam and Eve.

For one restraint,[205] Lords of the World besides?[206]
Who first seduc'd them to that foul revolt?
Th' infernal Serpent;[207] he it was, whose guile[208]
Stird up with Envy and Revenge, deceiv'd [35]
The Mother of Mankind,[209] what time his Pride
Had cast him out from Heav'n, with all his Host
Of Rebel Angels,[210] by whose aid aspiring
To set himself in Glory above his Peers,
He trusted to have equal'd the most High, [40]
If he oppos'd; and with ambitious aim
Against the Throne and Monarchy of God
Rais'd impious War in Heav'n and Battle proud
With vain attempt. Him the Almighty Power
Hurld headlong flaming from th' Ethereal Sky [45]
With hideous ruin and combustion down
To bottomless perdition,[211] there to dwell
In Adamantine Chains and penal Fire,

---

[205] One restraint refers to the one tree from which Adam and Eve were forbidden to eat.

[206] This refers to the Angels, who held lordship over the domains of the earth. Milton is referring to Satan as the cause of the fall of man as well as the cause of revolt of the angels.

[207] In the Bible, the serpent comes to deceive Eve. Traditionally, it has been looked that the Serpent was Satan in disguise.

[208] guile = deception

[209] i.e., Eve.

[210] Satan, previously known as Lucifer, had led one third of the angels of heaven to revolt against the Almighty. They were all cast to hell.

[211] This is a reference to "the bottomless pit" in the Book of Revelations.

Who durst defy th' Omnipotent to Arms.
Nine times the Space that measures Day and Night [50]
To mortal men, he with his horrid crew
Lay vanquisht,[212] rowling in the fiery Gulf
Confounded though immortal:[213] But his doom
Reserv'd him to more wrath;[214] for now the thought
Both of lost happiness and lasting pain [55]
Torments him;[215] round he throws his baleful eyes
That witness'd huge affliction and dismay
Mixt with obdurate pride and stedfast hate:
At once as far as Angels kenn[216] he views
The dismal Situation waste and wild, [60]
A Dungeon horrible, on all sides round
As one great Furnace flam'd, yet from those flames
No light, but rather darkness visible[217]
Serv'd only to discover sights of woe,
Regions of sorrow, doleful shades,[218] where peace [65]

---

[212] Milton gives an approximate measure of the distance from heaven to hell, rather, the length of time it took for them to fall from heaven to hell. This is with reference to *The Divine Comedy*, where Dante talks of the distance it takes to go from hell to heaven.

[213] Though Satan is immortal, being an angel, he is bound up and his powers are shaken, and he lies in the agony of hell.

[214] His torture makes him angrier with God.

[215] It must be made clear right from the start that the torment of hell that Milton mentions is not just physical; it is psychological also.

[216] Ken = saw. Over here, it means "As far as angels can see".

[217] Darkness visible = oxymoron.

[218] "doleful shades" is a reference to *The Divine Comedy*, where the spirits are mentioned as "shades" in the sense that they are mere shadows. Here, Milton means that the shades which are there

> And rest can never dwell, hope never comes
> That comes to all; but torture without end
> Still urges, and a fiery Deluge, fed
> With ever-burning Sulphur unconsum'd:[219]
> Such place Eternal Justice had prepar'd[220] [70]
> For those rebellious, here their Prison ordain'd
> In utter darkness, and their portion set
> As far remov'd from God and light of Heav'n
> As from the Center thrice to th' utmost Pole.
> O how unlike the place from whence they fell! [75]
> There the companions of his fall,[221] o'rewhelm'd
> With Floods and Whirlwinds of tempestuous fire,
> He soon discerns, and weltring by his side
> One next himself in power, and next in crime,
> Long after known in Palestine,[222] and nam'd [80]
> Beelzebub. To whom th' Arch-Enemy,

In this flaming place are sad – they do not offer respite from torture. Once more, this is psychological.

[219] This is a reference to the Bible, where Jesus tells of the eternal fire of hell and the tortured souls in this way: "Where their worm never dies and the fire is not quenched".

[220] This is once more a reference to *The Divine Comedy*, where Dante talks about an inscription on the gate of hell, where it Is stated that hell was created by "Eternal Justice".

[221] This refers to the other fallen angels.

[222] Milton, from now onwards, will mention the names of various pagan gods and demi-gods and the places where they are worshipped, and state that they were all fallen angels who deceived men to think they were gods.

In a lot of places, Satan and Beelzubub are attributed to be one, but here, they are different beings.

And thence in Heav'n call'd Satan, with bold words
Breaking the horrid silence thus began.

If thou beest he; But O how fall'n! how chang'd
From him, who in the happy Realms of Light [85]
Cloth'd with transcendent brightness didst out-shine
Myriads though bright: If he Whom mutual league,
United thoughts and counsels, equal hope
And hazard in the Glorious Enterprise,[223]
Joined with me once, now misery hath joined [90]
In equal ruin: into what Pit thou seest
From what height fall'n, so much the stronger prov'd
He with his Thunder:[224] and till then who knew
The force of those dire Arms? yet not for those,
Nor what the Potent Victor in his rage [95]
Can else inflict, do I repent or change,[225]
Though chang'd in outward lustre;[226] that fixt mind
And high disdain, from sense of injur'd merit,
That with the mightiest rais'd me to contend,
And to the fierce contention brought along [100]
Innumerable force of Spirits[227] arm'd

---

[223] This refers to the enterprise of revolting against God, which they felt was glorious. Milton wants to tell that Satan still thinks this to be glorious.

[224] Satan does not wish to acknowledge the superiority of God even now. He says that it is because of the power of thunder that God overcame them.

[225] This hubris of Satan is what led to his fall and to his further suffering. He does not wish to repent of his deeds, and prefers to be out of heaven than to express remorse.

[226] As will be told in later books, Satan's appearance has changed with his bad action. He is no longer a glorious angel in appearance, but is hideous.

[227] This refers to the other angels who revolted.

That durst dislike his reign, and me preferring,
His utmost power with adverse power oppos'd
In dubious Battle on the Plains of Heav'n,
And shook his throne.[228] What though the field be lost? [105]
All is not lost; the unconquerable Will,
And study of revenge, immortal hate,
And courage never to submit or yield:
And what is else not to be overcome?
That Glory never shall his wrath or might [110]
Extort from me. To bow and sue for grace
With suppliant knee, and defy his power,
Who from the terror of this Arm so late
Doubted his Empire, that were low indeed,
That were an ignominy and shame beneath [115]
This downfall; since by Fate the strength of Gods
And this Empyreal substance cannot fail,
Since through experience of this great event
In Arms not worse, in foresight much advanc't,
We may with more successful hope resolve [120]
To wage by force or guile eternal War
Irreconcileable, to our grand Foe,
Who now triumphs, and in th' excess of joy
Sole reigning holds the Tyranny of Heav'n.[229]

---

[228] Satan is exaggerating. He wishes to maintain his dignity as a leader, even though he is fallen.

[229] In this speech, Satan says that he will wage eternal war against God, whom he holds as their "Foe", and says that though they have been cast down and physically conquered, their will cannot be conquered, and their will is to still wage war against God. This shows his arrogance. Readers should not mistake this to be Milton's assertion of heroism, but rather, how beguiling Satan can be. As told elsewhere in the topics, Satan is not the hero of this epic…Milton's subject is man, and he views Satan as the "infernal serpent".

So spake th' Apostate Angel,[230] though in pain, [125]
Vaunting aloud, but rackt with deep despare:
And him thus answer'd soon his bold Compeer.[231]

O Prince, O Chief of many Throned Powers,
That led th' imbattelld Seraphim to War
Under thy conduct, and in dreadful deeds [130]
Fearless, endanger'd Heav'ns perpetual King;
And put to proof his high Supremacy,
Whether upheld by strength, or Chance, or Fate,
Too well I see and rue the dire event,
That with sad overthrow and foul defeat [135]
Hath lost us Heav'n, and all this mighty Host
In horrible destruction laid thus low,
As far as Gods and Heav'nly Essences
Can perish: for the mind and spirit remains
Invincible, and vigour soon returns, [140]
Though all our Glory extinct, and happy state
Here swallow'd up in endless misery.
But what if he our Conquerour, (whom I now
Of force believe Almighty, since no less
Then such could hav orepow'rd such force as ours)[232] [145]
Have left us this our spirit and strength intire
Strongly to suffer and support our pains,[233]

---

[230] This tells us in which lowly condition he is placed, and the fact that even though he is apostate, he does not cease his deception, but urges further hatred against God.

[231] i.e., Beelzebub.

[232] Beelzebub acknowledges the truth and can see through the vanity of fighting against God, and has understood that God is the Almighty. However, his loyalty is still with Satan, and it is in this choice that they all remain devils.

[233] Beelzebub feels that the strength of spirit is there in them still so that they are able to bear the pain of hell.

> That we may so suffice his vengeful ire,
> Or do him mightier service as his thralls
> By right of War, what e're his business be [150]
> Here in the heart of Hell to work in Fire,
> Or do his Errands in the gloomy Deep;[234]
> What can it then avail though yet we feel
> Strength undiminisht, or eternal being
> To undergo eternal punishment?[235] [155]
> Whereto with speedy words th' Arch-fiend[236] reply'd.
>
> Fall'n Cherube,[237] to be weak is miserable
> Doing or Suffering: but of this be sure,
> To do ought good never will be our task,
> But ever to do ill our sole delight,[238] [160]
> As being the contrary to his high will[239]

---

[234] Beelzebub is of the opinion that God will make them slaves now, and they will now have to run His errands, whatever they be, in hell.

[235] As they were angels, they were immortal. SO, Beelzebub says that their punishment will be eternal, which again has a psychological implication. It is the duration of the punishment to eternity that makes the suffering more tedious than it is physically, for physically, as Beelzebub remarks, the strength is "undiminish'd".

[236] i.e., Satan.

[237] Cherub is the short-form of Cherubim, which refers to an angelic creature of very high order.

[238] This is where (perhaps) the hamartia of Satan lies, in his decision to persist in evil, when he has the chance to change, repent and be good. He chooses to be evil and suffer, and this error in judgement brings woe for him as well as mankind.

[239] i.e., the high will of God.

Whom we resist. If then his Providence
Out of our evil seek to bring forth good,[240]
Our labour must be to pervert that end,
And out of good still to find means of evil; [165]
Which oft times may succeed, so as perhaps
Shall grieve him, if I fail not, and disturb
His inmost counsels from thir destind aim.[241]
But see the angry Victor hath recall'd
His Ministers of vengeance and pursuit[242] [170]
Back to the Gates of Heav'n: The Sulphurous Hail
Shot after us in storm, oreblown hath laid
The fiery Surge, that from the Precipice
Of Heav'n receiv'd us falling, and the Thunder,
Wing'd with red Lightning and impetuous rage, [175]
Perhaps hath spent his shafts,[243] and ceases now

---

[240] Satan understands that their evil will be turned by God so that the end is something good, but he will do his best to thwart that good end.

[241] It will be Satan's aim to see that the goodness directed by God does not reach its destination. He wishes to prevent it. Here, he once more shows his folly, for he has been defeated in the first place, and so, knows it quite well that he cannot prevent that which God ordains. His stubbornness to fight, knowing quite well he cannot win has often been commented upon as his act of heroism. However, such comments stray from the purpose which Milton sets out right at the start. Milton's purpose is to "justify the ways of God to men", where he views Satan as the "infernal serpent". Readers must not forget this.

[242] Milton makes Satan state that God has withdrawn his angels from chasing the fallen angels, and they have now gone back to heaven.

[243] Shafts refer to arrows, here, figuratively referring to the lightning streaks. Satan looks upon the cessation of lightning as if they are now "spent", that is, there is no more lightning in God's hand to strike with, so they cease. Here again we see his constant

> To bellow through the vast and boundless Deep.
> Let us not slip th' occasion, whether scorn,
> Or satiate fury yield it from our Foe.[244]
> Seest thou yon[245] dreary Plain, forlorn and wild, [180]
> The seat of desolation, void of light,
> Save what the glimmering of these livid flames
> Casts pale and dreadful? Thither let us tend[246]
> From off the tossing of these fiery waves,
> There rest, if any rest can harbour there, [185]
> And reassembling our afflicted Powers,
> Consult how we may henceforth most offend
> Our Enemy, our own loss how repair,
> How overcome this dire Calamity,
> What reinforcement we may gain from Hope, [190]
> If not what resolution from despare.
>
> Thus Satan talking to his neerest Mate
> With Head up-lift above the wave, and Eyes
> That sparkling blaz'd, his other Parts besides
> Prone on the Flood, extended long and large [195]
> Lay floating many a rood, in bulk as huge
> As whom the Fables name of monstrous size,[247]
> Titanian, or Earth-born, that warr'd on Jove,

---

tendency to look down upon his superior. He does not acknowledge that God has decided not to pursue them any more, but has left them in that state, and states that there is no more lightning with which he can strike.

[244] He wishes to utilizes this chance when they are not pursued by the forces of God.

[245] i.e., yonder = over there

[246] They wish to fly to that plain of darkness, and rest there.

[247] Milton compares the size of Satan with other mythological creatures.

Briareos or Typhon, whom the Den
By ancient Tarsus held, or that Sea-beast [200]
Leviathan,[248] which God of all his works
Created hugest that swim th' Ocean stream:
Him haply slumbring on the Norway foam
The Pilot of some small night-founder'd Skiff,
Deeming some Island, oft, as Sea-men tell, [205]
With fixed Anchor in his skaly rind[249]
Moors by his side under the Lee, while Night
Invests the Sea, and wished Morn delays:
So stretcht out huge in length the Arch-fiend lay
Chain'd on the burning Lake, nor ever thence [210]
Had ris'n or heav'd his head, but that the will
And high permission of all-ruling Heaven
Left him at large to his own dark designs,[250]

---

[248] Leviathan is a legendary creature, which is supposed to be a beast inside the sea, which man cannot tame, which is mentioned in The Bible. Some have tried to state that this creature refers to the Lochness Monster, whose whereabouts are near Ireland, and some say that this refers to the crocodile, but as no proper description of the creature is given in The Bible, the creature remains in the shrouds of mystery.

[249] Some captain once mistook the creature to be an island and anchored there. The whale has often been mistaken for an island, and Milton might be fusing the legend of the Leviathan with tales of the whale being mistaken for an island.

[250] Milton states that it was the will of God to let Satan move about there, and without God permitting it, Satan would not be able to move also. This is an allusion to The Bible, where Pilate, astounded by the silence of Jesus to his questions, asks, "Do you not answer me? Don't you know that I have the power to punish you and the power to release you?" to which Jesus answers, "You would have no power against me unless it had been granted to you from above." Milton wishes to state that Satan is under God, but critics have often used such lines to mean that Milton is hinting that the evil was permitted by God. However, as that is not what

> That with reiterated crimes he might
> Heap on himself damnation,[251] while he sought [215]
> Evil to others, and enrag'd might see
> How all his malice serv'd but to bring forth
> Infinite goodness, grace and mercy shewn
> On Man by him seduc't, but on himself
> Treble confusion, wrath and vengeance pour'd.[252] [220]
> Forthwith upright he rears from off the Pool
> His mighty Stature; on each hand the flames
> Drivn backward slope thir pointing spires, and rowld
> In billows, leave i'th' midst a horrid Vale.
> Then with expanded wings he stears his flight [225]
> Aloft, incumbent on the dusky Air
> That felt unusual weight,[253] till on dry Land
> He lights, if it were Land that ever burn'd
> With solid, as the Lake with liquid fire;
> And such appear'd in hue, as when the force [230]
> Of subterranean wind transports a Hill
> Torn from Pelorus, or the shatter'd side
> Of thundring Ætna, whose combustible
> And fewel'd entrals thence conceiving Fire,
> Sublim'd with Mineral fury, aid the Winds, [235]
> And leave a singed bottom all involv'd
> With stench and smoak: Such resting found the sole

Milton set out to do, one must not be lead astray by interpretations which forget contexts.

[251] Milton states that the purpose to let Satan be by himself was to make him more and more condemned by his continual crimes.

[252] Satan would tend to bring evil upon Mankind, but would be infuriated to see that it would result in ultimate grace and mercy (with the coming of the Saviour) for Mankind and condemnation for himself.

[253] The air was dense.

Of unblest feet.²⁵⁴   Him followed his next Mate,
Both glorying to have scap't the Stygian flood
As Gods, and by thir own recover'd strength, [240]
Not by the sufferance of supernal Power.²⁵⁵

Is this the Region, this the Soil, the Clime,
Said then the lost Arch-Angel, this the seat
That we must change for Heav'n, this mournful gloom
For that celestial light? Be it so, since he [245]
Who now is Sovran can dispose and bid
What shall be right: farthest from him is best
Whom reason hath equalled, force hath made supreme
Above his equals. Farewell happy Fields
Where Joy for ever dwells: Hail horrors, hail [250]
Infernal world, and thou profoundest Hell
Receive thy new Possessor: One who brings
A mind not to be chang'd by Place or Time.
The mind is its own place, and in it self
Can make a Heav'n of Hell, a Hell of Heav'n.²⁵⁶ [255]
What matter where,²⁵⁷ if I be still the same,
And what I should be, all but less then he
Whom Thunder hath made greater?²⁵⁸ Here at least
We shall be free; th' Almighty hath not built
Here for his envy, will not drive us hence: [260]

---

²⁵⁴ What Milton means is that Satan did not really find rest.

²⁵⁵ Satan and Beelzebub boasted that they escaped from the pool upon dry land by their will and power, and not by the permit of Heaven.

²⁵⁶ Compare this with Marlowe's *Dr. Faustus*, where Mephistophilis tells Dr. Faustus, "Whither we go is hell; Myself am hell, nor am I out of it".

²⁵⁷ i.e., it does not matter to which place I go to…

²⁵⁸ Satan still refuses to acknowledge the natural superiority of God, and tells that it is because of Thunder that God is greater.

> Here we may reign secure, and in my choice[259]
> To reign is worth ambition though in Hell:
> Better to reign in Hell, then serve in Heav'n.[260]
> But wherefore let we then our faithful friends,
> Th' associates and copartners of our loss [265]
> Lye thus astonisht on th' oblivious Pool,[261]
> And call them not to share with us their part
> In this unhappy Mansion,[262] or once more
> With rallied Arms to try what may be yet
> Regaind in Heav'n, or what more lost in Hell?[263] [270]
>
> So Satan spake, and him Beelzebub
> Thus answer'd. Leader of those Armies bright,[264]

---

[259] i.e., opinion

[260] This decision of his once more reinforces his hamartia of not acknowledging his mistake and asking for forgiveness. He wishes to reign as a devil instead of serving as an angel in heaven. This also brings out his trait as a leader – his ultimate motive is actually not the good of the other fallen angels, but to be a leader. As long as he reigns, it does not matter to him, even if the place is hell.

[261] Here, it does not mean Pool which is oblivious, but Pool of Oblivion. Milton once more brings in classical mythology, and alludes to the River Styx, one of the five rivers surrounding Hades, the underworld. Styx was the river of oblivion, that is, nothingness. It would make the bathers forget everything. All the dead souls had to bathe in this river to forget their earthly life.

[262] The "unhappy Mansion" refers to Hell.

[263] Satan wants to call the other fallen angels, who are still lying in the pool. He wants them to come and be where he is, in the "unhappy Mansion", and also thinks of the possibility of another attack on Heaven.

[264] The word "bright" is an irony, for the once-bright angels are no longer in their angelic forms.

Which but th' Onmipotent none could have foild,²⁶⁵
If once they hear that voice, their liveliest pledge
Of hope in fears and dangers, heard so oft [275]
In worst extremes, and on the perilous edge
Of battle when it rag'd, in all assaults
Their surest signal, they will soon resume
New courage and revive, though now they lie
Groveling and prostrate on yon Lake of Fire,²⁶⁶ [280]
As we erewhile,²⁶⁷ astounded and amaz'd,
No wonder, fall'n such a pernicious height.

He scarce had ceas't when the superiour Fiend
Was moving toward the shore; his ponderous shield
Ethereal temper, massy, large and round, [285]
Behind him cast; the broad circumference
Hung on his shoulders like the Moon, whose Orb
Through Optic Glass the Tuscan Artist views
At Ev'ning from the top of Fesole,²⁶⁸
Or in Valdarno, to descry new Lands, [290]
Rivers or Mountains in her spotty Globe.

---

²⁶⁵ This is to be read as "Which none but the Omnipotent could have foiled". This shows that Beelzebub understands the superiority of God.

²⁶⁶ Beelzebub asks Satan to call and rouse the other fallen angels, telling that just as his voice kept on giving them hope during battle, it would again give them hope when they hear him call to them when they are lying in the Lake of Fire.

²⁶⁷ i.e., as Satan and Beelzebub were themselves in that state a while ago.

²⁶⁸ This refers to Galileo, viewing the moon with his telescope. One of the characteristics of the epic is that there is oscillation. The lines move in past, present and future. So, Milton here alludes to the events of future, when Galileo would view the moon with his telescope.

His Spear, to equal which the tallest Pine
Hewn on Norwegian hills, to be the Mast
Of some great Ammiral, were but a wand,
He walkt with to support uneasy steps [295]
Over the burning Marle,[269] not like those steps
On Heavens Azure, and the torrid Clime
Smote on him sore besides, vaulted with Fire;
Nathless[270] he so endur'd, till on the Beach
Of that inflamed Sea, he stood and call'd [300]
His Legions, Angel Forms, who lay intrans't
Thick as Autumnal Leaves that strow the Brooks
In Vallombrosa, where th' Etrurian shades
High overarch't imbowr; or scatterd sedge
Afloat, when with fierce Winds Orion arm'd [305]
Hath vext the Red-Sea Coast, whose waves orethrew
Busiris and his Memphian Chivalry,
While with perfidious hatred they pursu'd
The Sojourners of Goshen, who beheld
From the safe shore thir floating Carkases [310]
And broken Chariot Wheels, so thick bestrown
Abject and lost lay these, covering the Flood,
Under amazement of thir hideous change.
He call'd so loud, that all the hollow Deep
Of Hell resounded. Princes,[271] Potentates, [315]
Warriers, the Flowr of Heav'n, once yours, now lost,
If such astonishment as this can sieze
Eternal spirits; or have ye chos'n this place
After the toil of Battle to repose
Your wearied virtue, for the ease you find [320]

---

[269] Satan walked with the support of his spear, as the steps were difficult. His spear was so tall that in comparison to it, a mast made from the tallest pine for some admiral would look like a wand.

[270] i.e., Nonetheless

[271] Satan's speech towards his fallen angels begins from "Princes".

To slumber here, as in the Vales of Heav'n?[272]
Or in this abject posture have ye sworn
To adore the Conqueror? who now beholds
Cherub and Seraph[273] rowling in the Flood
With scatter'd Arms and Ensigns, till anon [325]
His swift pursuers from Heav'n Gates discern
Th' advantage, and descending tread us down
Thus drooping, or with linked Thunderbolts
Transfix us to the bottom of this Gulf.
Awake, arise, or be for ever fall'n.[274] [330]

They heard, and were abasht, and up they sprung
Upon the wing, as when men wont to watch
On duty, sleeping found by whom they dread,
Rouse and bestir themselves ere well awake.
Nor did they not perceive the evil plight [335]
In which they were, or the fierce pains not feel;
Yet to their General's Voice they soon obeyed
Innumerable. As when the potent Rod
Of Amrams So[275] in Egypt's evil day

---

[272] Satan speaks in such a provoking manner so that they are roused. He asks if they have chosen to rest in this place, being tired from the battle. He intends that hearing this, they will immediately rouse up.

[273] Seraph is the short form of Seraphim. Cherubim and Seraphim were both higher orders of angels.

[274] Satan tells that if they do not rise now, God might send his thunders again, and fix them to the bottom of the gulf. He urges them to arise at once, or remain in a fallen state forevermore. This speech brings out the leader-like qualities in him. He cleverly speaks in such a manner so that they are roused up, being provoked. They do not understand that even if they rouse up, they remain "fallen" angels, for they will never go to heaven again.

[275] This refers to Moses and his staff, by which he did wonders in Egypt.

Wav'd round the Coast, up call'd a pitchy cloud [340]
Of Locusts, warping on the Eastern Wind,
That ore the Realm of impious Pharaoh hung
Like Night, and darken'd all the Land of Nile:[276]
So numberless were those bad Angels seen
Hovering on wing under the Cope of Hell [345]
'Twixt upper, nether, and surrounding Fires;
Till, as a signal giv'n, th' uplifted Spear
Of their great Sultan waving to direct
Their course, in even balance down they light
On the firm brimstone, and fill all the Plain;[277] [350]
A multitude, like which the populous North
Pour'd never from her frozen loins, to pass
Rhene or the Danaw, when her barbarous Sons
Came like a Deluge on the South, and spread
Beneath Gibralter to the Lybian sands. [355]
Forthwith from every Squadron and each Band
The Heads and Leaders thither hast where stood
Their great Commander; Godlike shapes and forms
Excelling human, Princely Dignities,
And Powers that erst in Heaven sat on Thrones; [360]
Though of their Names in heav'nly Records now
Be no memorial blotted out and ras'd
By their Rebellion, from the Books of Life.[278]
Nor had they yet among the Sons of Eve

---

[276] This refers to the darkness that befell Egypt as one of the plagues.

[277] Satan raises his spear as a signal and they follow that course and land in safety.

[278] Milton states that the names of the fallen angels were blotted out of the records of Heaven, and the Book of Life did not have their names any more.

Got them new Names,[279] till wandring ore the Earth, [365]
Through Gods high sufferance for the trial of man,
By falsities and lies the greatest part
Of Mankind they corrupted to forsake
God their Creator, and th' invisible
Glory of him that made them, to transform [370]
Oft to the Image of a Brute,[280] adorn'd
With gay Religions full of Pomp and Gold,
And Devils to adore for Deities:
Then were they known to men by various Names,
And various Idols through the Heathen World. [375]
Say, Muse, their Names then known, who first, who last,
Rous'd from the slumber, on that fiery Couch,
At their great Emperors call, as next in worth
Came singly where he stood on the bare strand,
While the promiscuous croud stood yet aloof? [380]
The chief were those who from the Pit of Hell
Roaming to seek their prey on earth, durst fix
Their Seats long after next the Seat of God,
Their Altars by his Altar, Gods ador'd
Among the Nations round, and durst abide [385]
Jehovah thundring out of Sion, thron'd
Between the Cherubim;[281] yea, often plac'd
Within his Sanctuary it self their Shrines,
Abominations; and with cursed things

---

[279] What Milton tries to tell is that these fallen angels began to be worshipped by men under various names. They were actually demons, whom men worshipped under other names. Milton will now proceed to list various tribal gods and goddesses and state that they were all coming from various fallen angels.

[280] Many tribal religions practice worshipping animals, and Milton here states that they were fallen angels, changing shapes and appearing as great beasts to men, whom men mistook to be gods.

[281] This is a reference to various passages of The Bible, where the throne of God is between Cherubims.

His holy Rites, and solemn Feasts profan'd, [390]
And with their darkness durst affront his light.
First Moloch,[282] horrid King besmear'd with blood
Of human sacrifice, and parents tears,
Though for the noise of Drums and Timbrels loud
Thir childrens cries unheard, that past through fire [395]
To his grim Idol. Him the Ammonite
Worshipt in Rabba[283] and her watry Plain,
In Argob and in Basan, to the stream
Of utmost Arnon. Nor content with such
Audacious neighbourhood, the wisest heart [400]
Of Solomon he led by fraud to build
His Temple right against the Temple of God[284]
On that opprobrious Hill, and made his Grove
The pleasant Vally of Hinnom,[285] Tophet thence
And black Gehenna call'd, the Type of Hell. [405]
Next Chemos, th' obscene dread of Moabs Sons,
From Aroar to Nebo,[286] and the wild
Of Southmost Abarim;[287] in Hesebon[288]
And Horonaim, Seon's Realm, beyond
The flowry Dale of Sibma clad with Vines, [410]

---

[282] God of the sun, seen as a destructive power.

[283] Capital of Ammonites

[284] Solomon, persuaded by his wives, built "high places" on the Mount of Olives to Moloch, Chemos and Astarte.

[285] The garden in this valley was where rites to Moloch were performed, and so, it was defiled.

[286] Aroer was a small town on the bank of the Arnon. Nebo was the mountain from the top of which Moses saw the Promised Land.

[287] This was the mountain range of which Nebo was a mount.

[288] This was the city of Sihon, the King of the Amorites.

And Eleale to th' Asphaltick Pool.[289]
Peor[290] his other Name, when he entic'd
Israel in Sittim on their march from Nile
To do him wanton rites, which cost them woe.[291]
Yet thence his lustful Orgies[292] he enlarg'd [415]
Even to that Hill of scandal,[293] by the Grove
Of Moloch[294] homicide, lust hard by hate;
Till good Josiah drove them thence to Hell.[295]
With these came they, who from the bordering flood
Of old Euphrates to the Brook that parts [420]
Egypt from Syrian ground,[296] had general Names
Of Baalim and Ashtaroth, those male,
These Feminine.[297] For Spirits when they please

---

[289] The Dead Sea.

[290] Found in The Bible as Baal-Peor, or simply, Baal.

[291] The people of Israel, returning from Egypt, often erred. This refers to the time when they offered sacrifice to Baal in the region of Moab, because of which God destroyed "twenty and four thousand" (Numb. 25:9)

[292] i.e., rites

[293] Refers to the Mount of Olives, where rites to Chemos were performed.

[294] See note 101.

[295] Josiah put and end to this and the place was turned to the common refuse-place of Jerusalem.

[296] The Besor.

[297] Baalim = Baal. Also known as Baal-Berith, Baal-Zebub and Baal-Peor. Baalim was the collective name of his various manifestations. Ashtaroth was the collective name of the moon goddess. As singular, her name is Ashtoreth. Baal and Ashtoreth were the sun and moon deities, respectively, and very important for the Phoenicians and the Cannanites.

Can either Sex assume, or both; so soft
And uncompounded is their Essence pure, [425]
Not ti'd or manacl'd with joint or limb,
Nor founded on the brittle strength of bones,
Like cumbrous flesh; but in what shape they choose
Dilated or condens't, bright or obscure,
Can execute their aerie purposes, [430]
And works of love or enmity fulfil.
For those the Race of Israel oft forsook
Their living strength,[298] and unfrequented left
His righteous Altar, bowing lowly down
To bestial Gods; for which their heads as low [435]
Bow'd down in Battle,[299] sunk before the Spear
Of despicable foes. With these in troop
Came Astoreth, whom the Phoenicians call'd
Astarte, Queen of Heav'n, with crescent Horns;[300]
To whose bright Image nightly by the Moon [440]
Sidonian Virgins paid their Vows and Songs,
In Sion also not unsung, where stood
Her Temple on th' offensive Mountain, built
By that uxorious King,[301] whose heart though large,
Beguil'd by fair Idolatresses, fell [445]
To Idols foul. Thammuz[302] came next behind,

---

[298] That is, Jehovah, their only God, the Creator, against whom Satan rebels and is thrown to Hell.

[299] Milton states that because they went after other gods and goddesses, the Almighty gave them to their enemies in battle. As is written in The Bible, God tells that because of their idol-worship, He will "carry them beyond Babylon", which did happen, and they were scattered all over the earth.

[300] See note 100 and 113.

[301] See note 100.

[302] Thammuz was the son of Cyneras, King of Byblus in Phoenicia. He was slain by a boar in Lebanon. It was held that every year, his

Whose annual wound in Lebanon allur'd
The Syrian Damsels to lament his fate
In amorous dittyes all a Summer's day,
While smooth Adonis from his native Rock [450]
Ran purple to the Sea, suppos'd with blood
Of Thammuz yearly wounded: the Love-tale
Infected Sion's daughters with like heat,
Whose wanton passions in the sacred Porch
Ezekiel[303] saw, when by the Vision led [455]
His eye survey'd the dark Idolatries
Of alienated Judah. Next came one
Who mourn'd in earnest, when the Captive Ark
Maim'd his brute Image, head and hands lopt off
In his own Temple, on the grunsel[304] edge, [460]
Where he fell flat, and sham'd his Worshipers:[305]
Dagon his Name, Sea Monster, upward Man
And downward Fish: yet had his Temple high

---

blood flowed anew and he came to life. Annual festivals were held to celebrate the occasion. His death was lamented at first, and his revival was celebrated next. In Greek myth, Thammuz is identical with Adonis, and represents the seasons of summer (revival) and winter (death). The River Adonis would redden each year in summer, due to the mixing of the water with red soil, brought by the spring torrents from the Lebanon heights. This gave the concept of the flowing of blood each year.

[303] One of the Jewish prophets.

[304] threshold

[305] This refers to Dagon, the god of the Philistines. The Philistines had once defeated Israel, and had captured the Ark of the Covenant, where The Ten Commandments were kept. This Ark was placed before the idol of Dagon, and the next day, it was found that the idol had fallen to the ground, it's face and the palms of the hands broken. (1 Sam. 5:4)

Rear'd in Azotus,[306] dreaded through the Coast
Of Palestine, in Gath and Ascalon [465]
And Accaron and Gaza's frontier bounds.
Him follow'd Rimmon, whose delightful Seat
Was fair Damascus, on the fertile Banks
Of Abbana and Pharphar,[307] lucid streams.
He also against the house of God was bold: [470]
A Leper once he lost and gain'd a King,[308]
Ahaz his sottish[309] Conqueror, whom he drew
Gods Altar to disparage and displace
For one of Syrian mode, whereon to burn
His odious off'rings, and adore the Gods [475]
Whom he had vanquished. After these appear'd
A crew who under Names of old Renown,
Osiris, Isis, Orus[310] and their Train[311]
With monstrous shapes and sorceries abus'd
Fanatic Egypt and her Priests, to seek [480]
Their wandering Gods disguis'd in brutish forms
Rather than human. Nor did Israel scape
Th' infection when their borrow'd Gold compos'd
The Calf in Oreb:[312] and the Rebel King[313]

---

[306] Greek spelling of Ashdod, one of the important cities of Patestine.

[307] These were two rivers. Damascus lay between them.

[308] Naaman was the leper and Ahaz was the King. See 2 Kings. 5.

[309] foolish

[310] Osiris was the chief god of the Egyptians, and was worshipped as a bull. Isis was a goddess with the body of a woman but horns like a cow. Orus, or, Horus, was their sun-god.

[311] i.e., the other gods and goddesses of Egypt.

[312] This refers to Israel's idol-worshipping in the desert, when Moses was on Mount Sinai. They melted their gold and shaped it

Doubl'd that sin in Bethel and in Dan, [485]
Lik'ning his Maker to the Grazed Ox,
Jehovah, who in one Night when he pass'd
From Egypt marching, equal'd with one stroke
Both her first born and all her bleating Gods.[314]
Belial[315] came last, then whom a Spirit more lewd [490]
Fell not from Heaven, or more gross to love
Vice for it self: To him no Temple stood
Or Altar smok'd; yet who more oft then he
In Temples and at Altars, when the Priest
Turns Atheist, as did Ely's Sons,[316] who fill'd [495]
With lust and violence the house of God.
In Courts and Palaces he also Reigns
And in luxurious Cities, where the noise
Of riot ascends above their loftiest Towers,
And injury and outrage: And when Night [500]

---

to that of a bull-calf, and worshipped that. God commanded Moses to go down, and Moses, seeing their idolatry, was angered to such an extent that he threw the tablets where the commandments were written, and they broke. The offenders were all put to death, and the tablets were made again.

[313] Jeroboam, who rebelled against Rehoboam. He made the calves of gold, and so, Milton says that he "doubled" the sin. One was set in Bethel and the other, in Dan.

[314] This is again oscillation. Milton suddenly goes back in time from Jeroboam to Moses, and refers to the tenth and the last plague of Egypt, when all the first-born children of Egypt were killed in one night, man and animals. As the gods of Egypt all had animal-like forms, and as the first born of the animals were also killed, Milton states that both the Egyptians and their gods were equalled in death in one night in the last plague of Egypt.

[315] Belial was no deity, but was a word which meant worthlessness profitless or wickedness. Milton connects it with lust.

[316] See 1 Samuel 2:12-17.

Darkens the Streets, then wander forth the Sons
Of Belial, flown with insolence and wine.
Witness the Streets of Sodom, and that night
In Gibeah, when the hospitable door
Expos'd a Matron to avoid worse rape. [505]
These were the prime in order and in might;
The rest were long to tell, though far renown'd,
Th' Ionian Gods, of Javans Issue held
Gods, yet confest later then Heav'n and Earth
Their boasted Parents; Titan Heav'n's first born [510]
With his enormous brood, and birthright seiz'd
By younger Saturn, he from mightier Jove
His own and Rhea's Son like measure found;
So Jove usurping reign'd:[317] these first in Crete
And Ida known, thence on the Snowy top [515]
Of cold Olympus rul'd the middle Air
Their highest Heav'n; or on the Delphian[318] Cliff,
Or in Dodona, and through all the bounds
Of Doric Land;[319] or who with Saturn old

---

[317] Milton now moves to Greek mythology. As per Greek and Roman mythology, Uranus and Gyae (Earth) were the oldest, whose intercourse led to the birth of Cronos (Time), also known as Saturn in Roman and 11 other Titans. Cronos came to power and Uranus receded in the sky. Cronos lay with Earth, which led to the birth of Zeus and others. However, Cronos buried them inside the earth, for he feared his throne might be lost. Rhea, another name for Earth, counselled them to revolt, and one time, when Cronos came to make love to Rhea, Zeus and the others revolted and he was defeated. Zeus, called Jupiter (shortened to Jove in Roman myth) took his father's place. When Milton refers to Titan, he means the oldest of the 12 Titans, who was overthrown by Cronos.

[318] Delphi is famous for the Temple of Apollo, and the Delphian oracles were famous for the powers of prophesy.

[319] Refers to Greece.

Fled over Adria to th' Hesperian Fields,[320] [520]
And ore the Celtic roam'd the utmost Isles.[321]
All these and more came flocking; but with looks
Down cast and damp, yet such wherein appear'd
Obscure some glimps of joy, to have found their chief
Not in despair, to have found themselves not lost [525]
In loss it self; which on his count'nance cast
Like doubtful hue: but he his wonted pride
Soon recollecting, with high words, that bore
Semblance of worth, not substance,[322] gently rais'd
Their fainting courage, and dispel'd their fears. [530]
Then straight commands that at the warlike sound
Of Trumpets loud and Clarions be upreard
His mighty Standard; that proud honour claim'd
Azazel as his right, a Cherube tall:
Who forthwith from the glittering Staff unfurld [535]
Th' Imperial Ensign, which full high advanc'd
Shone like a Meteor streaming to the Wind
With Gemms and Golden lustre rich imblaz'd,
Seraphic arms and Trophies: all the while
Sonorous metal blowing Martial sounds: [540]
At which the universal Host upsent
A shout that tore Hells Concave, and beyond
Frighted the Reign of Chaos and old Night.
All in a moment through the gloom were seen
Ten thousand Banners rise into the Air [545]
With Orient Colours waving: with them rose

---

[320] As per Greek and Roman mythology, Saturn fled to Italy ("Hesperian fields")

[321] Britain.

[322] Milton tells very clearly that Satan's speech sounded grand, but lacked actual power.

A Forest huge of Spears:³²³ and thronging Helms
Appear'd, and serried shields in thick array
Of depth immeasurable: Anon they move
In perfect Phalanx to the Dorian mood³²⁴ [550]
Of Flutes and soft Recorders; such as rais'd
To hight of noblest temper Hero's old
Arming to Battle, and in stead of rage
Deliberate valour breath'd, firm and unmov'd
With dread of death to flight or foul retreat, [555]
Nor wanting power to mitigate and swage
With solemn touches, troubl'd thoughts, and chase
Anguish and doubt and fear and sorrow and pain
From mortal or immortal minds. Thus they
Breathing united force with fixed thought [560]
Mov'd on in silence to soft Pipes that charm'd
Their painful steps³²⁵ o're the burnt soile; and now
Advanc'd in view, they stand, a horrid Front
Of dreadful length and dazling Arms, in guise
Of Warriers old with order'd Spear and Shield, [565]
Awaiting what command their mighty Chief
Had to impose: He through the armed Files
Darts his experienc'd eye, and soon traverse
The whole Battalion views, their order due,
Their visages and stature as of Gods, [570]
Their number last he sums. And now his heart
Distends with pride, and hardening in his strength
Glories: For never since created man,

---

[323] So many spears that it looked like a forest. Compare once more the appearance of each spear with "tallest pine", as Milton remarked in the previous lines.

[324] This was a special type of marching order. Milton is stating that the fallen angels are now marching in ranks to go to Satan.

[325] Contrast the "soft Pipes" with the "painful steps" and once more, the psychological aspect is revealed.

Met such imbodied force, as nam'd with these
Could merit more then that small infantry [575]
Warr'd on by Cranes:[326] though all the Giant brood
Of Phlegra[327] with th' Heroic Race[328] were join'd
That fought at Theb's and Ilium,[329] on each side
Mixt with auxiliar Gods; and what resounds
In Fable or Romance of Uthers Son [580]
Begirt with British and Armoric Knights;[330]
And all who since, Baptiz'd or Infidel
Jousted in Aspramont or Montalban,
Damasco, or Marocco, or Trebisond,
Or whom Biserta sent from Afric shore [585]
When Charlemain with all his Peerage fell
By Fontarabbia.[331] Thus far these beyond
Compare of mortal prowess, yet observ'd

---

[326] Any other army would look like an army of pygmies before the army of Satan. The purpose of stating this is two-fold. In the first place, it would add to the epic style of grandness, and in the second place, it would assert God's superiority that such a great army was thrown out of Heaven by the Power of God.

[327] Old name of Pallene peninsula, where, as per mythology, the giants were born.

[328] This refers to the Greeks.

[329] Milton refers to all the Greek warriors who fought in Thebes and Ilium.

[330] Milton refers to the Arthurian legends. "Uther's son" refers to King Arthur, who was the son of Uther Pendragon. From Greek heroes, Milton now moves to English heroes.

"Armoric" means "of Armorica", which was another name for Brittany (now Britain).

[331] Milton now alludes to several medieval romances, mainly Italian in origin.

Their dread commander: he above the rest
In shape and gesture proudly eminent [590]
Stood like a Tower; his form had yet not lost
All her Original brightness,[332] nor appear'd
Less then Arch Angel ruind, and th' excess
Of Glory obscur'd: As when the Sun new ris'n
Looks through the Horizontal misty Air [595]
Shorn of his Beams, or from behind the Moon
In dim Eclips disastrous twilight sheds
On half the Nations, and with fear of change
Perplexes Monarchs.[333] Dark'n'd so, yet shone
Above them all th' Arch Angel: but his face [600]
Deep scars of Thunder had intrencht, and care[334]
Sat on his faded cheek, but under Brows
Of dauntless courage, and considerate Pride
Waiting revenge: cruel his eye, but cast
Signs of remorse and passion to behold [605]
The fellows of his crime,[335] the followers rather
(Far other once beheld in bliss) condemn'd
For ever now to have their lot in pain,
Millions of Spirits for his fault amerc'd
Of Heav'n, and from Eternal Splendors flung [610]
For his revolt, yet faithful how they stood,
Their Glory withered. As when Heaven's Fire
Hath scath'd the Forest Oaks, or Mountain Pines,
With singed top their stately growth though bare

---

[332] Satan's form had not yet fully changed, but was changing. He lost his brightness, though not fully. It must be noted that before his fall, he was known as Lucifer, which meant bearer of light.

[333] Eclipses were held to be ill omens, and Milton means that even kings used to be worried during eclipses.

[334] i.e., worry

[335] Satan is inwardly aware of his "crime".

Stands on the blasted Heath.[336] He now prepar'd [615]
To speak; whereat their doubl'd Ranks they bend
From wing to wing, and half enclose him round
With all his Peers: attention held them mute.
Thrice he assayd, and thrice in spight of scorn,[337]
Tears such as Angels weep,[338] burst forth: at last [620]
Words interwove with sighs found out their way.

O Myriads of immortal Spirits, O Powers
Matchless, but with th' Almighty, and that strife
Was not inglorious, though th' event was dire,
As this place testifies, and this dire change [625]
Hateful to utter: but what power of mind
Foreseeing or presaging, from the Depth
Of knowledge past or present, could have fear'd,
How such united force of Gods, how such
As stood like these, could ever know repulse? [630]
For who can yet beleeve, though after loss,
That all these puissant Legions, whose exile
Hath emptied Heav'n, shall fail to re-ascend

---

[336] The state of the other fallen angels has been compared with tall trees which has been blasted in forest fire, and have now become black. This darkness of the angels is literal as well as figurative. Literally, they have lost their glory and brightness, and figuratively, they have become "dark" with their evil ensigns.

[337] The significance of the number three must not go unnoticed. Three, Seven and Nine are held to be numbers associated with divinity or something supernatural, and sometimes, ominous. So, here, Satan performs his action three times. Pope turns this to mock-usage in his mock-epic 'The Rape of the Lock'.

[338] Here, Milton brings out how depressed Satan is. However, his description does not dwell upon the tears, but is simply like a passing comment, for Milton does not wish the readers to feel pity for Satan. His words serve to bring out the miserable condition of Satan more than the pitiful condition.

Self-rais'd, and repossess thir native seat?
For mee be witness all the Host of Heav'n, [635]
If counsels different, or danger shun'd
By me, have lost our hopes. But he who reigns
Monarch in Heav'n, till then as one secure
Sat on his Throne, upheld by old repute,
Consent or custome, and his Regal State [640]
Put forth at full, but still his strength conceal'd,
Which tempted our attempt, and wrought our fall.[339]
Henceforth his might we know, and know our own
So as not either to provoke, or dread
New war, provok'd; our better part remains [645]
To work in close design, by fraud or guile
What force effected not:[340] that he no less
At length from us may find, who overcomes
By force, hath overcome but half his foe.
Space may produce new Worlds;[341] whereof so rife [650]
There went a fame in Heav'n that he ere long
Intended to create, and therein plant
A generation,[342] whom his choice regard

---

[339] Satan says that God had not shown to them his full power, and so, they underestimated him and attempted to overcome Him in the rebellion. In the rebellion, their inferiority was seen, and they were cast into hell.

[340] Satan says that now, they will not work against God by use of force, but by guile, that is, by means of deception.

[341] The rebellion of the angels was supposed to have taken place before the creation mentioned in the Bible. In other words, this happens before the Seven Days of Creation, and the Seven Days of Creation, as found in the Bible, does not refer to the entire creation. The angels were created before, and so, it seems, was hell. So, Satan over here prophesies that new "Worlds" might be created later, as he did hear a rumour of that sort when he was still in heaven.

Should favour equal to the Sons of Heaven:
Thither, if but to pry, shall be perhaps
Our first eruption, thither or elsewhere: [655]
For this Infernal Pit shall never hold
Cælestial Spirits in Bondage, nor th' Abyss
Long under darkness cover. But these thoughts
Full Counsel must mature: Peace is despaird, [660]
For who can think Submission? War then, War
Open or understood must be resolv'd.

He spake: and to confirm his words, out-flew
Millions of flaming swords, drawn from the thighs
Of mighty Cherubim; the sudden blaze [665]
Far round illumin'd hell: highly they rag'd
Against the Highest, and fierce with grasped arms
Clash'd on their sounding Shields the din of war,
Hurling defiance toward the vault of Heav'n.[343]

There stood a Hill not far whose griesly top [670]
Belch'd fire and rowling smoke; the rest entire
Shone with a glossy scurff, undoubted sign
That in his womb was hid metallic Ore,
The work of Sulphur. Thither wing'd with speed
A numerous Brigade hasten'd. As when Bands [675]
Of Pioners with Spade and Pickax arm'd
Forerun the Royal Camp, to trench a Field,
Or cast a Rampart. Mammon[344] led them on,
Mammon, the least erected Spirit that fell
From heav'n, for ev'n in heav'n his looks and thoughts [680

---

[342] This refers to human beings.

[343] Upon hearing Satan, the other fallen angels all took out their swords and raised them high, and shouted defiance (once more) to Heaven and God.

[344] Mammon was the pagan god of money. Milton makes him a fallen angel also.

]
Were always downward bent, admiring more
The riches of Heav'ns pavement, trod'n Gold,
Then aught divine or holy else enjoy'd
In vision beatific: by him first
Men also, and by his suggestion taught, [685]
Ransack'd the Center,[345] and with impious hands
Rifl'd the bowels of their mother Earth
For Treasures better hid. Soon had his crew
Op'nd into the Hill a spacious wound
And dig'd out ribs of Gold. Let none admire [690]
That riches grow in Hell;[346] that soil may best
Deserve the precious bane. And here let those
Who boast in mortal things, and wond'ring tell
Of Babel, and the works of Memphian Kings
Learn how their greatest Monuments of Fame, [695]
And Strength and Art are easily out-done
By Spirits reprobate, and in an hour
What in an age they with incessant toil
And hands innumerable scarce perform.
Nigh on the Plain in many cells prepar'd, [700]
That underneath had veins of liquid fire[347]
Sluc'd from the Lake, a second multitude
With wondrous Art found out the massy Ore,
Severing each kind, and scum'd the Bullion dross:
A third as soon had form'd within the ground [705]
A various mould, and from the boiling cells

---

[345] i.e., Men began to dig under the earth ('Centre') for diamond and other precious stones.

[346] The readers might be awed in thinking that Hell has riches, and so, Milton warns the readers that they should not be greedy of the gold which is found in Hell, for they would serve as "bane" to those who seek the gold of Hell.

[347] i.e., Lava

By strange conveyance fill'd each hollow nook,
As in an Organ from one blast of wind
To many a row of Pipes the sound-board breaths.
Anon out of the earth a Fabric huge [710]
Rose like an Exhalation, with the sound
Of Dulcet[348] Symphonies and voices sweet,
Built like a Temple, where Pilasters round
Were set, and Doric pillars overlaid
With Golden Architrave; nor did there want [715]
Cornice or Freeze, with bossy Sculptures grav'n,
The Roof was fretted Gold. Not Babylon,
Nor great Alcairo such magnificence
Equal'd in all their glories, to inshrine
Belus or Serapis their Gods, or seat [720]
Their Kings, when Egypt with Assyria strove
In wealth and luxury. Th' ascending pile
Stood fixt her stately highth, and strait the dores
Op'ning thir brazen foulds discover wide
Within, her ample spaces, o're the smooth [725]
And level pavement: from the arched roof
Pendant by suttle Magic many a row
Of Starry Lamps and blazing Cressets fed
With Naphtha and Asphaltus yeilded light
As from a sky. The hasty multitude [730]
Admiring enter'd, and the work some praise
And some the Architect: his hand was known
In Heav'n by many a Towred structure high,
Where Scepter'd Angels held thir residence,
And sat as Princes, whom the supreme King [735]
Exalted to such power, and gave to rule,
Each in his Hierarchie, the Orders bright.
Nor was his name unheard or unador'd
In ancient Greece; and in Ausonian land
Men call'd him Mulciber; and how he fell [740]
From Heav'n, they fabl'd, thrown by angry Jove
Sheer o're the Chrystal Battlements: from Morn

---

[348] i.e., Sweet

To Noon he fell, from Noon to dewy Eve,
A Summers day; and with the setting Sun
Dropt from the Zenith like a falling Star, [745]
On Lemnos th' Ægean Ile: thus they relate,
Erring; for he with this rebellious rout
Fell long before; nor aught avail'd him now
To have built in Heav'n high Towrs; nor did he scape
By all his Engins, but was headlong sent [750]
With his industrious crew to build in hell.
Mean while the winged Haralds by command
Of Sovran power, with awful Ceremony
And Trumpets sound throughout the Host proclaim
A solemn Councel forthwith to be held [755]
At Pandæmonium, the high Capital
Of Satan and his Peers: thir summons call'd
From every Band and squared Regiment
By place or choice the worthiest; they anon
With hunderds and with thousands trooping came [760]
Attended: all access was throng'd, the Gates
And Porches wide, but chief the spacious Hall
(Though like a cover'd field, where Champions bold
Wont ride in arm'd, and at the Soldans chair
Defi'd the best of Paynim chivalry [765]
To mortal combat or carreer with Lance)
Thick swarm'd, both on the ground and in the air,
Brusht with the hiss of russling wings. As Bees
In spring time, when the Sun with Taurus rides,
Pour forth thir populous youth about the Hive [770]
In clusters; they among fresh dews and flowers
Flie to and fro, or on the smoothed Plank,
The suburb of thir Straw-built Cittadel,
New rub'd with Baum, expatiate and confer
Thir State affairs. So thick the aerie crowd [775]
Swarm'd and were straitn'd; till the Signal giv'n.
Behold a wonder! they but now who seemd
In bigness to surpass Earths Giant Sons
Now less then smallest Dwarfs, in narrow room

Throng numberless, like that Pigmean Race [780]
Beyond the Indian Mount, or Faerie Elves,
Whose midnight Revels, by a Forrest side
Or Fountain some belated Peasant sees,
Or dreams he sees, while over-head the Moon
Sits Arbitress, and neerer to the Earth [785]
Wheels her pale course, they on thir mirth and dance
Intent, with jocond Music charm his ear;
At once with joy and fear his heart rebounds.
Thus incorporeal Spirits to smallest forms
Reduc'd thir shapes immense, and were at large, [790]
Though without number still amidst the Hall
Of that infernal Court. But far within
And in thir own dimensions like themselves
The great Seraphic Lords and Cherubim
In close recess and secret conclave sat [795]
A thousand Demy-Gods on golden seats,
Frequent and full. After short silence then
And summons read, the great consult began.

The invocation

John Milton, the great Puritan poet, mentions his intention of justifying "the ways of God to Men" in his invocation of the English epic Paradise Lost. These words may seem like a distant echo of the lines "Prepare the way of the Lord," to "make its paths straight" (Matthew 3:3). It is quite evident from the start that Milton, though he talks of men of all races, that is men in general, he is actually concerned about a particular section of people -- the Christians. The opening lines of the epic, "Of Man's first disobedience, and the fruit/Of that forbidden tree" draws our image to the Biblical tale of the fall of man as a result of the temptation by Satan. The image continues, and becomes stronger with the words "one greater Man restore us, and regain the blissful seat". The image of Christ is too prominent to be missed by any reader. Here, too, Milton rearranges the words of the Bible "... as by one man's disobedience many were made sinners, so also by one Man's obedience many will be made righteous" (Romans 5:`19). Milton also voices similar thoughts in his treatise *Of Education*, where he writes, "The end then of Learning to repair the ruins of our first Parents by regaining to know God aright, and out of that knowledge to love him".

As is the convention of the epic poem, Milton calls upon a Muse to aid him in his invocation, but it is not one of the classical muses who dwelt on Mt. Helicon, from whom Homer and Virgil got inspiration, rather, it is the "Heavenly Muse", the Holy Spirit, whose aid Milton asks for. So, though he follows the Greek "pagan" poets in following the epic convention, he makes his own. In fact, he calls upon the Holy Spirit to make him "soar above the Aonian mount", above the reach of the pagan gods and goddesses, and makes the Christian element superior to that of the Greeks, or any other religion. He, thus, pursues the cause of Christianity as a religion set above others by the Sovereign and Omnipotent God.

By invoking the "Heavenly Muse" to inspire him, Milton also takes on the honour of self-asserted prophethood, or even that of a human saviour. He draws a parallel between his task of writing the epic and that of Moses (of leading the Israelites out of Egypt) and even that of Christ Himself (saving the people from sin and leading them towards the path of salvation). Whether the latter claim is sure or not, whether it was Milton's idea to compare himself with his Lord, the Saviour, it is certain that Milton does think of himself in high terms, to perform "Things unattempted yet in prose or rhyme". We will never know if God had actually told Milton to "justify" His ways before men by taking the "unattempted" task through means of poetry. In Book II of *The Reason of Church Government*, Milton declares his desire to write a great work that will serve to glorify England as earlier poets had glorified their native lands and culture.

However, after the analogy with Moses, Milton commits his first act of heresy. He says: "In the beginning how the Heavens and Earth/Rose out of Chaos". The raising of creation from chaos is basically the Greek concept; Christianity lays down that God created the universe *ex nihilos* (out of nothing). But he quickly repents for his heresy by going back to dog or the temple of God on Sion (now Zion) Hill. He makes the "Sion Hill" equivalent and superior to Mount Helicon ("intends to soar/Above the Aonian mount"). Milton then talks of Siloa's brook, which is mentioned in Isaiah 7:6, "the waters of Siloa that go softly" and in the description of "pool" in John 9:7-11. One of the reasons why Milton might have referred to Siloa may be to compare its waters with the waters of Aganippe ("the dark-coloured") which is frequented by the Classical Muses. Indicating the passage in *Lyc. 15, 16*, Milton addresses the Muses as "Sisters of the sacred well, that from beneath the seat of Jove doth spring". He takes Hesiod's thoughts, and gives it a scriptural investiture. The focus is on the complete parallel between the classical muses on the spring that rises by the altar of Zeus, and the Heavenly Muse Who haunts the stream that flows by the Temple ("the oracle") of the Almighty.

Milton wants to be lifted for higher inspiration, so as to treat of higher things, higher than the classical poets whose inspiration came from the Muses of antiquity. By saying "no middle flight", he intends to "soar" to the highest "Empyrean". The Aonian Mount is actually Mount Helicon, in Boeotia, sacred to the Muses, hence their title Aonides.

It is in the following lines Milton's puritan spirit expresses itself. "…O Spirit, dost prefer/Before all temples the upright heart and pure". He lashes his pen against the corrupt practices of the Anglican Church. Again, we find an echo of the lines in the Gospel of Christ according to John, where Christ says, "For the Father is Spirit" and that "the day is coming, when" people "would worship the Father" "neither" in the temple, nor on the mountain", but " in spirit and in truth" for God "is seeking such to worship Him". In a treatise, *On Christian Doctrine*, Milton relied solely on the text of the Bible to formulate his ideas, even at the risk of denying commonly accepted Church doctrine.

Milton seeks the instruction of the Heavenly Muse, the Holy Spirit, for it "know'st". Here, we see Milton's acceptance of his ignorance and his subjection before God. He not only accepts that he does not know what happened at that time – and before Creation – but also acknowledges that God was there at the very beginning. "I am the Alpha and the Omega, the Beginning and the End, the First and the Last." (Rev. 22:13) Milton then proceeds to build the imagery by talking about the dove. He writes, "...with mighty wings outspread,/Dove-like sat'st brooding on the vast Abyss, and mad'st it pregnant:" The concept of Dove is historical and religious. When Christ was baptized, the Sprit of God was supposed to have descended upon Him as a Dove ("...the heaven was opened. And the Holy Spirit descended in bodily form like a Dove upon Him," – Luke 3:21-22). In fact, doves were considered bi-sexual. So, by using the image of the dove, Milton universalises the age-old religious belief. He carefully chooses his words. He writes "brooded", which can have so many connotations. The first connotation of the word, to associate it with making pregnant, is quite clear. Brooding is also associated with deep thinking. So, Milton might have also tried to say that God created the universe in perfect calculation – there is much thought and wisdom in it. But there is also another image which lurks out from reading between the lines. Milton is also talking about his poetic ability. He wants to tell the Holy Spirit that just as God has made all things – given life to all things, created everything – so may he endow Milton with the power of creating art through poetry. He seeks that spark of creativity from the Holy Spirit, to make him carry out his "unattempted yet" task. This is made stronger by his next words: "what in me is dark/Illumine, what is low raise and support". He is definitely talking about his poetic genius, and also referring to the fact that he was near-blind when writing the epic. Here, he wishes for divine insight.

The last two lines of the invocation reveal Milton's true purpose – to "assert Eternal Providence,/And Justify the ways of God to men". Whether Milton had any right or authority to "Justify" such a great thing, it is certain that he has at least made this a Christian epic and given us a masterpiece.

The character of Satan

The character of Satan has aroused much debate through the ages. There is an increasing number of critics who view Satan in a rather positive light, hailing him as the revolting leader, who opposes tyranny.

However, such views do not go with Milton's puritan outlook, and it would be preposterous to state that Milton makes Satan the leader who fights against tyranny. Indeed, those who hold such views read the text from their coloured glasses, and not really by keeping the author in mind. While the post-modern age does talk about "Death of the author", this cannot be taken as a liberty to make any sort of interpretation and justifying it by claiming that the text is autonomous. So, I stress once more, that critics who present Satan as a heroic character do much injustice to the work of Milton. Milton's poetry has always been religious, and it would be blasphemy to state that he would make Satan the protagonist of the tale.

The correct approach to understanding Satan is through the words of Milton, "Of man's first disobedience and the fruit of that forbidden tree…".The chief character of *Paradise Lost* is man, and not Satan. The tale is not about Satan's heroism, but about "man's first disobedience"; the purpose of the tale is "to justify the ways of God to men". If Satan is seen in a positive light, it makes the very purpose of the poem futile.

Satan, therefore, is the deceiving "serpent"; the devil, as he is viewed in Christianity. However, it is true that he does exaggerate what is there in a few pages into a long epic. In such an exaggeration, the character is bound to differ from what is seen in *The Bible*. In *Paradise Lost*, Satan appears as the fallen leader. He was once one of the Archangels, and had the name Lucifer, meaning, bearer of light. However, his *hamartia* was his *hubris*. Filled with a mighty ambition, he led one third of the Angels in Heaven to revolt against God, and were, obviously, defeated and thrown into hell. The epic begins from this state of their being in "darkness visible" in hell. From this state of physical and psychological torture, Satan (he loses his name of Lucifer after his act of rebellion and gets the name Satan, which means "the devil") rouses the other fallen angels and tells them that they must be content to rule in hell ("Better to rule in hell, than serve in heaven"). From the depths of hell, Pandemonium arises, which becomes the palace of the devils. Book I ends here.

Satan no doubt appears as a leader in giving morale boosting speeches to his fallen comrades. However, he must not be confused as a good leader; the speeches he gives are speeches of deception. Knowing that if they ask for forgiveness, they would be given that, for God is always merciful to those who repent, he refuses to acknowledge his wrong in rebelling against the Supreme. He prevents the others from asking for forgiveness from God, and tells them that they must now make their future in their states of being devils.

He is filled with bitterness at his defeat, and decides that his way to seek revenge would be to destroy the creation of God. It is told to him that a new creation is made "the earth" and that a new creature is placed there "man", on whom God has placed a lot of importance. Satan decides that he will ruin this beautiful creation by making man sin. His envious decision is the mark of a fallen leader; a truly great leader would not do this – this is the mark of a petty leader, and in is here that Satan falls in character as well as actions.

The art of oratory cannot be denied to him, and it has already been said that he gives great speeches like a leader. This can be looked upon as his unwillingness to accept defeat and his desire to fight on, having undaunted will. He keeps his comrades with him and is able to keep his team together even after facing defeat. However, the practical part of it must also be examined. Satan has no option but to give good speeches, for if he does not do so, he will certainly be condemned by his own comrades. Therefore, his speeches should also be viewed as his tactic to keep the fallen angels from rebelling against him by diverting their attention towards hating God all the more, and to make them think that their tasks now lie in ruining his creation.

In Book II, he undertakes the task of journeying all by himself to find the way to the earth, and that is no doubt, courageous of him. There can be no doubt about his courage, for had he not courage, he could have never led the rebellion. In later books, he is told that his grand form has changed and he appears vulgar, and that is also a mark of his vulgar thoughts. When he deceives Eve in the guise of a Serpent, he is lowly in shape as well as in action, and on returning to hell to give the news of his success, he finds that all the devils have been converted into serpents by his action. So, he leads not only mankind, but one-third of the angels of heaven to sin as well. The positive traits which he otherwise might have retained are lost in him by his actions. So, he becomes a vile serpent, and there is a fall in his character.

Satan's Speeches in "Paradise Lost" Book-I

Introduction

Satan of Book-I *Paradise Lost*, is one of the glorious examples of political leadership and political oratory. His speeches are the key to his character and his art of oratory excels the best of Roman rhetoric. He is the leader of the rebel-angels in Heaven and the uncrowned monarch of Hell. By following his lead, the fallen angels are deprived of "happy fields, where joy forever dwells." Satan has now the task of retaining their loyalty and does so by the sheer magic of his high-pitched oratory. There is a certain pathetic grandeur of injured merit in them which wins the hearts of his followers. Around the character of Satan, Milton has thrown a singularity of daring, a grandeur of sufferance and a ruined splendour, which constitute the very height of poetic sublimity.

Satan is the first to recover from the stupor into which all the rebel angels fall. Soon he notices his first lieutenant, Beelzebub, weltering by his side. He finds that his compeer is much changed. So he makes a cautious approach, for he is not sure whether his friend is in a mood to blame him or he still loves him.

First Speech. Satan's speeches reveal pure Miltonic lyricism. His opening speech to Beelzebub is a magnificent set-piece. It reveals the character of Satan - a defiant rebel and a great leader. He encourages and sympathizes with his followers with bold words and sentiments.

Satan first takes pity on the change in his friend. Then he refers to their friendship of the hazardous enterprise in heaven and in their present misery. He is ashamed to admit the might of God. But he will not allow it to change his mind. He has nothing but contempt for God who insulted his merits. It is a sense of injured merit that makes him wage war against the tyrant of Heaven. As for the battle, it has been an equal match and the issue uncertain. It is not their want of merit but God's new and secret weapon that won the war. There is an irony through Satan's speech which continually reduces his stature even when apparently it seems to be building it up. Satan's historical of "high disdain" and "sense of injured merit" have overtones of the ludicrous. It seems weak and childish.

A single victory does not permanently ensure God's victory. For the present, they may have lost the field, but that does not mean they have lost everything.

> What though the field be lost?
> All is not lost-the unconquerable will.
> And study of revenge, immoral hate,
> And courage never to submit or yield.
> And what is else not to be overcome?

He, who failed to conquer these things cannot be said to be victor at all. Defeat is complete only when the spirit and the will too are subjugated. The bow down before God is worse than defeat. So he is determined to wage eternal war by force or guile.

Satan's question "what though the field be lost?" is "an exposure of himself and his inability to act in any other way other than what he enumerates."

Though the speech is one of high rhetorics there is barrenness; no suggestion of action at all except to brood on revenge and hate. Revenge will be eternally "studied" and have sustained yet it is so grandly expressed that we are thrilled by the implied suggestion to wage ceaseless war against hopeless odds, this appears as admirable.

Second Speech. With his second speech, Satan sweeps off all doubts from his friend's mind. "To be weak is miserable, doing or suffering." If God attempts to turn evil into good, it must be the sacred duty of the fallen angels to foil his attempts and turn all good to evil. God has now withdrawn all his forces and is in a confounded state. They should not let this opportunity slip. It is imperative that all of them should assemble and consult how they may hereafter most offend their enemy, best repair their own loss.

The audacity and superb self-confidence of Satan are well brought out in these words. He seizes the opportunity to mobilize his forces once again, conscious of the crushing defeat that he and his followers have suffered. Satan is trying to infuse fresh courage into them. His speech shows a heroic quality.

Third Speech. After winning over Beelzebub and putting new courage in him, Satan asks him whether they are forced to exchange this mournful gloom for celestial light. Now that they have become avowed enemies of God, the farther they are from him the better. So he welcome the dismal horrors of the infernal world. For him Hell is as good a place as Heaven, for his mind remains unchanged by place or time.

> The mind is its own place, and in itself
> Can make a Heaven of Hell, a Hell of Heaven.

In Hell they are free from servitude. It is "better to reign in Hell than serve in Heaven."

"Farthest from him is best" is a statement of heroic defiance and of moral alienation. Once again the appeal is to the law of nature and God's monarchy is presented to be based on force not on reason.

The line "Receive thy new Possessor" is characteristic of the Satanic mind and its passion for over lordship.

Satan's speech is "full of ringing phrases expressed with a deliberate sonority." The brief elegiac note gives way to rhetorical assertions of self-confidence. Again irony underlies the rhetoric. The ringing line "Better to reign in Hell than serve in Heaven" with its melodramatic tone scarcely conceals the mixture of pride and spite which it expresses.

Fourth Speech. Taking Beelzebub with him, he addresses other angels, with a resounding voice. He directly touches their ego by calling them, "Princes, Potentates, Warriors, the Flower of Heaven." He ask them whether they are sleeping thus on account of physical exhaustion or in despair. He exhorts them to "wake, arise or be forever fallen."

Initially, Satan sarcastically addresses his fallen angels and then he tries to revive their detached spirits. His speech is so commanding and fiery that his followers are roused out of their stupor.

Fifth Speech. Satan addresses the assembled angels. He is filled with pride to have so many comrades. It is impossible that these vast numbers are vanquished. They are all powerful and still there is every hope of regaining their native seat. God has conquered them by use of force, but such success is only a partial success. Hell cannot contain so many valiant spirits for long. Peace of course, is despaired and therefore ruled out. The only course open to them is war. "War open or understood." Satan invites all of them to the great council.

Satan choked with emotion and tears, begins his speech, like a politician he indulges in rhetoric. Without distorting facts he turns them to a different light and gives his defeated host a margin of hope. Throughout, Satan resolves "to wage by force or guile eternal war." Later he places an alternative before the infernal council "op'n war or covert guile." But now one finds that the emphasis is on war not guile. Satan is determined to combat with

God to save his own pride. Satan makes a warlike speech full of contradictions and absurdities when examined closely but admirable and impressive on the face of it ending with an appeal to continue conflict.

> "War then, War
> Open or understood must be resolv'd"

Satan's Speeches and Character – Was Milton of 'the Devil's party'?[349]

As a reader of Milton's Paradise Lost Book-1, its usual that one will mistake Satan as the epic Hero, because of his strong speeches. The impression that one gets after examining Santan's speeches is that of nobility and greatness. But if we carefully examine Satan's speeches we will find that he is the personification of evil.

Beelzebub is the First person to whom Satan addresses " and till then who knew the force of those dire arms?" Satan tells that God eventuallyproved stronger because of his power of Thunder. He then tells that he is not repentant of his rebellion against God, and his mind is "fixed". "What though the field be lost? All is not lost: the unconquerable will, and study of revenge, immortal hate, and courage never to submit or yield"- This speech gives Satan a true heroic stature, he says that they didnt lost everything, they still have there unconquerable will power, and the courage never to submit or surrender.

Satan second speech is again made to Beelzebub, he says "to be weak is miserable, doing or suffering", this speech undoubtedly have heroic texture in it, but immediately after this speech Satan evil nature comes out, when he says "to do ought good never will be our task, but ever to do ill our sole delight". If God seeks "to bring forth good" out of good they will still find means of evil.

---

[349] Reprinted by permission of eNotes.com

With such statement only a handful of readers and critics can symphathise with Satan.

Satan's third and the most important speech is also made to Beelzebub, his only listener. The third speech of Satan is very popular and impressive, it acts on the conscience of the reader. In this speech Satan shows his love of freedom and hatred of slavery. He refers himself as a "new possessor" of hell and claims to be "One who brings a mind not to be changed by place or time", he further talks about the power of mind "the mind is in its own place, and in itself can make a heven of hell, a hell of heaven". His love for freedom is depicted in his speech where he says. "Here atleast we shall be free" "To reign is worth ambition though in hell, it is better to reign in hell than to serve in heaven". Such remarks undoubtedly will inspire and impress any reader.

Satan fourth and fifth speech is addressed to the fallen angels. These speeches undoubtedly shows Satan's leadership quality and power of his words. Satan refers fallen angels as "princes, potentates, and warriors". Satan with his words made the fallen angels ashamed for there immobilty. He further flatters fallen angels by refering them as "power matchless, but with the Almighty"

Blake said that, in writing Paradise Lost, Milton was of the devil's party without knowing it. Undoubtedly the portrayel of Satan through his speeches are grand and worthy of highest admiration, but also we cannot skip the hollowness os Satan's evil character, presented by his own speeches and comments on chanracter of Satan by Milton himself.

9. Alexander Pope

(1688-1744)

The Rape of the Lock

Introduction to The Mock-Epic or the Heroi-Comical Poem

The Mock-Epic came up as a genre in the Neo-Classical Age, also known as the Augustan Age. Alexander Pope took this form to its zenith. The Mock-Epic is a narrative poem, whose purpose is not to mock the epic, but to satirise the society and its behaviour. The grand style of the epic was followed to mock the grand lifestyle of the English men and women of the time. The characters are presented in the grand manner in which they would be presented in an epic, and the inability of the characters to put on the shoes of the epic heroes brings out the mockery all the more. The artificially grand narrative style also exposes and critisises the artificiality of the times.

Batrachomyomachia, or *The Battle of the Frogs and Mice* is the earliest surviving mock-epic, and satirises Homer's *Iliad*.[350] *Hudibras, Mac Flecnoe, Absalom and Achitophel* are other notable mock-epics.

---

[350] The authorship has been attributed to Homer and to Pigres, the brother of Queen Artemisia, but so far, the authorship remains unknown.

The Rape[351] of the Lock

An Heroi-Comical Poem In Five Cantos

Nolueram, Belinda, tuos violare capillos;
Sed juvat, hoc precibus me trebuisse tuis. – Martial[352]

To MRS. ARABELLA FERMOR[353]

MADAM,

It will be vain to deny that I have some Value for this Piece, since I dedicate it to You. Yet You may bear me Witness, it was intended only to divert a few young Ladies, who have good Sense and good Humour enough, to laugh not only at their Sex's little unguarded Follies, but at their own. But as it was communicated with the Air of a Secret, it soon found its Way into the World. An imperfect Copy having been offered to a Bookseller, You had the good-Nature for my Sake to consent to the Publication of one more correct: This I was forced to before I had executed half my Design, for the *Machinery* was entirely wanting to compleat it.

---

[351] In Latin, the word is *rapere*, which means "to carry away".

[352] This is from Martial's *Epigrams*, 12.84.1-2. Martial of course, does not mention Belinda. He writes 'Polytime' (Tillotson, 2003). Here's my translation of it:

"I was unwilling to violate your hair,
But I am joyful to have granted that to your request."

[353] The "Mrs." serves to indicate that Arabella was a lady. Unlike the present form of the addres, "Mrs." in Pope's time would refer to both married and unmarried ladies (it was in opposition to "Master, or, Mr.). Children and prostitutes would be labelled as "Miss". Arabella was in fact twenty-two and single at the time Lord Petre cut off a lock of her hair, the event which served as the basis for the poem.

The *Machinery*, Madam, is a term invented by the Criticks, to signify that Part which the Deities, Angels, or Daemons, are made to act in a Poem: For the ancient Poets are in one Respect like many modern Ladies: Let an Action be never so trivial in itself, they always make it appear of the utmost Importance. These Machines I determin'd to raise on a very new and odd Foundation, the *Rosicrucian* Doctrine of Spirits.

I know how disagreeable it is to make use of hard Words before a Lady: but 'tis so much the Concern of a Poet to have his works understood, and particularly by your Sex, that You must give me leave to explain two or three difficult Terms.

The *Rosicrucians* are a People I must bring You acquainted with. The best Account I know of them is in a French book called *Le Comte de Gabalis,* which both in its Title and Size is so like a Novel, that many of the Fair Sex have read it for one by Mistake. According to these Gentlemen the four Elements are inhabited by Spirits, which they call *Sylphs, Gnomes, Nymphs,* and *Salamanders.* The *Gnomes,* or Daemons of Earth, delight in Mischief: but the *Sylphs*, whose Habitation is Air, are the best-conditioned Creatures imaginable. For they say, any Mortals may enjoy the most intimate Familiarities with these gentle Spirits, upon a Condition very easy to all true *Adepts,* an inviolate Preservation of Chastity.

As to the following Canto's, all the Passages of them are as Fabulous, as the Vision at the Beginning, or the Transformation at the End; (except for the Loss of your Hair, which I always name with Reverence.) The Human Persons are as Fictitious as the Airy ones; and the Character of *Belinda,* as it is now manag'd, resembles You in nothing but in Beauty.

If this Poem had as many Graces as there are in Your Person, or in Your Mind, yet I could never hope it should pass thro' the World half so Uncensured as You have done. But let its Fortune be what it will, mine is happy enough, to have given me this Occasion of assuring You that I am, with the truest Esteem,

Madam,
Your most Obedient
Humble Servant,
A. POPE

Canto I

What dire Offence[354] from am'rous Causes springs,[355]
What mighty Contests rise from trivial Things,
I sing-This verse to CARYL, Muse![356] is due;
This, ev'n *Belinda* may vouchsafe to view:[357]
Slight is the Subject, but not so the Praise,[358]   [5]
If She inspire, and He approve, my Lays.[359]

---

[354] Readers should note that until recently, it was the custom to write all nouns by beginning them in upper case (capital letters). Editions which do not display the nouns in upper case simply modernise the spelling rules. Readers should not, therefore, be confused, or try to look for hidden meanings behind the use of these upper case letters.

[355] The epigram should not be missed. The "dire Offense" comes not from dire things, but from "am-rous Causes". Right from the start of the poem, Pope breaks, or rather, uses the tone of seriousness to talk of "trivial Things", thereby bringing the mock-heroic aspect in it.

[356] Pope satirises the epic convention of dedicating the song to an inspiring Muse. The Muse for Pope is a human. John Caryll (or Caryl), a close friend of Pope, asked Pope to write the poem to help reconcile the Fermor and Petre families.

[357] i.e., Even Belinda, the heroine, would agree to it.

[358] i.e., the issue is trivial, but the praise (importance) given to it is of epic proportions.

[359] The "She" and "He" refer to the persons concerned with the event which occasioned this poem.

Say what strange Motive, Goddess! cou'd compel
A well-bred *Lord* t'assault a gentle *Belle?*[360]
Oh say what stranger Cause, yet unexplor'd,
Cou'd make a gentle *Belle* reject a *Lord?*[361]   [10]
In tasks so bold, can little Men engage,
And in soft Bosoms, dwell such mighty Rage?

Sol[362] through white Curtains shot a tim'rous Ray,
And ope'd those Eyes that must eclipse the Day:[363]
Now Lap-dogs give themselves the rouzing Shake,[364][15]

---

[360] "Say what...cou'd compel" is a satiric use of the beginning of *The Iliad*, where Homer talks asks the Muse about the reason of the "baneful wrath" of Achilles, and so, begins the poem. Here, this line is rather serious, but in the very next line, Pope tells that the issue was that of a genteelman assaulting a lady, which just takes away the garb of seriousness and makes the matter ludicrous, and thereby, mock-heroic.
Belle is French for Girl.
[361] Pope goes on to say that it the issue of a lord assualting a lady might seem "strange", but there is a stranger issue – that of a lady rejecting the proposal of a gentleman. Readers might be reminded of the opening of *Pride and Prejudice*, written much later, where Austen tells of ayoung bachelor being the cause of attraction among the maidens. What Pope tells over here is that the "strange" reasons point at the shallowness of the society.
[362] i.e., Sun
[363] The Sun's rays, coming through the curtains, awakens Belinda, but the readers must not miss the satire of "must eclipse the day". What Pope hints at is that the eyes, being opened, do not perform their task of seeing the day. Belinda, and all such coquettes, are so precooupied with their superficiality that they cover up (eclipse) the natural brightness of the day. Belinda is more attracted towards the jewels and make-up than in seeing the bright day.
[364] The watchful dogs are no longer to be seen; they are replaced with the lap-dogs, which were in vogue among the ladies at that time, and continued to be so for many a century.

And sleepless Lovers, just at Twelve, awake:[365]
Thrice[366] rung the Bell, the Slipper knock'd the Ground,
And the press'd Watch return'd a silver sound,[367]
Belinda still her downy Pillow prest,
Her guardian *Sylph*[368] prolng'd the balmy rest.   [20]
'Twas he had summon'd to her silent Bed
The Morning Dream that hover'd o'er her Head.[369]
A Youth more glitt'ring than a *Birth-night Beau*[370]
(That ev'n in slumber caus'd her Cheek to glow)
Seem'd to her Ear his winning Lips[371] to lay,   [25]
And thus in Whispers said, or seemed to say.

Fairest of Mortals, thou distinguish'd Care
Of thousand bright Inhabitants of Air![372]
If e'er one Vision touch'd thy infant Thought,
Of all the Nurse and all the Priest have taught,   [30]
Of airy Elves by Moonlight Shadows seen,
The silver Token, and the Circled Green,
Or Virgins visited by Angel-powers
With Golden Crowns and Wreaths of heav'nly Flow'rs;
Hear and believe! thy own Importance know,   [35]

---

[365] The *carpe diem* theme is satirized here.
[366] Satirical use of the ominous number Three. This will be seen later also.
[367] Pope indulges in a lot of personifications in this poem.
[368] In the occult philosophy of Paracelsus, a being that has air as its element. Also, read the introductory letter of Pope.
[369] Compare this with *Iliad*, where Iris sends a dream in the morning.
[370] A boy from an aristocratic class.
[371] Belinda dreams of a lovely young man, and in her sleep, she is charmed by him. His lips have already won Belinda's heart, even before any physical meeting.
[372] Ariel, the sylph, speaks to Belinda in the dream in this way, and tells that there are thousands of sylphs who are placed to take care of her.

Nor bound thy narrow Views to things below.
Some secret Truths, from Learned Pride conceal'd,
To Maids alone and Children are reveal'd:[373]
What tho' no Credit doubting Wits may give?[374]
The Fair and Innocent shall still believe.[375]   [40]
Know then, unnumber'd Spirits round thee fly,
The light *Militia*[376] of the lower sky:
These, tho' unseen, are ever on the Wing,
Hang o'er the *Box,* and hover round the *Ring.*[377]
Think what an Equipage[378] thou hast in Air,   [45]
And view with scorn *Two Pages* and a *Chair.*[379]
As now your own, our Beings were of old,
And once inclos'd in Woman's beauteous Mold;

---

[373] Compare this with the verse from The Bible, "Out of the mouths of babes and nursing infants, You have perfected praise". Pope over here, satirically tells that Belinda is too filled with conceit, and even in her dreams, she feels she is visited by spirits who tell her that she is fairest of all, and is a very important figure.

[374] People in general would of course, not believe if Belinda says that a sylph has told this to her in a dream.

[375] What Pope means that that the ladies who are fair are naïve enough to believe in such things.

[376] Military order. Belinda feels that an entire military order of supernatural creatures fly about her to take care of her.

[377] The Ring was in Hyde Park. It was on the northern side of the eastern end of the place now known as Serpentine.

[378] A horse-driven carriage, with an attendant and footmen to help the person get up and down the carriage. The sylphs over here serve this purpose. They take care of her every detail.

[379] Compare this with the second set of prophecies made by the witches to Macbeth, where they ask him "Learn to scorn" the power of man.

Here, the Pages refer to the attendant and the footman, at whom Belinda would look with scorn, and not with an eye of gratitude for their service. The Chair refers to the sedan chair on which she would sit. She is so filled with vanity that she would scorn even this expensive chair.

Thence, by a soft Transition, we repair[380]
From earthly Vehicles to these of Air.[381]   [50]
Think not, when Woman's transient Breath is fled,
That all her Vanities at once are dead.
Succeeding Vanities she still regards,
And tho' she plays no more, o'erlooks the Cards.[382]
Her Joy in gilded[383] Chariots, when alive,   [55]
And love of *Ombre*[384], after Death survive.
For when the Fair in all their Pride expire,
To their first Elements the Souls retire:
The Sprites of fiery Termagants in Flame[385]
Mount up, and take a *Salamander's* name.   [60]
Soft yielding Minds to Water glide away,
And sip, with *Nymphs,* their elemental Tea.[386]
The graver Prude sinks downward to a *Gnome,*
In search of Mischief still on Earth to roam.
The light Coquettes in *Sylphs* aloft repair,   [65]
And sport and flutter in the Fields of Air.

---

[380] Transform, and also note the sense of being made better.

[381] The sylphs originate from women. I other words, Pope means that they are figments of imagination of women.

[382] The sylphs, originating into "light inhabitants of Air" after the death of woman, look into the affairs of men and women and dictate their actions, which the humans are not aware of. To humans, winning or losing at a game of cards would seem to be a matter of luck, but it is the sylphs who play a role in this. What Pope means is that in life, the women of the Restoration times indulged in vanities, like that of playing cards, and after death, the originating sylphs also cannot let go of this vanity. They hang about and around, overlooking these actions.

[383] i.e., of gold

[384] A game of cards.

[385] Johnson describes this as "A scold; a brawling turbulent woman".

[386] In those days, this would be pronounced as /ti/+/ei/.

Know further yet; Whoever fair and chaste
Rejects Mankind, is by some *Sylph* embrac'd:
For Spirits, freed from mortal Laws, with ease
Assume what Sexes and what Shapes they please.[387] [70]
What guards the Purity of melting Maids,
In Courtly Balls, and Midnight Masquerades,
Safe from the treach'rous Friend, the daring Spark,
The Glance by Day, the Whisper in the Dark;
When kind Occasion prompts their warm Desires, [75]
When Music softens, and when Dancing fires?[388]
'Tis but their *Sylph,* the wise Celestials know,
Tho' *Honour* is the Word with Men below.

Some Nymphs there are, too conscious of their Face,
For Life predestin'd to the *Gnomes'* Embrace. [80]
Who swell their Prospects and exalt their Pride,
When Offers are disdain'd, and Love deny'd.
Then gay[389] Ideas crowd the vacant Brain,
While Peers and Dukes, and all their sweeping Train,
And Garters, Stars, and Coronets appear, [85]
And in soft sounds, *Your Grace* salutes their Ear.
'Tis these that early taint the Female Soul,[390]
Instruct the eyes of young *Coquettes* to roll,

---

[387] This is an allusion to *Paradise Lost*, Book I, lines 423-424:
  "For Spirits when they please
  Can either Sex assume, or both,"
[388] This is a description of the ballroom dances and the flirting that would take place when "occasion" arose.
Ariel might say that even though the Maids are "melting", that is, they fall to the charms of the men, they remain pure and chaste because the sylphs protect them, the sylphs are actually helpless, as Pope describes in the following cantos.
[389] i.e., happy
[390] Pope over here tries to balance the scale a bit, for it would appear that he is lashing against the females only. So, he tells here that it is the men of high class who instruct the females to behave thus.

> Teach Infant Cheeks a bidden Blush to know,
> And little Hearts to flutter at a *Beau*. [90]
>
> Oft when the World imagine Women stray,
> The *Sylphs* through Mystic mazes guide their Way.
> Thro' all the giddy Circle they pursue,
> And old Impertinence expel by new.[391]
> What tender Maid but must a Victim fall [95]
> To one Man's Treat, but for another's Ball?
> When *Florio* speaks, what Virgin could withstand,
> If gentle *Damon* did not squeeze her Hand?[392]
> With varying Vanities, from ev'ry Part,
> They shift the moving Toyshop of their Heart;[393] [100]
> Where Wigs with Wigs, with Sword-knots Sword-knots strive,
> Beaux banish Beaux, and Coaches Coaches drive.[394]
> This erring Mortals Levity may call,
> Oh blind to Truth! the *Sylphs* contrive it all.
>
> Of these am I, who thy Protection claim, [105]
> A watchful Sprite,[395] and *Ariel* is my name.
> Late, as I rang'd the crystal Wilds of Air,

---

[391] It should be noted that their previous acts of Impertinence are not expelled by their present acts of pernitence, but by newer acts of Impertinence. In other words, they remain "stray" and do not correct themselves, despite all claims by the sylphs.

[392] Pope tells that if a "tender Maid" rejects the love of one man, it is only because there is someone else whom she will accept. In other words, there is no chaste woman in the Restoration period, as per Pope.

[393] Readers should be reminded of Hamlet's utterance, "Frailty, thy name is woman".

[394] An allusion to *Iliad*, iv. 508-9:
> Now Shield with Shield, with Helmet Helmet clos'd,
> To Armour Armour, Lance to Lance oppos'd.

[395] i.e., Spirit.

In the clear Mirror of thy ruling *Star*
I saw, alas! some dread Event impend,
Ere to the Main this morning's Sun descend,[396]   [110]
But Heav'n reveals not what, or how, or where:[397]
Warn'd by thy *Sylph,* oh pious Maid beware!
This to disclose is all thy Guardian can.
Beware of all, but most beware of Man!

He said: when *Shock,*[398] who thought she slept too long, [115]
Leap'd up, and wak'd his Mistress with his Tongue.
'Twas then, *Belinda!* if Report say true,[399]
Thy Eyes first open'd on a *Billet-doux;*[400]
Wounds, Charms, and *Ardors,* were no sooner read,
But all the Vision vanish'd from thy Head.[401]   [120]

And now, unveil'd, the *Toilet* stands display'd,
Each Silver Vase in mystic Order laid.
First, rob'd in White, the Nymph intent adores
With Head uncover'd, the *Cosmetic* Pow'rs.

---

[396] i.e., before Sunset
[397] This exposes the actual lack of knowledge of the sylphs, who claim to "contrive it all".
[398] This refers to a kind of lap-dog, supposed to have been brought to England from Iceland.
[399] Pope here satirises the circulation of fake reports, for if this were to be considered true, it means that there were others watching her sleep saw her awake. So, this is a false report, and like all false reports, are said in a most convincing tine of seriousness.
[400] There are several meanings of *billet-doux*. Literally, *billet* means note (as in a short letter) and *doux* means sweet. So, it has been taken to mean love-note or love letter (sweet as a synonym of lovely).

[401] Belinda totally forgot about her dream. No doubt, the "moving toyshop of" her "heart" has been shifted.

A heav'nly Image in the Glass appears,[402]   [125]
To that she bends, to that her Eyes she rears;
Th' inferior Priestess,[403] at her Altar's side,
Trembling, begins the sacred Rites of Pride.
Unnumber'd Treasures ope[404] at once, and here
The various Off'rings of the World appear;   [130]
From each she nicely culls with curious Toil,
And decks the Goddess with the glitt'ring Spoil.
This casket *India's* glowing Gems unlocks,
And all *Arabia* breathes from yonder Box.[405]
The Tortoise here and Elephant unite,   [135]
Transform'd to *Combs*[406], the speckled and the white.
Here Files of Pins extend their shining Rows,
Puffs, Powders, Patches, Bibles, Billet-doux.[407]
Now awful Beauty puts on all its Arms;
The Fair each moment rises in her Charms,[408]   [140]
Repairs[409] her Smiles, awakens ev'ry Grace,
And calls forth all the Wonders of her Face;

---

[402] The Image is that of Belinda herself, and she feels herself to be divine. She adores herself in the mirror, and so, one can say this is narcissist.

[403] This is Betty, the servant, who begins to dress Belinda.

[404] i.e., open

[405] A reference to the perfumes of Arabia.

[406] The teeth of the comb were made of ivory, and the part which joined them was made of tortoise shell.

[407] Readers should look at the arrangement. The Bible is placed with other material possessions, which means that Belinda does not really care for religion at all, and it is just a book to fashionably display, to put on her the guise of being a very "pious Maid", which she is not actually.

[408] Compare this with Shakespeare's Sonnet 18, "And every fair from fair sometime declines".

[409] Belinda practises her smiles to see which smiling face will suit her.

Sees by Degrees a purer Blush arise,[410]
And keener Lightnings quicken in her Eyes.[411]
The busy *Sylphs* surround their darling Care;   [145]
These set the Head, and those divide the Hair,
Some fold the Sleeve, whilst others plait the Gown;
And *Betty's* prais'd for labours not her own.[412]

Canto II

Not with more Glories, in th' Ethereal Plain,
The Sun first rises o'er the purpled Main,
Than issuing forth, the Rival of his Beams
Launch'd on the Bosom of the Silver *Thames*.[413]
Fair Nymphs, and well-drest Youths around her shone, [5]
But ev'ry Eye was fix'd on her alone.
On her white Breast a sparkling *Cross* she wore,
Which *Jews* might kiss, and Infidels adore.[414]
Her lively Looks a sprightly Mind disclose,[415]
Quick as her Eyes, and as unfix'd as those: [10]
Favours to none, to all she Smiles extends,
Oft she rejects, but never once offends.
Bright as the Sun, her Eyes the Gazers strike,

---

[410] Readers must not fail to see the sarcasm here. It is not at all pure, but is coloured by make-up.

[411] i.e., her eyes are sparkling. Tillotson notes that Belinda applies the juice of Belladonna "to enlarge the pupil of her eye or darkens the surrounding skin" (Tillotson 28).

[412] This is ironical, for it is Betty who does it and not the sylphs.

[413] This refers to the Barge, on which Belinda is, and also to Belinda, who appeared like a sparkling sun "on the Bosom of the Silver Thames".

[414] The Jews and Infidels would kiss the cross not out of conversion, but out of the lust for gold and Belinda. Pope mocks the shallow religious mentality of the people, and also of coquettes like Belinda, who would use objects associated with religion to serve such petty purpose.

[415] Notice the epigram.

And, like the Sun, they shine on all alike.
Yet graceful Ease, and Sweetness void of Pride, [15]
Might hide her Faults, if *Belles* had Faults to hide:
If to her share some Female Errors fall,
Look on her Face, and you'll forget 'em all.[416]

This Nymph, to the Destruction of Mankind,
Nourish'd two Locks which graceful hung behind [20]
In equal Curls, and well conspir'd to deck
With shining Ringlets the smooth Iv'ry Neck.[417]
Love in these Labyrinths his Slaves detains,
And mighty Hearts are held in slender Chains.
With hairy sprindges we the Birds betray, [25]
Slight lines of Hair surprise the Finny Prey,[418]
Fair Tresses Man's Imperial Race insnare,
And Beauty draws us with a single Hair.

Th' Advent'rous *Baron* the bright Locks admir'd,
He saw, he wish'd, and to the Prize aspir'd: [30]
Resolv'd to win, he meditates the way,
By Force to ravish, or by Fraud betray;
For when Success a Lover's Toil attends,
Few ask, if Fraud or Force attain'd his Ends.

For this, ere *Phoebus*[419] rose, he had implor'd [35]
Propitious Heav'n, and ev'ry Power ador'd,
But chiefly *Love* – to *Love* an Altar built,

---

[416] If there is any fault in the character, it will be forgotten on seeing the face. In other words, the coquettes would give such a fake countenance that the ones who are wronged will forgive them. It also means that the people are so shallow that they will forget the offense when they behold a beautiful face.
[417] The neck of Belinda is so white that it seems like ivory.
[418] i.e., the fish
[419] The classical god of Sun.

Of twelve vast *French* Romances,[420] neatly gilt.
There lay three Garters, half a Pair of Gloves,
And all the Trophies of his former Loves.[421] [40]
With tender *Billet-doux* he lights the Pyre,[422]
And breathes three am'rous Sighs to raise the Fire.[423]
Then Prostrate falls,[424] and begs with ardent Eyes

---

[420] The French Romances bore the stigma of being rather vulgar in content (as well as the esteem of being rather romantic). The suggestion of the romances being in French is perhaps to allude to the intensity of passion that will be found in them.

I have not found any suitable explanation for the presence of the number of "twelve", and so, offer my own explanation:

a) They represent the twelve months, implying that throughout the year, Lord Peter behaves in a similar manner (as he would, with Belinda). This is supported in the next few lines, by stating hiss "trophies" which he has secured from other ladies.

b) They are a Biblical allusion to the twelve gates of the new Jerusalem, serving the purpose of mock-epic here.

c) They are a Biblical allusion to the number of disciples Jesus chose to be with him. The twelve French romances are his companions. In this view also, the purpose which is served is that of mock-epic.

[421] This shows that he is not really steadfast in love.

[422] i.e., a stack of woods arranged in a particular manner for burning something/someone on it.

[423] He does not literally set anything on fire. The fire is his passion inside.

[424] While his posture suggests someone who is ardently worshipping, the lines suggest he indulges in self-love. His sighs were to work himself to a state of passion, where he burns with fire inside.

Soon to obtain, and long possess the Prize:
The Pow'rs gave Ear, and granted half his Pray'r, [45]
The rest, the Winds dispers'd in empty Air.[425]

But now secure[426] the painted Vessel[427] glides,
The Sun-beams trembling on the floating Tydes,
While Musick steals upon the Sky,
And soften'd Sounds along the Waters die. [50]
Smooth flow the Waves, the Zephyrs gently play,
Belinda smil'd, and all the World was gay.
All but the *Sylph* – With careful Thoughts opprest,
Th' impending Woe sat heavy on his Breast.
He summons straight his Denizens of Air; [55]
The lucid Squadrons round the Sails repair:
Soft o'er the Shrouds Aerial Whispers breath,
That seem'd but Zephyrs to the Train beneath.[428]
Some to the Sun their Insect-Wings unfold,[429]
Waft on the Breeze, or sink in Clouds of Gold. [60]
Transparent Forms, too fine for mortal Sight,
Their fluid Bodies half dissolv'd in Light.
Loose to the Wind their airy Garments flew,
Thin glitt'ring Textures of the filmy Dew;
Dipt in the richest Tincture of the Skies, [65]
Where Light disports in ever-mingling Dies,
While ev'ry Beam new transient Colours flings,

---

[425] This is a reference to *The Iliad*.
[426] The irony lies in the word "secure".
[427] The word "painted" tells us that the "Vessel" does not refer to the Barge, but to Belinda, who is totally "painted" with make-up. The word "Vessel" has got a sexual innuendo.
[428] Ariel spoke to the other "Sylphs and Sylphids", but that seemed like the blowing of the gentle Zephyr to the humans.
[429] Allusion to the moths, who open their wings and fly towards the sun and any other source of fire, and burn themselves in it. Here, Pope means that Belinda's open display of beauty would cause her more harm that good.

Colours that change whene'er they wave their Wings.
Amid the Circle, on the gilded mast,
Superiour by the Head,[430] was *Ariel* plac'd: [70]
His Purple Pinions op'ning to the Sun,
He rais'd his Azure Wand, and thus begun.[431]

Ye *Slyphs* and *Sylphids,* to your Chief give ear,
Fays, Fairies, Genii, Elves, and *Daemons* hear![432]
Ye know the Spheres and various Tasks assign'd   [75]
By Laws Eternal to th' Aerial Kind.
Some in the Fields of purest *Aether* play,
And bask and whiten in the Blaze of Day.
Some guide the Course of wand'ring Orbs on high,
Or roll the Planets through the boundless Sky.   [80]
Some less refin'd, beneath the Moon's pale Light
Pursue the Stars that shoot athwart the Night;
Or suck the Mists in grosser Air below,
Or dip their Pinions in the painted Bow,
Or brew fierce Tempests on the wintry Main,   [85]
Or o'er the Glebe distil the kindly Rain.
Others on Earth o'er human Race preside,

---

[430] Note the satire on superiority. Ariel is not superior by means of merit, but by being taller. Pope here satirises the society where merit is sadly not given prominence in deciding ranks.

[431] Readers should not fail to notice the similarity with *Paradise Lost*, Book I, where Satan raises his tall sword before addressing his fallen angels after they gather together to hear him.

[432] Pope perhaps deliberately adds all these names to heighten the sense of absurdity? There seems to be hierarchy in the order of these creatures, with sylphs being on top, followed by sylphids. Daemons are at the bottom of the order. There seems to be seven divisions and an obvious allusion to the order of heavenly beings, as believed in medieval times, which is even found in *Paradise Lost* (Seraphim, Cherubim and Thrones in the First Hierarchy; Dominations, Virtues and Powers in the Second Hierarchy; Principalities, Archangels and Angels in the Third Hierarchy).

Watch all their Ways, and all their Actions guide:
Of these the Chief the Care of Nations own,[433]
And guard with Arms Divine the *British Throne*. [90]

Our humbler Province is to tend the Fair,
Not a less pleasing, tho' less glorious Care.[434]
To save the Powder from too rude a Gale,
Nor let th' imprison'd Essences exhale;
To draw fresh Colours from the vernal Flow'rs, [95]
To steal from Rainbows ere they drop in Show'rs
A brighter Wash;[435] to curl their waving Hairs,
Assist their Blushes, and inspire their Airs;[436]
Nay oft, in Dreams, Invention[437] we bestow,
To change a *Flounce*, or add a *Furbelo!*[438] [100]

This Day, black Omens threat the brightest Fair
That e'er deserv'd a watchful Spirit's Care;
Some dire Disaster, or by Force, of Slight,
But what, or where, the Fates have wrapt in Night.
Whether the Nymph shall break *Diana's* law,[439] [105]
Or some frail *China* jar receive a Flaw,[440]

---

[433] i.e., it is human chief of nations (here, the British Monarch) is given under the care of the chief of the Aiery creatures.

[434] In the following lines, Pope lists the extremely trivial aspects which the sylphs guard in their duty towards "the Fair".

[435] i.e., "A medial or cosmetic lotion" (Johnson).

[436] i.e., pride

[437] i.e., imagination (invent that which is not there)

[438] i.e., "A piece of stuff plaited and puckered together, either below or above, on the petticoats or gowns of women" (Johnson).

[439] i.e., lose her chastity.

[440] Notice how Pope makes Ariel speak of two entirely different matters in the same tone of seriousness. A maid losing her chastity and a China jar breaking or cracking do not deserve the same attention.

Or stain her Honour, or her new Brocade,[441]
Forget her Pray'rs, or miss a Masquerade,
Or lose her Heart,[442] or Necklace, at a Ball;
Or whether Heav'n has doom'd that *Shock* must fall.[443][110]
Haste then ye Spirits! to your Charge repair;
The flutt'ring Fan be *Zephyretta's* Care;
The Drops[444] to thee, *Brillante,* we consign;
And, *Momentilla,* let the Watch be thine;
Do thou, *Crispissa,* tend her fav'rite Lock;   [115]
Ariel himself shall be the guard of *Shock.*

To Fifty chosen *Sylphs,* of special Note,
We trust th' important Charge, the *Petticoat:*
Oft have we known that sev'nfold Fence to fail,[445]
Tho' stiff with Hoops, and arm'd with Ribs of Whale.[120]
Form a strong Line about the Silver Bound,
And guard the wide Circumference around.

Whatever Spirit, careless of his Charge,
His Post neglects, or leaves the Fair at large,
Shall feel sharp Vengeance soon o'ertake his Sins,   [125]
Be stop'd in *Vials,* or transfixt with *Pins;*[446]
Or plung'd in Lakes of bitter *Washes* lie,[447]

---

[441] The "Honour" would be stained by the loss of chastity and the "new Brocade" would be stained if the liquid from inside the China jar falls on it.

[442] i.e., lose her heart to a man.

[443] Once more, the excessive importance on lap-dogs.

[444] i.e., "Diamond(s) hanging in the ear" (Johnson).

[445] Compare this with the shield of Achilles, which had seven layers, and which was bound by silver.

[446] Compare this with the torture of Prometheus by Zeus. Prometheus was bound with chains upon a rock and birds of prey would peck at his entrails, which would grow again, and so, the torture would continue.

[447] Compare this with the lake of fire as found in the Bible, and the dark lake of hell as found in *Paradise Lost.*

> Or wedg'd whole Ages in a *Bodkin's* Eye:[448]
> *Gums* and *Pomatums*[449] shall his Flight restrain,
> While clog'd he beats his silken Wings in vain;   [130]
> Or Alom-*Stypticks*[450] with contracting Pow'r
> Shrink his thin Essence like a rivell'd Flower.
> Or, as *Ixion* fix'd, the Wretch shall feel
> The giddy Motion of the whirling Mill,[451]
> Midst Fumes of burning Chocolate shall glow,   [135]
> And tremble at the Sea that froaths below!
>
> He spoke; the Spirits from the Sails descend;
> Some, Orb in Orb, around the Nymph extend,
> Some thrid the mazy Ringlets of her Hair,
> Some hang upon the Pendants of her Ear;   [140]
> With beating Hearts the dire Event they wait,
> Anxious, and trembling for the Birth of Fate.

Canto III

> Close by those Meads for ever crown'd with Flow'rs,
> Where *Thames* with Pride surveys his rising Tow'rs,
> There stands a Structure[452] of Majestic Fame,
> Which from the neighb'ring *Hampton* takes its Name.
> Her *Britain's* Statesmen oft the Fall foredoom   [5]
> Of foreign Tyrants, and of Nymphs at home;

---

[448] Compare this with Mars' imagination in the *Iliad*, book viii, about being condemned to pain for ages and ages, pierced with Grecian darts. Also compare this state with the condition of Ariel in *The Tempest*, before being freed from black magic.

[449] i.e., Ointments

[450] It prevents bleeding.

[451] Ixion was banished by Zeus, who further punished him by tying him on a wheel. As the wheel rolled continually, his punishment was also continual.

[452] This refers to Hampton Court.

Here Thou, great *Anna!*[453] whom three Realms[454] obey,
Dost sometimes Counsel take-and sometimes *Tea*.[455]

Hither the Heroes and the Nymphs resort,
To taste awhile the Pleasures of a Court;   [10]
In various Talk th' instructive Hours they past,
Who gave a *Ball,*[456] or paid the *Visit* last:
One speaks the Glory of the *British Queen,*
And one describes a charming *Indian Screen;*[457]
A third interprets Motions, Looks, and Eyes;[458]   [15]
At every Word a Reputation dies.[459]
Snuff, or the *Fan,* supply each Pause of Chat,[460]
With singing, laughing, ogling, *and all that.*
Mean while, declining from the Noon of Day,
The Sun obliquely shoots his burning Ray;   [20]
The hungry Judges soon the Sentence sign,
And Wretches hang that Jury-men may Dine;[461]

---

[453] i.e., Queen Anne

[454] The three realms would be England, Scotland and Ireland, which together formed Great Britain or The United Kingdom. Ireland had not separated at that time.

[455] This is an anti-climax.

[456] It was the custom in contemporary society that Balls would be given in a particular season, and that too, from one family to another family.

[457] i.e., a curtain

[458] What Pope actually means is that someone sits and criticizes others.

[459] The people engage in slanderous gossip.

[460] They take snuff or fan themselves for pleasure when they do not gossip. In other words, they are not at all involved in any serious task of decision making.

[461] The judges are not concerned about giving a proper sentence after proper inspection; they just wish to complete their tasks quickly and head to eat. Pope satirises the sorry state of administrative affairs in this part.

The Merchant from th' *Exchange*⁴⁶² returns in Peace,
And the long Labours of the Toilet cease.
Belinda now, whom Thirst of Fame invites,   [25]
Burns to encounter two adventrous Knights,⁴⁶³
At *Ombre* singly to decide their Doom;⁴⁶⁴
And swells her Breast with Conquests yet to come.
Straight the three Bands prepare in Arms to join,⁴⁶⁵
Each Band the number of the Sacred Nine.   [30]
Soon as she spreads her Hand, th' Aerial Guard
Descend, and sit on each important Card:⁴⁶⁶
First *Ariel* perch'd upon a *Matadore*,⁴⁶⁷
Then each, according to the Rank they bore;
For *Sylphs,* yet mindful of their ancient Race,   [35]
Are, as when women, wond'rous fond of Place.

Behold, four *Kings,* in Majesty rever'd,⁴⁶⁸
With hoary Whiskers and a forky Beard;
And four fair *Queens* whose Hands sustain a Flow'r,
Th' expressive Emblem of their softer Pow'r;   [40]
Four *Knaves* in Garbs succinct, a trusty Band;

---

⁴⁶² i.e. Stock Exchange

⁴⁶³ Compare this with the desire of Achilles to get fame in *The Iliad*. Just as Achilles would be eager to encounter other warriors, Belinda desires to encounter to men.

⁴⁶⁴ The parody is that of a single encounter between warriors. Here, it is not actual battle, but a game of cards which has been presented so satirically, and Pope wishes to state that the people are more concerned about a card game than a game of ombre.

⁴⁶⁵ The parody is of soldiers who form ranks and squardrons.

⁴⁶⁶ Compare this with the gods and goddesses of the *Iliad*, who take sides and support their favourite warrior.

⁴⁶⁷ Compare this with Zeus, in the shape of an eagle, perching on top of a mountain.

⁴⁶⁸ In this and in the following lines of the stanza, notice the description of the cards. Pope refers to the Kings, Queens and Jacks of all the four bands of cards.

Caps on their heads, and Halberds in their hand;
And particolour'd Troops, a shining Train,
Draw forth to combat on the Velvet Plain.

The skilful Nymph reviews her Force with Care; [45]
Let Spades be Trumps! she said, and Trumps they were.[469]

Now move to War her Sable *Matadores,*[470]
In show like Leaders of the swarthy *Moors.*
Spadillio first, unconquerable Lord!
Let off two captive Trumps, and swept the Board. [50]
As many more *Manillio* forc'd to yield,
And march'd a Victor from the verdant Field.
Him *Basto* follow'd, but his Fate more hard
Gain'd but one Trump and one *Plebian* card.
With his broad Sabre next, a Chief in Years, [55]
The hoary Majesty of *Spades* appears;
Puts forth one manly Leg, to sight reveal'd,
The rest, his many-colour'd Robe conceal'd.
The Rebel-*Knave,* that dares his Prince engage,
Proves the just Victim of his Royal Rage. [60]
Ev'n mighty *Pam,* that Kings and Queens o'erthrew,
And mow'd down Armies in the Fights of *Lu,*
Sad Chance of War! now, destitute of Aid,
Falls undistinguish'd by the Victor *Spade!*

Thus far both Armies to *Belinda* yield; [65]
Now to the *Baron* Fate inclines the Field.[471]
His warlike *Amazon* her Host invades,
Th' Imperial Consort of the Crown of *Spades.*
The *Club's* black Tyrant first her Victim dy'd,

---

[469] This is an allusion to the words of the Bible, "And God said, 'Let there be light' and all was light".
[470] In this and in the following lines, Pope personifies the cards and assigns them names and describes their action in the battle.
[471] This is again a parody of *The Iliad*, where the gods and goddesses are whimsical and change their favours.

Spite of his haughty Mien, and barb'rous Pride: [70]
What boots the Regal Circle on his Head,
His Giant Limbs, in State unwieldy spread;
That long behind he trails his pompous Robe,
And of all Monarchs only grasps the Globe?

The *Baron* now his *Diamonds* pours apace; [75]
Th' embroider'd *King* who shows but half his Face,
And his refulgent *Queen,* with pow'rs combin'd,
Of broken Troops an easy Conquest find.
Clubs, Diamonds, Hearts, in wild Disorder seen,
With Throngs promiscuous strew the level Green. [80]
Thus when dispers'd a routed Army runs,
Of *Asia's* Troops, and *Afric's* Sable Sons,
With like Confusion different Nations fly,
In various Habits, and of various Dye,
The pierc'd Battalions dis-united fall, [85]
In Heaps on Heaps; one Fate o'erwhelms them all.

The *Knave* of *Diamonds* tries his wily Arts,
And wins (oh shameful Chance!) the *Queen* of *Hearts.*
At this, the Blood the Virgin's Cheek forsook,
A livid Paleness spreads o'er all her Look; [90]
She sees, and trembles at th' approaching Ill,
Just in the Jaws of Ruin, and *Codille.*
And now (as oft in some distemper'd State)
On one nice *Trick* depends the gen'ral Fate,
An *Ace* of Hearts steps forth: The *King* unseen [95]
Lurk'd in her Hand, and mourn'd his captive *Queen.*
He springs to Vengeance with an eager Pace,
And falls like Thunder on the prostrate *Ace*
The Nymph exulting fills with Shouts the Sky;
The Walls, the Woods, and long Canals reply. [100]

Oh thoughtless Mortals! ever blind to Fate,
Too soon dejected, and too soon elate!

Sudden these Honours shall be snatch'd away,
And curs'd for ever this Victorious Day.

For lo! the Board with Cups and Spoons is crown'd, [105]
The Berries crackle, and the Mill turns round;
On shining Altars of *Japan* they raise
The silver Lamp, and fiery Spirits blaze:
From silver Spouts the grateful Liquors glide,
And *China's* earth receives the smoking Tyde. [110]
At once they gratify their Scent and Taste,
While frequent Cups prolong the rich Repast.
Strait hover round the Fair her Airy Band;
Some, as she sipp'd, the fuming Liquor fann'd,
Some o'er her Lap their careful Plumes display'd, [115]
Trembling, and conscious of the rich Brocade.
Coffee (which makes the Politician wise,
And see through all things with his half-shut Eyes)
Sent up in Vapours to the *Baron's* Brain
New Stratagems, the radiant Lock to gain. [120]
Ah cease rash Youth! desist ere 'tis too late,
Fear the just Gods, and think of *Scylla's* Fate!
Chang'd to a Bird, and sent to flit in Air,
She dearly pays for *Nisus'* injur'd Hair!

But when to Mischief Mortals bend their Will, [125]
How soon they find fit Instuments of Ill!
Just then, *Clarissa* drew with tempting Grace
A two-edg'd Weapon[472] from her shining Case;
So Ladies in Romance assist their Knight,
Present the Spear, and arm him for the Fight. [130]
He takes the Gift with rev'rence, and extends
The little Engine on his Fingers' Ends;
This just behind *Belinda's* Neck he spread
As o'er the fragrant Steams she bends her Head:
Swift to the Lock a thousand Sprights repair, [135]
A thousand Wings, by turns, blow back the Hair;

---

[472] i.e., a pair of scissors

And thrice they twitch'd the Diamond in her Ear,
Thrice she look'd back, and thrice the Foe drew near.
Just in that instant, anxious *Ariel* sought
The close Recesses of the Virgin's thought;[473]   [140]
As on the Nosegay in her Breast reclin'd,
He watch'd th' Ideas rising in her Mind,
Sudden he view'd, in spite of all her Art,
An Earthly Lover lurking at her Heart.[474]
Amaz'd, confus'd, he found his Power expir'd,[475]   [145]
Resign'd to Fate, and with a Sigh retir'd.

The *Peer* now spreads the glittering *Forfex* wide,
T' inclose the Lock; now joins it, to divide.
Ev'n then, before the fatal Engine clos'd,
A wretched *Sylph* too fondly interpos'd;   [150]
Fate urged the Sheers, and cut the *Sylph* in twain,[476]
(But Airy Substance soon unites again)

---

[473] i.e., Ariel went inside her mind to know her thoughts. Why Ariel would choose this crucial moment to know Belinda's thoughts is beyond answer, but Pope does this to show the total lack of proper sense among the sylphs, and later, the total lack of power to prevent the lock from being cut.

[474] The satire lies in "in spite of all her Art". Belinda tries to hide all thoughts of a lover, but is unable to prevent, sa she desires a male company.

[475] There is no reason why Ariel's powers should go away, but Pope makes this happen to hint at the actual inefficiency of the sylphs.

[476] If there were any doubts about the powers of the sylphs, that is washed away in this part. One sylph comes to protect the lock and gets cut itself!

This part is also a satirical presentation of Satan being "cut asunder" by the sword of an archangel, in *Paradise Lost*.

The meeting Points the sacred Hair dissever[477]
From the fair Head, for ever and for ever!

Then flah'd the living Lightnings from her Eyes, [155]
And Screams of Horror rend th' affrighted Skies.
Not louder Shrieks to pitying Heav'n are cast,
When Husbands, or when Lapdogs breathe their last,[478]
Or when rich *China* Vessels, fal'n from high,
In glitt'ring Dust and painted Fragments lie! [160]

Let Wreaths of Triumph now my Temples twine,
(The Victor cry'd) the glorious Prize is mine!
While Fish in Streams, or Birds delight in Air,
Or in a Coach and Six the *British* Fair,
As long as *Atalantis* shall be read, [165]
Or the small Pillow grace a Lady's Bed,
While *Visits* shall be paid on solemn Days,
When num'rous Wax-lights in bright Order blaze,
While Nymphs take Treats, or Assignations give,
So long my Honour, Name, and Praise shall live![479] [170]

What Time would spare, from Steel receives its date,
And Monuments, like Men, submit to Fate!
Steel cou'd the Labour of the Gods destroy,[480]
And strike to Dust th' Imperial Tow'rs of *Troy;*

---

[477] The blades of the scissors (The Forfex) meet, which cuts the hair.

[478] Note the third use of the Lapdog. Pope does not demean the husbands or elevate the lapdogs. He merely satirises the shallowness of the society where two very different aspects are given the same importance.

[479] Compare this with the words of the conspirators in *Julius Caesar*, after the assassination of Julius Caesar in Act III.
Also compare this with Shakespeare's Sonnet 18.

[480] This refers to the destruction of Troy, which rose up by the music of Apollo. So, steel weapons destroyed something which a god made.

> Steel cou'd the Works of mortal Pride confound,   [175]
> And hew Triumphal Arches to the Ground.
> What Wonder then, fair Nymph! thy Hair shou'd feel
> The conqu'ring Force of unresisted Steel?

The Opening as a Mockery of The Epic Invocation

Tillotson has commented, "The title and opening of a poem often contain a kernel of the whole…they are devised so as to anchor the wandering wits of the reader".

The Rape of the Lock begins with these lines:

> What dire Offence from am'rous Causes springs,
>
> What mighty Contests rise from trivial Things,

and immediately, the reader understands Pope is treading the road taken by Homer, Virgil and Milton in order to reach their destination: The Epic. Homer's *Iliad* begins:

> Achilles' baneful wrath – resound – O goddess – that imposed
> Infinite sorrows on the Greeks, and many brave souls loos'd
> From breasts heroic; (Chapman's translation)

Milton begins *Paradise Lost* with:

> Of Man's first disobedience, and the fruit
> Of that forbidden Tree…

It is clear that they all talk of the *cause* – the subject matter – of the epic first. For Pope, it is "dire Offence from am'rous Causes". But though there is a striking similarity in the way in which they all begin, no reader will miss the fact that *The Rape of the Lock* is different. Though its presentation is rather formal and serious (with lots of spondees for heavy stress), the subject matter is rather "trivial". It is not Achilles' wrath, or of arms and the man, or of Man's first disobedience, sung by Homer, Virgil and Milton respectively, which are all serious in presentation as well as subject-matter, but of cutting off of a lock of hair which Pope is concerned about. He says, "I sing," "arranging the heavy singing robes of Milton about him" (Tillotson), but not with religious solemnity; rather, he plays the role of a Shakespearean Fool, who makes us laugh all the way with a talk which is apparently devoid of sense, but is said with a foresight deeper than the wisest men.

So, it is clear that *The Rape of the Lock* begins with lines which are pretty sarcastic, and therefore, tends to mock. Yet, Pope maintains the formality of the epic structure. The opening is clearly his invocation. However, it is not a prayer to the nine muses of Homer and Virgil, or the heavenly Muse of Milton, but to a mortal – Pope's friend, John Caryll! The mocking mimicry of Pope is perfectly achieved in the line:

> I sing – This Verse to Caryll, Muse! is due.

Homer talks about the character around whom his task revolves – Achilles; Milton mentions his poem deals with Man; Pope, too, mentions his character in his invocation – not a warrior, or the great parents of human race, but a young coquette – Belinda. The "subject" is thus, justly "slight", and Pope remarks:

> Slight is the Subject, but not so the Praise,
>
> If She inspire, and He approve my Lays.

These two lines are borrowed from Virgil's *Georgis*, where we get (in Dryden's translation):

> <u>Slight is the subject</u>, but the praise not small,
>
> <u>If</u> Heav'n assist, <u>and</u> Phoebus hear <u>my</u> Call.

and in Shelley's translation:

> The Subjects humble, <u>but not so the Praise</u>,
>
> <u>If</u> any Muse assist the Poets <u>Lays</u>.

The underlined parts of the translation shows how freely Pope borrowed from them and combined them.

For the source of Pope's next line, we do not have to travel across the seas to Greece and Rome, for it is in his homeland. Pope writes:

> Say what strange Motive, Goddess! Cou'd compel

In *Paradise Lost*, Milton writes:

> ...say first what cause
>
> Moved our grand parents, in that happy state...

But whereas Milton talks of the great cause which made Adam and Eve "transgress" and fall from God's favour, Pope talks of the "strange motive" for which a "well-bred Lord" assaulted a "gentle Belle"! And to top it over his predecessors, he mentions of yet another cause – a "stranger Cause", where a

> ...gentle Belle reject a Lord?

Pope talks of the indecent action of assaulting a "gentle Belle" as "Tasks so bold," equating it with great jobs which the epic heroes had to carry out. In the next line, which is the last line of the invocation, Pope writes:

> And in soft Bosoms dwells such mighty Rage?

There is an uncanny similarity with Belinda's rage, coming out of her heart – her beautiful breasts – and that of Juno's constant fuming. But where is a goddess, and where is she!

In the last few lines of what can be called Pope's invocation, the reader begins to question the direction of mockery – is it towards the epic form, or towards the society? The poem confirms that it is the society which Pope is mocking. The purpose of Pope's mock-epic is not to mock the form of the epic, but to mock the Augustan society in its very failure to rise to the epic standards. The contemporary society prized itself for maintaining formality everywhere. It was an era of "restraint", where people held back their natural feelings, behaving by putting on the dress of imposed manners, which was only superficial. Pope, and the other satirists of the age, found this ridiculous. Pope exposes the pettiness of the society, juxtaposing it against the grandeur of the traditional epic heroes. Pope's invocation makes us imagine the picture of a society which has lost all proportion, and where the trivial is handled with the gravity and solemnity that ought to be reserved only for important issues.

So, to conclude, one might say that the opening lines of *The Rape of the Lock* are mock-heroic in style. Pope includes the conventional epic subjects of love and war, but in a "trivial" form. The "am'rous Causes" are not the grand love of Greek heroes, but the selfish desires of men and women. The "mighty Contests" are brought down to the level of card-games and general foolery of men and women in cutting off of a lock of hair. So, the opening is not a mockery of the epic form, but a mockery of the society through the epic form.

Portrayal of 18th Century London Life in *The Rape of the Lock*

The Rape of the Lock is a humorous – and rather sarcastic – indictment of the vanities and idleness of the 18th century aristocratic society. The poem has been traditionally read as a mock-heroic criticism of the superficiality inherent within Pope's culture of the time – the Augustan era. The Augustan age characterized itself on its ability to restrain emotions. Pope is bent upon exposing the absurdity found predominantly in the aristocratic society, as a result of the conservative lifestyle of the people.

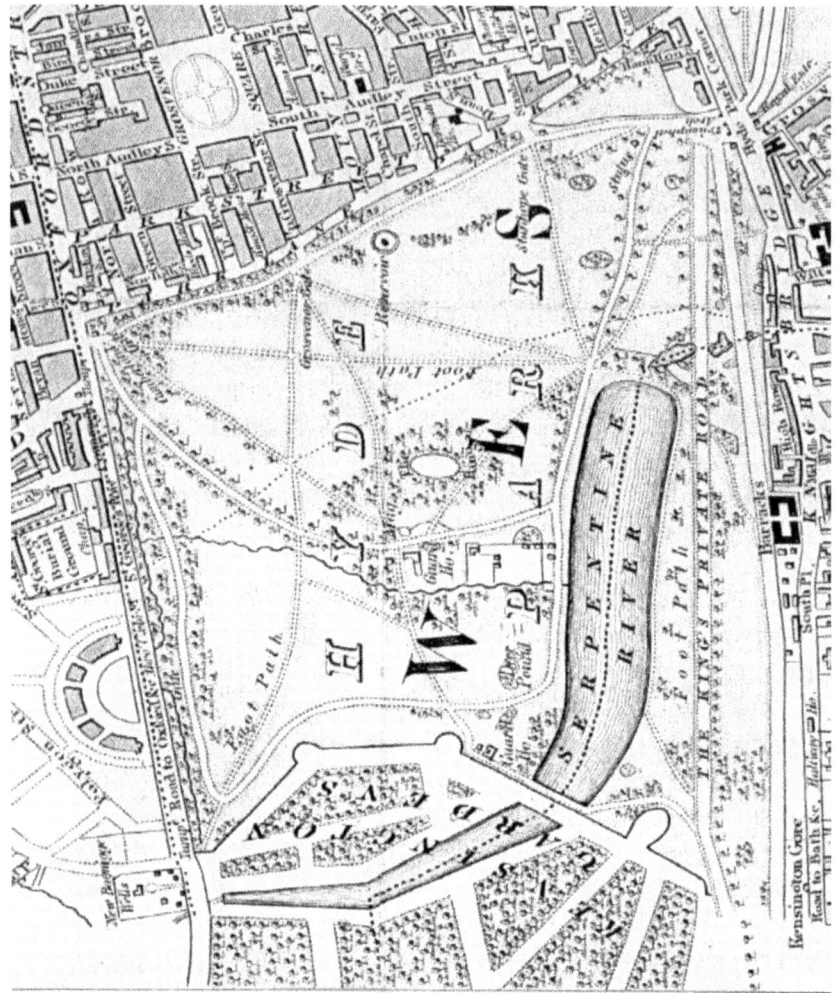

Fig. 2: 18th Century Map of London[481]

However, this conservationist approach was with respect to morality and behaviour and emotions; in expenditure, there was no restraint. The people lived a luxurious lifestyle, avoiding excess of emotions, and this came under the attack of the satirists, who sought to right the wrongly moving society.

---

[481] This image is in the public domain in its country of origin and does not require permission.

In criticizing, Pope saves himself from accusations of his victims through his refuge in the supernatural machinery – which seem to control everything. So, Pope is just a narrator – an apparently disinterested narrator – who narrates what has come to pass, and glorify the machinery of the sylphs, salamanders, gnomes and nymphs, who have brought about the actions.

Pope's first comment comes from his apparent confusion and inability to understand the cause of the quarrel, and so, he feels compelled to ask his "Goddess" about it:

> Say what strange Motive, Goddess! cou'd compel
> A well-bred Lord t' assault a gentle Belle?
> Oh say what stranger Cause, yet unexplor'd
> Cou'd make a gentle Belle reject a Lord?

In truth, Pope hints at the fact that it is the society which is "strange", and the confusion looms large in the minds of the people, whose behaviour cannot be justified by rationality. If a lord who is "well-bred" insults a lady, it is a matter of shame; on the other hand, a "gentle Belle" should be extremely fortunate if a lord asks her hand in marriage (without issues of feminist thinking), and she should accept it, not reject him! Only her vanity would make her commit such an act.

Pope goes on to say that right from a girl's childhood, the patriarchal society instructs the female gender in the art of superficiality, and deprives their chances of leading a freer, normal and natural life"

> 'Tis these that early taint the Female Soul,
> Instruct the eyes of young Coquettes to roll,

The superficial customs which the society follows are laid down by those in authority in the society, and they love to lead a lavish and sophisticated lifestyle.

> While Peers and Dukes, and all their sweeping Train,

> And Garters, Stars, and Coronets appear,
> And in soft Sounds, Your Grace salutes their Ear.

The chief concern of the ones in authority is to receive praise, and be flattered, and Pope has depicted this with a lot of care. He describes the inside activities of the Hampton Court, where he talks of Statesmen predicting the fall of "Foreign Tyrants". Predicting the fall of "Foreign Tyrants" was actually a favourite preoccupation of astrologers like Partridge. Pope describes the Hampton Court as "a Structure of Majestick France". In Evelyn's Diary, we find the comment, "Hampton Court is as noble and uniform a pile, and as capricious as any Gothic architecture can have made it." So, we are assured of Pope's honesty and accuracy. He talks of Queen Anne to visit the place ("Great Anna"). Croker writes, "Queen Anne only went there occasionally," and in keeping with it, Pope adds the word, "sometimes". Here, the judges and jury-men hurry the legal proceedings in order to enjoy a luxurious dinner (that is, midday meal), so, the impartiality of the Judiciary body is very much questioned!

But what Pope is really concerned about is the depiction of the social groups which gather at and on specific places and times. A popular practice at such social gatherings was the Card-game "Ombre". As for the group, it widely varied:

> One speaks the Glory of the British Queen,
> And one describes a charming Indian Screen;
> A third interprets Motions, Looks and Eyes;

so, one can imagine no one will run out of topic! But no matter the subject,

> At ev'ry Word a Reputation dies.

In this one line, Pope brings in the entire picture of the thing in which the society loves to indulge: defaming others. The people, in other words, are scandalous and back-biting, despite their pretended dignified look.

While Pope criticizes both men and women, it is beyond a doubt that the fairer sex gets most of the blame. While the ridiculous behaviour of the lords seem "strange", those of the ladies are "stranger". While he blames the patriarchal society for instructing the girls in the art of superficiality, he makes it clear that they let the males dominate and instruct them, showing they have not enough wit to manage things on their own. So, the butt of ridicule is the female race, who, in spite of all "art", desires an "earthly lover".

While talking of the "Pleasures of the Court", Pope describes vividly the rising popularity of coffee. It was during the Augustan era that a large number of coffee-houses were set up in England, and the political men of the age, along with writers and poets, used to cluster around the coffee table and discuss things over their drinks. Tea, too, was had, but it was expensive, and coffee was more popular. Pope keeps this in mind and makes Queen Anne take the more expensive "Tea", while making Belinda and the others take "Coffee". Tillotson comments that "The coffee houses had long been the chief haunt of amateur politicians".

Pope does not miss to talk about the exquisiteness of the people for fancy articles. He gives a very sarcastic description of the cups, spoons and dishes:

> For lo! The Board with Cups and Spoons is crown'd,
> The Berries crack, and the Mill turns round.
> On shining Alters of Japan they raise
> The silver Lapm; the fiery Spirits blaze.
> From silver Spouts the grateful Liquors glide,
> While China's Earth receives the smoking Tyde.

In the toilette scene also, Pope attacks this exquisite taste:

> This Caskets India's glowing Gems unlocks,
> And all Arabia breathes from yonder Box.

In describing a variety of objects, Pope also turns humans into commodities – especially women. Ellen Pollak explains, "Pope criticizes the sterility of a world in which the signs of things have actually become substitutes for the things themselves, where virtue has been reduced to reputation and men themselves into swordknots, where in effect people live in a materialistic and metonymic void," and where "female sexuality is a material property over which man has natural claim."

In depicting the contemporary man-woman relationship, Pope shows a world where women are valued for their beauty, and yet, all of them – whether beautiful or not – strive towards perfecting their make-up in order to attain peak performance, and appear in a beauty which is not natural. With the help of "Cosmetic Pow'rs," they aim at creating a "purer blush". They work and re-work their smiles – and smile at everybody. This shows their lack of focus.

> Favours to none, to all she Smiles extends,
> Oft she rejects, but never once offends.

To these women, their desires are as inconsistent as the inconstant gods and goddess of Homer and Virgil, who keep on taking and changing sides. Their desires are like toys, and

> They ship the moving Toyshop of their heart

and to top it all, give equal importance to lap-dogs and their husbands!

The men play about with such women – who shamelessly let them do so, and each of them becomes "a Victim" to the advances made by men. However, Pope criticizes the men to some extent in saying,

> And Beauty draws us with a single Hair

and points at the shallowness of men, who are drawn by so light a thing.

To conclude, it can be said that in *The Rape of the Lock*, Pope paints an accurate picture of the Augustan era, and presents it to the world – to its readers – to evaluate his work, which is itself an evaluation of the contemporary society with its vices (which are otherwise hidden in the restrained and conservative lifestyle by its artificiality and superficial politeness).

Supernatural Machinery in *The Rape of the Lock*

Alexander Pope added much of his "supernatural machinery"in the revised version of his heroi-comical poem, *The Rape of the Lock*, in the 1714 edition, enlarging it to five cantos from the what was previously in two cantos. He talks about its inclusion in his Dedication to the second edition, and mentions this was "wanting" in the first edition:

> for the machinery was entirely wanting to compleat it.

In the following lines of his Dedication, he tries to define this machinery as "a Term...signify that Part which the Deities, Angels or Daemons, are made to act in a Poem."

The use of supernatural machinery goes back to the time of Homer and Virgil, who had developed this device and made it an integral part of an epic. In fact, in the epics of Homer and Virgil, the supernatural creatures seem to guide the course of action. However, as Pope clearly states, *The Rape of the Lock* is "Heroi-Comical", in other words, mock-epic. In his enlarged edition of the poem, Pope has maximized the effect of the mock-heroic by maximizing the role of the supernatural machinery. In an epic, ethereal beings take active interest in the matters of human beings – the purpose being very serious. Pope indulges petty supernatural creatures to take care of every singular aspect of human activity – most of the activities being too trivial. So, just as the gods and goddesses prepare the armour of the epic hero with great care, innumerous Sylphs attend to Belinda – to dress her up:

> These set the Head, and those divide the Hair,
> Some fold the Sleeve, while others plait the Gown;

Great emphasis upon triviality is the feature of mock-epic, and the little gnomes, nymphs, salamanders and sylphs fulfil this greatly. In fact, *The Rape of the Lock* would have lost half its humour if the supernatural agencies were not present.

In *Iliad*, Jove sends Iris to bring a morning dream to the sleeping Agamemnon. In *Paradise Lost*, Satan tries to tempt Eve in her sleep before appearing later in the guise of a serpent. In *The Rape of the Lock*, Ariel appears to Belinda while she is dreaming. Homer talks of Pallas and Apollo sitting like Eagles and watching the battle between the Greeks and Trojans, and of their free help to the soldiers (Pallas guards Diomed while Venus saves Paris from Menelaus); Pope talks of the band of Sylphs descending upon Cards:

> …th' Aerial Guard
> Descend, and sit on each important Card.

Ariel, who overlooks everything, is comparable to Jove overlooking the fighting armies, while sitting on Ida. The mockery of the situation is intensified by comparing a card-game ('Ombre') with a battle, and gods and goddesses with little sylphs and nymphs. The sarcastic seriousness with which Pope narrates the tale is worth commenting. He seriously makes Belinda believe in the existence "Of thousand bright Inhabitants of Air", while sarcastically stating that only the innocent babies and fanciful maids will believe it:

> Some secret Truth from Learned Pride conceal'd,
> To Maids alone or Children are reveal'd.

He goes on to elaborate:

> What tho' no Credit doubting Wits may give?
> The Fair and Innocent shall still believe

Through Belinda's belief in these supernatural beings, Pope has been able to portray her inexperienced nature. Had he not talked of the supernatural machinery with respect to Belinda's faith, the readers would not have come to know about her dullness. So, while Betty dresses Belinda, Pope wants us to have a grand laugh at the fact that there might be people like her who think it is the sylphs who dress her up.

> And Betty's prais'd for Labours not her own.

So, the supernatural machinery is able to bring out a good character-sketch of Belinda, while at the same time making the text a good and decorative reading.

Pope makes it a point to bring out the total ineffectiveness of these creatures, in spite of all their controlling powers. Their intervention (unlike the intervention of Pallas or Jove in Homer or of Venus in Virgil), is of no avail. Ariel tries to warn her through the morning-dream, but Belinda simply forgets all about the dream once she gets up from bed. The sylphs who guard Belinda (or rather, cover up Belinda!) to protect her from the coming danger simply fail to prevent the scissors cutting the lock of hair. Moreover, the sylphs are aware of the imminent clipping of her lock, but know not what, how or where it is to happen:

> But Heav'n reveals not what, or how, or where:

As a result of this, Pope cunningly supplies Ariel with an excuse for their failure, that because Belinda nourished feelings for a man, they could not help her. But everyone knows better, and Pope humorously hints at it, by describing the sylph, who tries to save Belinda's lock by stepping in the path of the about-to-clasp scissors, but cannot save the lock. In addition, its body is cut into two parts! This shows that they cannot protect their charge, or even themselves!

Pope makes further fun of the epic features. Ethereal beings are supposed to be immortal, and so, when Satan suffers injury in battle in *Paradise Lost*, the body is quickly healed. Pope twists this idea and makes the unfortunate sylph, who was cut into two halves, one body again! Moreover, these creatures can take "any shape they please", as is characteristic of the classical gods and goddesses and as Satan also does. Following this pattern of mockery, Pope makes Lord Peter pray before the gods before his venture (as heroes do in the epics), and just like the whimsical gods and goddesses who have their own purpose in mind, and so, despite fervent prayers, may not grant the request fully, the gods of Lord Peter grant half his prayer. He is able to cut the lock, but not possess it:

> The Power's gave Ear, and granted half his Pray'r,
> The rest, the Winds dispers'd in empty Air.

Though Addison has criticized the revised use of the supernatural machinery as being excessive and by stating that it ruins the subject of the poem by turning attention elsewhere, there are few who side with him. In fact, it is through this supernatural machinery that our focus is magnified on certain aspects (like the portrayal of the character of Belinda, or the influence and popularity of the game of 'Ombre'). Without this machinery, *The Rape of the Lock* would not have been a mock-epic at all.

Cantos IV and V (unannotated)

Canto IV

But anxious Cares the pensive Nymph oppress'd,
And secret Passions labour'd in her Breast.
Not youthful Kings in Battle seiz'd alive,
Not scornful Virgins who their Charms survive,
Not ardent Lovers robb'd of all their Bliss,
Not ancient Ladies when refus'd a Kiss,
Not Tyrants fierce that unrepenting die,
Not *Cynthia* when her *Manteau's* pinn'd awry,
E'er felt such Rage, Resentment, and Despair,
As Thou, sad Virgin! for thy ravish'd Hair.

For, that sad moment, when the *Sylphs* withdrew,
And *Ariel* weeping from *Belinda* flew,
Umbriel, a dusky, melancholy Sprite,
As ever sully'd the fair Face of Light,
Down to the Central Earth, his proper Scene,
Repair'd to search the gloomy Cave of *Spleen.*

Swift on his sooty Pinions flits the *Gnome,*
And in a Vapour reach'd the dismal Dome.
No cheerful Breeze this sullen Region knows,
The dreaded *East* is all the Wind that blows.
Here in a Grotto, shelter'd close from Air,
And screen'd in Shades from Day's detested Glare,
She sighs for ever on her pensive Bed,
Pain at her Side, and *Megrim* at her Head.

Two Handmaids wait the Throne: Alike in Place,
But diffring far in Figure and in Face.
Here stood *Ill-nature* like an *ancient Maid,*
Her wrinkled form in *Black* and *White* array'd;
With store of Pray'rs, for Mornings, Nights, and Noons,
Her Hand is fill'd; her Bosom with Lampoons.

There *Affectation* with a sickly Mien,
Shows in her Cheek the Roses of Eighteen,
Practis'd to Lisp, and hang the Head aside,
Faints into Airs, and languishes with Pride;
On the rich Quilt sinks with becoming Woe,
Wrapt in a Gown, for Sickness, and for Show.
The Fair ones feel such Maladies as these,
When each new Night-Dress gives a new Disease.

A constant *Vapour* o'er the Palace flies;
Strange Phantoms rising as the Mists arise;
Dreadful, as Hermits' Dreams in haunted Shades,
Or bright, as Visions of expiring Maids.
Now glaring Fiends, and Snakes on rolling Spires,
Pale Spectres, gaping Tombs, and Purple Fires:
Now Lakes of liquid Gold, *Elysian* Scenes,
And Crystal Domes, and Angels in Machines.

Unnumber'd Throngs, on ev'ry side are seen,
Of Bodies chang'd to various forms by *Spleen.*
Here living *Teapots* stand, one Arm held out,
One bent; the Handle this, and that the Spout:
A Pipkin there like *Homer's Tripod* walks;
Here sighs a Jar, and there a Goose-pye talks;
Men prove with Child, as pow'rful Fancy works,
And Maids turn'd Bottels, call aloud for Corks.

Safe past the *Gnome* through this fantastic Band,
A branch of healing *Spleenwort* in his Hand.
Then thus addrest the Pow'r-Hail wayward Queen;
Who rule the Sex to Fifty from Fifteen,
Parent of Vapors and of Female Wit,
Who give th' *Hysteric* or *Poetic* Fit,
On various Tempers act by various Ways,
Make some take Physic, others scribble Plays;
Who cause the Proud their Visits to delay,
And send the Godly in a Pett, to pray.

A Nymph there is, that all thy pow'r disdains,
And thousands more in equal Mirth maintains.
But oh! if e'er thy *Gnome* could spoil a Grace,
Or raise a Pimple on a beauteous Face,
Like Citron-Waters Matrons' Cheeks inflame,
Or change Complexions at a losing Game;
If e'er with airy Horns I planted Heads,
Or rumpled Petticoats, or tumbled Beds,
Or cause'd Suspicion when no Soul was rude,
Or discompos'd the Head-Dress of a Prude,
Or e'er to costive Lap-Dog gave Disease,
Which not the Tears of brightest Eyes could ease:
Hear me, and touch *Belinda* with Chagrin;
That single Act gives half the World the Spleen.

The Goddess with a discontented Air
Seems to reject him, tho' she grants his Pray'r.
A wond'rous Bag with both her Hands she binds,
Like that where once *Ulysses* held the Winds;
There she collects the Force of Female Lungs,
Sighs, Sobs, and Passions, and the War of Tongues.
A Vial next she fills with fainting Fears,
Soft Sorrows, melting Griefs, and flowing Tears.
The *Gnome* rejoycing bears her Gift away,
Spreads his black Wings, and slowly mounts to Day.

Sunk in *Thalestris'* Arms the Nymph he found,
Her Eyes dejected, and her Hair unbound.
Full o'er their Heads the swelling Bag he rent,
And all the Furies issu'd at the Vent.
Belinda burns with more than mortal Ire,
And fierce *Thalestris* fans the rising Fire.
O wretched Maid! she spread her Hands, and cry'd,
(While *Hampton's* Ecchoes, wretched Maid! reply'd)
Was it for this you took such constant Care
The *Bodkin, Comb* and *Essence* to prepare;
For this your Locks in Paper-Durance bound,
For this with tort'ring Irons wreath'd around!

For this with Fillets strain'd your tender Head,
And bravely bore the double Loads of Lead?
Gods! shall the Ravisher display your Hair,
While the Fops envy, and the Ladies stare!
Honour forbid! at whose unrivall'd Shrine
Ease, Pleasure, Virtue, All, our Sex resign.
Methinks already I your Tears survey,
Already hear the horrid Things they say,
Already see you a degraded Toast,
And all your Honour in a Whisper lost!
How shall I, then, your hapless Fame defend?
'Twill then be Infamy to seem your Friend!
And shall this Prize, th' inestimable Prize,
Expos'd through Crystal to the gazing Eyes,
And heighten'd by the Diamond's circling Rays,
On that Rapacious Hand for ever blaze?
Sooner shall Grass in *Hide-Park Circus* grow,
And Wits take Lodgings in the sound of *Bow;*
Sooner let Earth, Air, Sea, to *Chaos* fall,
Men, Monkeys, Lap-dogs, Parrots, perish all!

She said; then raging to Sir *Plume* repairs,
And bids her *Beau* demand the precious Hairs:
(Sir *Plume,* of *Amber Snuff-box* justly vain,
And the nice Conduct of a *Clouded Cane*)
With earnest Eyes and round unthinking Face,
He first the Snuff-box open's, then the Case,
And thus broke out--"My Lord, why, what the Devil!
"Z----ds! damn the Lock! 'fore Gad, you must be civil!
"Plague on't! 'tis past a Jest--nay, prithee, Pox!
"Give her the Hair"--he spoke, and rapp'd his Box.

It grieves me much (replied the Peer again)
Who speaks so well shou'd ever speak in vain.
But by this Lock, this sacred Lock I swear,
(Which never more shall join its parted Hair;
Which never more its Honours shall renew,

Clipp'd from the lovely Head where late it grew)
That while my Nostrils draw the vital Air,
This Hand, which won it, shall for ever wear.
He spoke, and speaking, in proud Triumph spread
The long-contended Honours of her Head.

But *Umbriel,* hateful *Gnome!* forbears not so;
He breaks the Vial whence the Sorrows flow.
Then see! the Nymph in beauteous Grief appears,
Her Eyes half-languishing, half-drown'd in Tears;
On her heav'd Bosom hung her drooping Head,
Which with a Sigh, she rais'd; and thus she said.

For ever curs'd be this detested Day,
Which snatch'd my best, my fav'rite Curl away!
Happy! ah ten times happy had I been,
If *Hampton-Court* these Eyes had never seen!
Yet am not I the first mistaken Maid,
By love of *Courts* to num'rous Ills betray'd.
Oh had I rather unadmir'd remain'd
In some lone Isle, or distant *Northern* land;
Where the gilt *Chariot* never mark'd the way,
Where none learn *Ombre,* none e'er taste *Bohea!*
There kept my Charms conceal'd from the mortal Eye,
Like Roses that in Desarts bloom and die.
What mov'd my Mind with youthful Lords to rome?
O had I stay'd, and said my Pray'rs at home!
'Twas this the Morning *Omens* did foretel;
Thrice from my trembling Hand the *Patch-box* fell;
The tott'ring *China* shook without a Wind,
Nay, *Poll* sate mute, and *Shock* was most Unkind!
A *Sylph* too warn'd me of the Threats of Fate,
In mystic Visions, now believ'd too late!
See the poor Remnants of these slighted Hairs!
My Hands shall rend what ev'n thy Rapine spares.
These, in two sable Ringlets taught to break,
Once gave new Beauties to the snowy Neck.
The Sister-Lock now sits uncouth, alone,

And in its Fellow's Fate foresees its own;
Uncurl'd it hangs, the fatal Sheers demands;
And tempts once more thy sacrilegious Hands.
Oh hadst thou, Cruel! been content to seize
Hairs less in sight, or any Hairs but these!

Canto V

She said: The pitying Audience melt in Tears,
But *Fate* and *Jove* had stopp'd the *Baron's* Ears.
In vain *Thalestris* with Reproach assails,
For who can move when fair *Belinda* fails?
Not half so fix'd the *Trojan* could remain,
While *Anna* begg'd and *Dido* rag'd in vain.
Then grave *Clarissa* graceful wav'd her Fan;
Silence ensu'd, and thus the Nymph began.

Say, why are Beauties prais'd and honour'd most,
The Wise Man's Passion, and the Vain Man's Toast?
Why deck'd with all that Land and Sea afford,
Why Angels call'd, and Angel-like ador'd?
Why round our Coaches crowd the white-gloved Beaux,
Why bows the Side-box from its inmost Rows?
How vain are all these Glories, all our Pains,
Unless good Sense preserve what Beauty gains:
That Men may say, when we the Front-box grace,
Behold the first in Virtue as in Face!
Oh! if to dance all Night, and dress all Day,
Charm'd the Small-pox, or chas'd old Age away;
Who would not scorn what Housewife's Cares produce,
Or who would learn one earthly Thing of Use?
To patch, nay ogle, might become a Saint,
Nor could it sure be such a Sin to paint.
But since, alas! frail Beauty must decay,
Curl'd or uncurl'd, since Locks will turn to grey;

Since painted, or not painted, all shall fade,
And she who scorns a Man, must die a Maid,
What then remains but well our Pow'r to use,
And keep good Humour still whate'er we lose?
And trust me, dear! good Humour can prevail,
When Airs, and Flights, and Screams, and Scolding fail.
Beauties in vain their pretty Eyes may roll;
Charms strike the Sight, but Merit wins the Soul.

So spoke the Dame, but no Applause ensu'd:
Belinda frown'd, *Thalestris* call'd her Prude.
To Arms, to Arms! the fierce Virago cries,
And swift as Lightning to the Combate flies.
All side in Parties, and begin th' Attack;
Fans clap, Silks rustle, and tough Whalebones crack;
Heroes' and Heroins' Shouts confus'dly rise,
And base, and treble Voices strike the Skies.
No common Weapons in their Hands are found,
Like Gods they fight, nor dread a mortal Wound.

So when bold *Homer* makes the Gods engage,
And heav'nly Breasts with human Passions rage;
'Gainst *Pallas, Mars; Latona, Hermes,* Arms;
And all *Olympus* rings with loud Alarms.
Jove's Thunder roars, Heav'n trembles all around;
Blue *Neptune* storms, the bellowing Deeps resound;
Earth shakes her nodding Tow'rs, the Ground gives way,
And the pale Ghosts start at the Flash of Day!

Triumphant *Umbriel* on a Sconce's Height
Clapp'd his glad Wings, and sate to view the Fight,
Propp'd on their Bodkin Spears the Sprites survey
The growing Combat, or assist the Fray.

While through the Press enrag'd *Thalestris* flies,
And scatters Death around from both her Eyes,
A *Beau* and *Witling* perish'd in the Throng,
One dy'd in *Metaphor,* and one in *Song.*

O cruel Nymph! a living death I bear,
Cried *Dapperwit,* and sunk beside his Chair.
A mournful Glance Sir *Fopling* upwards cast,
Those eyes are made so killing--was his last:
Thus on *Meander's* flow'ry Margin lies
Th' expiring Swan, and as he sings he dies.

As bold Sir *Plume* had drawn *Clarissa down,*
Chloe stepp'd in, and kill'd him with a Frown;
She smil'd to see the doughty Hero slain,
But at her Smile, the Beau reviv'd again.

Now *Jove* suspends his golden Scales in Air,
Weighs the Men's Wits against the Lady's Hair;
The doubtful Beam long nods from side to side;
At length the Wits mount up, the Hairs subside.

See fierce *Belinda* on the *Baron* flies,
With more than usual Lightning in her Eyes:
Nor fear'd the Chief th' unequal Fight to try,
Who sought no more than on his Foe to die.
But this bold Lord, with manly Strength endu'd,
She with one Finger and a Thumb subdu'd:
Just where the Breath of Life his Nostrils drew,
A charge of *Snuff* the wily Virgin threw;
The *Gnomes* direct, to ev'ry Atome just,
The pungent Grains of titillating Dust,
Sudden, with starting Tears each Eye o'erflows,
And the high Dome re-ecchoes to his Nose.

Now meet thy Fate, incens'd *Belinda* cry'd,
And drew a deadly *Bodkin* from her Side.
(The same, his ancient Personage to deck,
Her great great Grandsire wore about his Neck
In three *Seal-Rings;* which after melted down,
Form'd a vast *Buckle* for his Widow's Gown:
Her infant Grandame's *Whistle* next it grew,

The Bells she gingled, and the *Whistle* blew;
Then in a *Bodkin* grac'd her Mother's hairs,
Which long she wore, and now *Belinda* wears.)

Boast not my Fall (he cry'd) insulting Foe!
Thou by some other shalt be laid as low.
Nor think, to die dejects my lofty Mind.
All that I dread, is leaving you behind!
Rather than so, ah let me still survive,
And burn in *Cupid's* Flames-but burn alive.

Restore the Lock! she cries; and all around
Restore the Lock! the Vaulted Roofs rebound.
Not fierce *Othello* in so loud a Strain
Roar'd for the Handkerchief that caus'd his Pain.
But see how oft Ambitious Aims are cross'd,
And Chiefs contend 'till all the Prize is lost!
The Lock, obtain'd with Guilt, and kept with Pain,
In ev'ry place is sought, but sought in vain:
With such a Prize no Mortal must be blest,
So Heav'n decrees! with Heav'n who can contest?

Some thought it mounted to the Lunar Sphere,
Since all things lost on Earth, are treasur'd there.
There Heroe's Wits are kept in pond'rous Vases,
And Beau's in *Snuff-boxes* and *Tweezer-cases.*
There broken Vows, and Death-bed Alms are found,
And Lovers' Hearts with Ends of Riband bound;
The Courtier's Promises, and the Sick Man's Pray'rs,
The Smiles of Harlots, and the Tears of Heirs,
Cages for Gnats, and Chains to Yoak a Flea;
Dried Butterflies, and Tomes of Casuistry.

But trust the Muse-she saw it upward rise,
Tho' marked by none but quick Poetic eyes:
(So *Rome's* great Founder to the Heav'ns withdrew,
To *Proculus* alone confess'd in view.)
A sudden Star, it shot through liquid Air,

And drew behind a radiant *Trail of Hair*.
Not *Berenice's* Locks first rose so bright,
The Skies bespangling with dishevel'd Light.
The *Sylphs* behold it kindling as it flies,
And pleas'd pursue its Progress through the Skies.

This the *Beau-monde* shall from the *Mall* survey,
And hail with *Musick* its propitious Ray.
This the blest Lover shall for *Venus* take,
And send up Vows from *Rosamonda's* Lake.
This *Partridge* soon shall view in cloudless Skies
When next he looks through *Gallileo's* Eyes;
And hence th' Egregious Wizard shall foredoom
The fate of *Louis,* and the fall of *Rome*.

Then cease, bright Nymph! to mourn the ravish'd Hair
Which adds new Glory to the shining Sphere!
Not all the Tresses that fair Head can boast
Shall draw such Envy as the Lock you lost.
For, after all the Murders of your Eye,
When, after Millions slain, yourself shall die;
When those fair Suns shall set, as set they must,
And all those Tresses shall be laid in dust;
This *Lock,* the Muse shall consecrate to fame,
And 'midst the stars inscribe *Belinda's* Name!

A KEY TO THE LOCK

Written in 1715 by Pope (using the pseudonym Esdras Barnivelt), this humorous interpretation of *The Rape of the Lock* serves as a warning to critics not to take the poem too seriously. In the Key Pope exposes his own poem as a dangerous political allegory (Belinda represents Great Britain, the Lock represents the Barrier Treaty...). The Key also shows Pope trying to placate Sir George Brown (the original for Sir Plume, Sir George was none too happy with the role he played in the poem) by indicating there were at least two possible originals for Sir Plume.

A KEY TO THE LOCK

Or a Treatise proving, beyond all Contradiction, the dangerous Tendency of a late Poem entitled *The Rape of the Lock* to Government and Religion by Esdras Barnivelt, Apothecary

THE EPISTLE DEDICATORY TO MR *POPE*

Though it may seem foreign to my Profession, which is that of making up and dispensing salutary Medicines to his Majesty's Subjects, (I might say my Fellow-Subjects, since I have had the Advantage of being naturalised) yet cannot I think it unbecoming me to furnish an Antidote against the Poyson which hath been so artfully distilled through your Quill, and conveyed to the World through the pleasing Vehicle of your Numbers. Nor is my Profession as an Apothecary so abhorrent from yours as a Poet, since the Ancients have thought fit to make the same God the Patron of Both. I have, not without some Pleasure, observ'd the mystical Arms of our Company, wherein is represented *Apollo* killing the fell Monster *Python;* this in some measure admonishes me of my Duty, to trample upon and destroy, as much as in me lies, that Dragon, or baneful Serpent, *Popery.*

I must take leave to make you my Patient, whether you will or no; though out of the Respect I have for you, I should rather Chuse to apply Lenitive than corrosive Medicines, happy, if they may prove an Emetic sufficient to make you cast up those Errors, which you have imbibed in your Education, and which, I hope, I shall never live to see this Nation digest.

Sir, I cannot but lament, that a Gentleman of your acute Wit, rectified Understanding, and sublimated Imagination, should misapply those Talents to raise ill Humours in the Constitution of the Body Politick, of which your self are a Member, and upon the Health whereof your Preservation depends. Give me leave to say, such Principles as yours would again reduce us to the fatal Necessity of the Phlebotomy of War, or the Causticks of Persecution.

In order to inform you of this, I have sought your Acquaintance and Conversation with the utmost Diligence; for I hoped in Person to persuade you to a publick Confession of your Fault, and a Recantation of these dangerous Tenets. But finding all my Endeavors ineffectual, and being satisfied with the Conscience of having done all that became a Man of an honest Heart and honourable Intention; I could no longer omit my Duty in opening the Eyes of the World by the Publication of this Discourse. It was indeed written some Months since, but seems not the less proper at this Juncture, when I find so universal an Encouragement given by both Parties to the Author of a libellous Work that is designed equally to prejudice them both. The uncommon Sale of this Book (for above 6000 of 'em have been already vended) was also a farther Progress, and to preserve his Majesty's Subjects, by exposing the whole Artifice of your Poem in Publick.

Sir, to address my self to so florid a Writer as you, without collecting the Flowers of Rhetorick, would be an unpardonable *Indecorum;* but when I speak to the World, as I do in the following Treatise, I must use a simple Stile, since it would be absurd to prescribe an universal Medicine, or *Catholicon,* in a Language not universally understood.

As I have always professed to have a particular Esteem for Men of Learning, and more especially for yourself, nothing but the Love of Truth should have engaged me in a Design of this Nature. *Amicus Plato, Amicus Socrates, sed magis Amica Veritas.* I am

Your most
Sincere Friend,

and Humble Servant,

E. Barnivelt.

A KEY TO THE LOCK

Since this unhappy Division of our Nation into Parties, it is not to be imagined how many Artifices have been made use of by Writers to obscure the Truth, and cover Designs, which may be detrimental to the Publick; in particular, it has been their Custom of late to vent their Political Spleen in Allegory and Fable. If an honest believing Nation is to be made a Jest of, we have a Story of *John Bull* and his Wife; if a Treasurer is to be glanced at, an *Ant* with a *white Straw* is introduced; if a Treaty of Commerce is to be ridiculed, 'tis immediately metamorphosed into a Tale of Count *Tariff.*

But if any of these Malevolents have never so small a Talent in Rhime, they principally delight to convey their Malice in that pleasing way, as it were, gilding the Pill, and concealing the Poyson under the Sweetness of Numbers. Who could imagine that an *Original Canto* of *Spenser* should contain a Satyr upon one Administration; or that *Yarhel's Kitchin,* or the *Dogs of Egypt,* should be a sarcasm upon another.

It is the Duty of every well designing Subject to prevent, as far as in him lies, the ill Consequences of such pernicious Treatises; and I hold it mine to warn the Publick of the late Poem, entituled, the *Rape of the Lock;* which I shall demonstrate to be of this nature. Many of these sort of Books have been bought by honest and well-meaning People purely for their Diversion, who have in the end found themselves insensibly led into the Violence of Party Spirit, and many domestick Quarrels have been occasioned by the different Application of these Books. The Wife of an eminent Citizen grew very noisy upon reading *Bob Hush; John Bull,* upon *Change,* was thought not only to concern the State, but to affront the City; and the Poem we are now treating of, has not only dissolved an agreeable Assembly of Beaus and Belles, but (as I am told) has set Relations at as great a distance, as if they were Married together.

It is a common and just Observation, that when the Meaning of any thing is dubious, one can no way better judge of the true Intent of it, than by considering who is the Author, what is his Character in general, and his Disposition in particular.

Now that the Author of this Poem is professedly a *Papist,* is well known; and that a Genius so capable of doing Service to that Cause, may have been corrupted in the Course of his Education by *Jesuits* of others, is justly very much to be suspected; notwithstanding that seeming *Coolness* and *Moderation,* which he has been (perhaps artfully) reproached with, by those of his own Profession. They are sensible that this Nation is secured with good and wholesome Laws, to prevent all evil Practices of the Church of *Rome*; particularly the Publication of Books, that may in any sort propagate that Doctrine: Their Authors are therefore obliged to couch their Designs the deeper; and tho' I cannot averr that the Intention of this Gentleman was directly to spread Popish Doctrines, yet it comes to the same Point, if he touch the Government: For the Court of *Rome* knows very well, that the Church at this time is so firmly founded on the State, that the only way to shake the one is by attacking the other.

What confirms me in this Opinion, is the accidental Discovery I made of a very artful Piece of Management among his Popish Friends and Abettors, to hide this whole Design upon the Government, by taking all the Characters upon themselves.

Upon the Day that this Poem was published, it was my Fortune to step into the *Cocoa Tree,* where a certain Gentleman was railing very liberally at the Author, with a Passion extremely well counterfeited, for having (as he said) reflected upon him in the Character of *Sir Plume.* Upon his going out, I enquired who he was, and they told me, *a Roman Catholick Knight.*

I was the same Evening at *Will's,* and saw a Circle round another Gentleman, who was railing in like manner, and shewing his Snuff-box and Cane, to prove he was satyrized in the same Character. I asked this Gentleman's Name, and was told, he was *a Roman Catholick Lord.*

A Day or two after I was sent for, upon a slight Indisposition, to the young Lady's to whom the Poem is dedicated. She also took up the Character of *Belinda* with much Frankness and good Humour, tho' the Author has given us a Key in his Dedication, that he meant something further. This Lady is also a *Roman Catholick.* At the same time others of the Characters were claim'd by some Persons in the Room; and all of them *Roman Catholicks.*

But to proceed to the Work itself.

In all things which are intricate, as Allegories in their own Nature are, and especially those that are industriously made so, it is not to be expected we should find the clue at first sight; but when once we have laid hold on that, we shall trace this our Author through all the Labyrinths, Doublings and Turnings of this intricate Composition.

First let it be observed, that in the most demonstrative Sciences, some *Postulata* are to be granted, upon which the rest is naturally founded. I shall desire no more than one *Postulatum* to render this obvious to the meanest Capacity; which being granted me, I shall not only shew the Intent of this Work in general, but also explain the very *Names,* and expose all his fictitious *Characters* in their true Light; and we shall find, that even his *Spirits* were not meerly contrived for the sake of *Machinary.*

The only Concession which I desire to be made me, is that by the *Lock* is meant

The BARRIER TREATY

I. First then I shall discover, that BELINDA represents GREAT BRITAIN, or (which is the same thing) her late MAJESTY. This is plainly seen in his Description of her.

   On her white Breast a sparkling Cross she bore.

Alluding to the ancient Name of *Albion,* from her *white Cliffs,* and to the *Cross,* which is the Ensign of *England.*
II. The BARON, who cuts off the Lock, or Barrier Treaty, is the E[arl] of O[xfor]d.
III. CLARISSA, who lent the Scissars, my Lady M[ashe]m.
IV. THALESTRIS, who provokes *Belinda* to resent the Loss of the Lock or Treaty, the D[uches]s of M[arlborou]gh.
V. SIR PLUME, who is mov'd by *Thalestris* to redemand it of *Great Britain,* P[rin]ce Eu[ge]ne, who came hither for that purpose.

There are other inferior Characters, which we shall observe upon afterwards; but I shall first explain the foregoing.

The first Part of the *Baron's* Character is his being *adventrous,* or enterprizing, which is the common Epithet given to the E[arl] of O[xfor]d by his Enemies. The Prize he aspires to is the T[reasur]y, in order to which he offers a Sacrifice.

   -----------------------------an Altar built
Of twelve vast *French* Romances neatly gilt.

Our Author here takes occasion maliciously to insinuate this Statesman's *Love to France;* representing the Books he chiefly studies to be vast *French Romances.* These are the vast Prospects from the Friendship and Alliance of *France,* which he satyrically calls *Romances,* hinting thereby, that these Promises and

Protestations were no more to be relied on than those idle Legends. Of these he is said to build an Altar; to intimate, that all the Foundation of his Schemes and Honours was fix'd upon the *French Romances* abovementioned.

A Fan, a Garter, Half a Pair of Gloves.

One of the Things he sacrifices is a *Fan,* which both for its *gaudy Show* and *perpetual Flutt'ring,* has been made the Emblem of *Woman.* This points at the Change of the *Ladies* of the *Bedchamber;* the *Garter* alludes to the Honours he conferr'd on some of his Friends; and we may without straining the Sense, call the Half Pair of Gloves, a *Gauntlet;* the Token of those Military Employments, which he is said to have sacrificed to his Designs. The Prize, as I said before, means the T[reasur]y, which he makes it his Prayers *soon to obtain,* and *long to possess.*

The Pow'rs gave ear, and granted half his Pray'r,
The rest the Winds dispers'd in empty Air.

In the first of these Lines he gives him the T[reasur]y, and in the last suggests that he should not long posses that Honour.

That *Thalestris* is the D[uches]s of M[arlborou]gh, appears both by her nearness to *Belinda,* and by this Author's malevolent Suggestion, that she is a Lover of War.

To Arms, to Arms, the bold *Thalestris* cries.

But more particlary in several Passages in her Speech to *Belinda,* upon the cutting off the Lock, or Treaty. Among other Things she says, *Was it for this you bound your Locks in Paper Durance?* Was it for this so much Paper has been spent to secure the Barrier Treaty?

Methinks already I your Tears survey,
Already hear the horrid Things they say;
Already see you a degraded Toast.

This describes the Aspersions under which that good Princess suffer'd, and the Repentance which must have followed the Dissolution of that Treaty, and particularly levels at the Refusal some People made to drink Her M[ajest]y's Health.

Sir Plume (a proper Name for a Soldier) has all the Circumstances that agree with P[rin]ce *Eu[ge]ne.*

Sir Plume of Amber Snuff-box justly vain,
And the nice Conduct of a clouded Cane,
With earnest Eyes-----------

'Tis remarkable, this General is a great Taker of Snuff as well as Towns; his Conduct of the clouded Cane gives him the Honour which is so justly his due, of an exact Conduct in Battle, which is figured by his Truncheon, the Ensign of a General. His earnest Eye, or the Vivacity of his Look, is so particularly remarkable in him, that this Character could be mistaken for no other, had not this Author purposely obscur'd it by the fictitious Circumstance of a *round, unthinking Face.*

Having now explained the chief Characters of his *Human Persons* (for there are some others that will hereafter fall in by the by, in the Sequel of this Discourse) I shall next take in pieces his *Machinary,* wherein his Satyr is wholly confined to Ministers of State.

The Slyphs and Gnomes at first sight appeared to me to signify the two contending Parties of this Nation; for these being placed in the *Air,* and those on the *Earth,* I thought agreed very well with the common Denomination, High and Low. But as they are made to be the first Movers and Influencers of all that happens, 'tis plain they represent promiscuiosly the *Heads of Parties,* whom he makes to be the Authors of all those Changes in the State, which are generally imputed to the Levity and Instability of the *British* Nation.

This erring Mortals Levity may call,
Oh blind to Truth! The Sylphs contrive it all.

But of this he has given us a plain Demonstration; for speaking of these Spirits, he says in express Terms,

---------The chief the Care of Nations own,
And guard with Arms Divine the *British* Throne.

And here let it not seem odd, if in this mysterious way of Writing, we find the same Person, who has before been represented by the *Baron,* again described in the Character of *Ariel;* it being a common way with Authors, in this fabulous Manner, to take such a Liberty. As for instance, I have read in the *English St. Evremont,* that all the different Characters in *Petronius* are but *Nero* in so many different Appearances. And in the Key to the curious Romance of *Barclay's Argenis,* that both *Polarchus* and *Archombrotus* mean only the *King* of *Navarre.*

We observe in the very Beginning of the Poem, that *Ariel* is possess'd of the Ear of *Belinda;* therefore it is absolutely necessary that this Person must be the Minister who was nearest the Queen. But whoever would be further convinc'd, that he meant the late T[reasure]r, may know him by his Ensigns in the following Line.

He rais'd his Azure Wand.--------

His sitting on the Mast of a Vessel shows his presiding over the S[ou]th S[e]a Tr[a]de. When *Ariel* assigns to his *Sylphs* all the Posts about *Belinda,* what is more clearly described, than the Tr[easure]r's disposing all the Places of the Kingdom, and particularly about her M[ajest]y? But let us hear the Lines.

-------Ye Spirits to your Charge repair,
The flutt'ring Fan be *Zephyretta's* Care;
The Drops to thee, *Brillant,* we consign,
And, *Momentilla,* let the Watch be thine:
Do thou, *Crispissa,* tend her fav'rite Lock.

He has here particularized the Ladies and Women of the Bed-Chamber, the keeper of the Cabinet, and her M[ajest]y's Dresser, and impudently given Nicknames to each.

To put this Matter beyond all Dispute, the *Sylphs* are said to be *wond'rous fond of Place,* in the Canto following, where *Ariel* is perched uppermost, and all the rest take their Places subordinately under him.

Here again I cannot but observe, the excessive Malignity of this Author, who could not leave this Character of *Ariel* without the same invidious Stroke which he gave him in the Character of the *Baron* before.

Amaz'd, confus'd, he saw his Power expir'd,
Resign'd to Fate, and with a Sigh retir'd.

Being another Prophecy that he should resign his Place, which it is probable all Ministers do with a Sigh.

At the Head of the *Gnomes* he sets *Umbriel,* a dusky melancholy Spright, who makes it his Business to give *Belinda* the Spleen; a vile and malicious Suggestion against some grave and worthy Minister. The Vapours, Fantoms, Visions, and the like, are the Jealousies, Fears, and Cries of Danger, that have so often affrighted and alarm'd the Nation. Those who are described in the House of Spleen, under those several fantastical Forms, are the same whom their Ill-willers have so often called the *Whimsical.*

The two fore-going Spirits being the only considerable Characters of the Machinary, I shall but just mention the *Sylph* that is wounded with the Scissars at the Loss of the Lock, by whom is undoubtedly understood my L[ord] *To[wnshen]d,* who at that Time received a Wound in his Character for making the Barrier Treaty, and was cut of his Employment upon the Dissolution of it: But that Spirit reunites, and receives no Harm; to signify, that it came to nothing, and his L[o]rdsh[i]p had no real Hurt by it.

But I must not conclude this Head of the Characters, without observing, that our Author has run through every Stage of Beings in search of Topicks for Detraction; and as he has characteriz'd some Persons under Angels and Men, so he has represented an eminent Clergy-man as a Dog, and a noted Writer as a Tool. Let us examine the former.

----But *Shock*, who thought she slept too long,
Leapt up, and wak'd his Mistress with his Tongue.
'Twas then, *Belinda*, if Report say true,
Thy Eyes first open'd on a Billet-doux.

By this *Shock*, it is manifest he has most audaciously and profanely reflected on Dr. *Sach[evere]ll*, who leap'd up, that is, into the Pulpit, and awaken'd *Great Britain* with his *Tongue*, that is, with his *Sermon*. which made so much *Noise;* and for which he has frequently been term'd by others of his Enemies, as well as by this Author, a Dog: Or perhaps, by his *Tongue*, may be more literally meant his *Speech* at his *Trial*, since immediately thereupon, our Author says, her Eyes open'd on a *Billet-doux; Billets-doux* being Addresses to Ladies from Lovers, may be aptly interpreted those Addresses of Loving Subjects to her M[ajest]y, which ensued that Trial.

The other Instance is at the End of the third Canto.

Steel did the Labours of the Gods destroy,
And strike to Dust th' Imperial Tow'rs of *Troy*.
Steel could the Works of mortal Pride confound,
And hew Triumphal Arches to the Ground.

Here he most impudently attributes the Demolition of *Dunkirk*, not to the Pleasure of her M[ajest]y, or her Ministry, but to the frequent Instigations of his Friend Mr. *Steel;* a very artful Pun to conceal his wicked Lampoonery!

Having now consider'd the general Intent and Scope of the Poem, and open'd the Characters, I shall next discover the Malice which is covered under the Episodes, and particular Passages of it.

The Game at *Ombre* is a mystical Representation of the late War, which is hinted by his making Spades the Trump; Spade in *Spanish* signifying a Sword, and being yet so painted in the Cards of that Nation; to which it is well known we owe the Original of our Cards. In this one Place indeed he has unawares paid a Compliment to the Queen, and her Success in the War; for *Belinda* gets the better of the two that play against her, the Kings of *France* and *Spain.*

I do not question but ev'ry particular Card has its Person and Character assign'd, which, no doubt, the Author has told his Friends in private; but I shall only instance the Description of the Disgrace under which the D[uke] of M[arlborou]gh then suffer'd, which is so apparent in these Verses.

Ev'n mighty *Pam,* that Kings and Queens o'erthrew,
And mow'd down Armies in the Fights of *Lu,*
Sad Chance of War! now destitute of Aid,
Falls undistinguish'd---------

That the Author here had an Eye to our modern Transactions, is very plain from an unguarded Stroke towards the End of this Game.

And now, as oft in some *distemper'd State,*
On *one nice Trick* depends the gen'ral Fate.

After the Conclusion of the War, the publick Rejoicings and*Thanksgivings* are ridiculed in the two following Lines.

The Nymph exulting , fills with Shouts the Sky,
The Walls, the Woods, and long Canals reply.

Immediately upon which there follows a malicious Insinuation, in the manner of a Prophecy, (which we have formerly observ'd this seditious Writer delights in) that the Peace should continue but a short Time, and that the Day should afterwards be curst which was then celebrated with so much Joy.

Sudden these Honours shall be snatch'd away,
And curst for ever this victorious Day.

As the Game at *Ombre* is a satyrical Representation of the late War; so is the Tea-Table that ensues, of the Council-Table and its Consultations after the Peace. By this he would hint, that all the Advantages we have gain'd by our late extended Commerce, are only Coffee and Tea, or Things of no greater Value. That he thought of the Trade in this Place, appears by the Passage where he represents the *Sylphs* particularly careful of the *rich Brocade;* it having been a frequent Complaint of our Mercers, that *French Brocades* were imported in too great Quantities. I will not say, he means those Presents of rich Gold Stuff Suits, which were said to be made for M[ajest]y by the K[ing] of *F[rance]*, tho' I cannot but suspect, that he glances at it.

Here this Author, as well as the scandalous *John Dunton,* represents the Mi[nist]ry in plain Terms taking frequent Cups.

And frequent Cups prolong the rich Repast.

Upon the whole, it is manifest he meant something more than common Coffee, by his calling it,

Coffee that makes the *Politician* wise.

And by telling us, it was this Coffee, that

Sent up in Vapours to the *Baron's* Brain
New *Strategems*---------

I shall only further observe, that 'twas at this Table the Lock was cut off; for where but at the Council Board should the Barrier Treaty be dissolved?

The ensuing Contentions of the Parties upon the Loss of that Treaty, are described in the Squabbles following the Rape of the Lock; and this he rashly expresses, without any disguise in the Words.

All sides in *Parties*--------

Here first you have a Gentleman who sinks beside his Chair: A plain Allusion to a Noble Lord, who lost his Chair of Pre[side]nt of the Co[unci]l.

I come next to the *Bodkin,* so dreadful in the Hand of *Belinda;* by which he intimates the *British Scepter,* so rever'd in the Hand of our late August Princess. His own Note upon this Place tells us he alludes to a Scepter and the Verses are so plain, the need no Remark.

The same (his ancient Personage to deck)
Her great great Grandsire wore about his Neck
In three Seal Rings, which, after melted down,
Form'd avast Buckle for his Widow's Gown;
Her Infant Grandame's Whistle next it grew,
The Bells she gingled, and the Whistle blew,
Then in a Bodkin grac'd her Mother's Hairs,
Which long she wore, and now *Belinda* wears.

An open Satyr upon *Hereditary Right.* The three Seal Rings plainly allude to the three Kingdoms.

These are the chief Passages in the Battle, by which, as hath before been said, he means the Squabble of Parties. Upon this Occasion he could not end the Description of them, without testifying his malignant Joy at those Dissentions, from which he forms the Prospect that *both* should be disappointed, and cries out with Triumph, as if it were already accomplished.

Behold how oft ambitious Arms are crost,
And Chiefs contend till all the Prize is lost.

The Lock at length is turn'd into a *Star*, or the Old Barrier Treaty into a new and glorious *Peace;* this no doubt is what the Author, at the time he printed his Poem, would have been thought to mean, in hopes by that Complement to excape Punishment for the rest of his

Piece. It puts me in mind of a Fellow, who concluded a bitter Lampoon upon the Prince and Court of his Days, with these Lines.

God save the King, the Commons, and the Peers,
And grant the Author long may wear his Ears.

Whatever this Author may think of that Peace, I imagine it the most *extraordinary Star* that ever appear'd in our Hemisphere. A Star that is to bring us all the Wealth and Gold of the *Indies;* and from whose Influence, not Mr. *John Partridge* alone, (whose worthy Labours this Writer so ungenerously ridicules) but all true *Britains* may, with no less Authority than he, prognosticate the Fall of *Lewis,* in the Restraint of the exorbitant Power of *France,* and the Fate of *Rome* in the triumphant Condition of the Church of *England.*

We have now considered this Poem in its Political View, wherein we have shewn that it hath two different Walks of Satyr, the one in the Story itself, which is a Ridicule on the late Transactions in general; the other in the Machinary, which is a Satyr on the Ministers of State in particular. I shall now show that the same Poem, taken in another Light, has a Tendency to Popery, which is secretly insinuated through the whole.

In the first place, he has conveyed to us the Doctrine of Guardian Angels and Patron Saints in the Machinary of his *Sylphs,* which being a Piece of Popish Superstition that hath been endeavoured to be exploded ever since the Reformation, he would here revive under this Disguise. Here are all the Particulars which they believe of those Beings, which I shall sum up in a few Heads.

1*st.* The Spirits are made to concern themselves with all human Acts in general.

2*dly.* A distinct Guardian Spirit of Patron is assigned to each Person in particular.

THE ENGLISH EPIC AND THE ENGLISH MOCK-EPIC

Of these am I, who thy Protection claim,
A watchful Sprite-------

3*dly*. They are made directly to inspire Dreams, Visions, and Revelations.

Her Guardian *Sylph* prolong'd her balmy Rest,
'Twas he had summon'd to her silent Bed
The Morning Dream--------

4*thly*. They are made to be subordinate, in different degrees, some presiding over others, So *Ariel* hath his several Under-Officers at command.

Superior by the Head was *Ariel* plac'd.

5*thly*. They are employed in various Offices, and each hath his Office assigned him.

Some in the Fields of purest Aether play,
And bask and whiten in the Blaze of Day.
Some guide the Course, &c.

6*thly*. He hath given his Spirits the Charge of the several Parts of Dress; intimating thereby, that the Saints preside over the several Parts of Human Bodies. They have one Saint to cure the Tooth-ach, another cures the Gripes, and another the Gout,and so all the rest.

The flutt'ring Fan be *Zephyretta's* Care,
The drops to thee, *Brillante,* we consign, &c.

7*thly*. They are represented to know the Thoughts of Men.

As on the Nosegay in her Breast reclin'd,
He watch'd th' Ideas rising in her Mind.

8*thly.* They are made Protectors even to Animals and irrational Beings.

Ariel himself shall be the Guard of *Shock.*

So St. *Anthony* presides over Hogs, &c.

9*thly.* Others are made Patrons of whole Kingdoms and Provinces.

Of these the chief the Care of Nations own.

So St. *George* is imagined by the *Papists* to defend *England:* St. *Patrick, Ireland:* St. *James, Spain,* &c. Now what is the Consequence of all this? By granting that they have this Power, we must be brought back again to pray to them.

The *Toilette* is an artful Recommendation of the *Mass,* and pompous Ceremonies of the *Church of Rome.* The *unveiling* of the *Altar,* the *Silver Vases* upon it, being *rob'd* in *White,* as the Priests are upon the chief Festivals, and the *Head uncover'd,* are manifest Marks of this.

A heav'nly Image in the Glass appears,
To that she bends--------

Plainly denotes *Image-Worship.*

The *Goddess,* who is deck'd with *Treasures, Jewels,* and the *various Offerings of the World,* manifestly alludes to the Lady of *Loretto.* You have Perfumes breathing from the *Incense Pot* in the following Line.

And all *Arabia* breaths from yonder Box.

The Character of *Belinda,* as we take it in this third View. represents the Popish Religion, or the Whore of *Babylon;* who is described in the State this malevolent Author wishes for, coming forth in all her Glory upon the *Thames,* and overspreading the Nation with Ceremonies.

Not with more Glories in th' aetherial Plain,
The Sun first rises o'er the purple Main,
Than issuing forth the Rival of his Beams,
Launch'd on the Bosom of the Silver *Thames*.

She is dress'd with a *Cross* on her Breast, the Ensign of Popery, the *Adoration* of which is plainly recommended in the following Lines.

On her white Breast a sparkling *Cross* she wore,
Which Jews might *kiss,* and Infidels *adore*.

Next he represents her as the *Universal Church,* according to the Boasts of the Papists.

And like the Sun she shines on all alike.

After which he tells us,

If to her Share some Female Errors fall,
Look on her Face, and you'll forget them all.

Tho' it should be granted some Errors fall to her Share, look on the pompous Figure she makes throughout the World, and they are not worth regarding. In the Sacrifice following soon after, you have these two Lines.

For this, e'er *Phoebus* rose, he had implor'd
Propitious Heav'n, and en'ry Pow'r ador'd.

In the first of them, he plainly hints at their *Matins;* in the second, by adoring ev'ry Power, the *Invocation of Saints*.

Belinda's Visits are described with numerous *Waxlights,* which are always used in the Ceremonial Parts of the *Romish* Worship.

----------Visits shall be paid on solemn Days,
When num'rous Wax-lights in bright Order blaze.

The *Lunar Sphere* he mentions, opens to us their *Purgatory,* which is seen in the following Line.

Since all Things lost on Earth are treasur'd there.

It is a Popish Doctrine, that scarce any Person quits this World, but he must touch at Purgatory in his Way to Heaven; and it is here also represented as the *Treasury* of the *Romish Church.* Nor is it much to be wonder'd at, that the *Moon* should be *Purgatory,* when a Learn'd Divine hath in a late Treatise proved *Hell* to be in the *Sun.*

I shall now before I conclude, desire the Reader to compare this Key with those upon any other Pieces, which are supposed to be secret Satyrs upon the State, either antient or modern; as with those upon *Petronius Arbiter, Lucian's* true History, *Barclay's Argenis,* or *Rablais's Garagantua;* and I doubt not he will do me the Justice to acknowledge, that the Explanations here laid down, are deduced as naturally, and with as little Force, both from the general Scope and Bent of the Work, and from the several Particulars, and are every Way as consistent and undeniable as any of those; and ev'ry way as candid as any modern Interpretations of either Party, on the mysterious State Treatises of our Times.

To sum up my whole Charge against this Author in a few Words: He has ridiculed both the present Ministry and the last; abused great Statesmen and great Generals; nay the Treaties of whole Nations have not escaped him, nor has the Royal Dignity itself been omitted in the Progress of his Satyr; and all this he has done just at the Meeting of a new Parliament. I hope a proper Authority may be made use of to bring him to condign Punishment: In the mean while I doubt not, if the Persons most concern'd would but order Mr. *Bernard Lintott,* the Printer and Publisher of this dangerous Piece, to be taken into Custody, and examin'd; many further Discoveries might be made both of this Poet's and his Abettor's secret Designs, which are doubtless of the utmost Importance to the Government.

THE ENGLISH EPIC AND THE ENGLISH MOCK-EPIC

SECTION 3

PRE-ROMANTIC AND ROMANTIC POETRY

PRE-ROMANTIC AND ROMANTIC POETRY

10. Introduction to Pre-Romantic Poetry

As the name suggests, Pre-Romantic poetry came before the Romantic poets made their presence felt on the English soil. The Pre-Romantic poetry can be seen as a transitional phase between the Neo-Classical poetry and the Romantic Poetry. The Neo-classicists maintained very strict principles for writing poetry; emotions were kept out from this kind of poetry. It was all an exercise of the mind, but the emotions of the heart were not felt in it.

The Pre-Romantic poets sought to change that. However, they were not very successful. The Pre-Romantic poets talked about the rural landscape and the beauty of the country side and other simple things of life, and that was a move away from the poetry of the city-life, as revealed in the Neo-Classical poetry. Grey's *Elegy Written in a Country Churchyard* is a famous poem which brings out the features that are found in the Pre-Romantic poetry.

So, in themes, the Pre-Romantics moved away from that of the Neo-Classical poets. Wordsworth was to later lay claim on this simple description as the subject of his poetry, and state that his poetry was about the common man, and the subjects were those of common men. However, the aspect in which the Pre-Romantics leaned towards the Neo-Classicists was in their continuation of the heroic couplet. If not the heroic couplet, they certainly wrote poems keeping the rhyme and meter in mind, something on whose role Wordsworth was to state a lot in his famous *Preface* to the *Lyrical Ballads*.

So, the Pre-Romantics tried to show that poems can be written which would be pleasant to read because of the rhyme, but they could also be written to describe the country side and not necessarily the city life. Emotions, thus, were not contrary to rhyme in their poetry, but something which can work in harmony with the mental faculties, to give shape to the poems.

11. WILLIAM BLAKE
(1757 – 1827)

About the Poet

William Blake was born on 28 November, 1757, in London, England, to Catherine *née* Wright and James Blake. As a child, he was very imaginative, and claimed to having seen visions, of God and angels. His parents encouraged his artistic side, and trained him as an artist.

At the age of ten Blake went to Henry Pars' drawing school. When he was a boy of fourteen, he became an apprentice to the engraver James Basire, of the Society of Antiquaries. In this period, he had to make sketches and drawings art and sculpture found in churches like Westminster Abbey. Blake developed a taste for Gothic and Medieval art forms. In 1780 he was employed as an engraver with publisher Joseph Johnson.

In 1782 Blake married Catherine Sophia Boucher (1762-1831). Together, they worked on many of Blake's publications. His *Poetical Sketches*, came out in 1783.Blake also started to paint the pictures that would go with his poems. His paintings and texts are found on the same plate. The paintings focus on human anatomy or imaginative figures, surrounded in nature. He employed techniques for decorative margins and manually coloured the scenes, or printed with the colour already on the wood or copper plate. He used to mix the paint himself. That is why, no two paintings of Blake are the same, even though the poems would be the same.

In 1803 Blake was charged with sedition after a violent confrontation with soldier John Scolfield in which Blake uttered treasonable remarks against the King. He was later released. He then worked for illustrating his other works. *Jerusalem: The*

Emanation of the Giant Albion (c.1820) is his longest illustarted work.

In 1821, the Blakes moved to lodgings in Fountain Court, Strand. He began to make illustrations for *The Divine Comedy,* but it was never finished. William Blake died on 12 August, 1827. Blake was buried in an unmarked grave in the Non-Conformist Bunhill Fields in London. His wife Catherine was also buried there after four years. A grave marker now stands near the place now, and in 1957, a memorial was erected for them in the Poet's Corner of Westminster Abbey, London.

Fig. 3: Blake's Painting of *The Lamb*.[482]

---

[482] This work is in the public domain and does not require permission for reproduction.

The Lamb

Little Lamb, who made thee
Dost[483] thou know who made thee
Gave thee life and bid thee feed?
By the stream and o'er the mead;[484]
Gave thee clothing of delight,[485]
Softest clothing woolly bright;
Gave thee such a tender voice,
Making all the vales rejoice:[486]
Little Lamb who made thee
Dost thou know who made thee?

Little Lamb, I'll tell thee,
Little Lamb, I'll tell thee:
He[487] is called by thy name,
For He calls Himself a Lamb:
He is meek and He is mild,
He became a little child:[488]

---

[483] *dost* – i.e., Do.

[484] *mead* – i.e., Meadow.

[485] *clothing...delight* – i.e., the wooly cover. Here, this is a source of delight, as this is of immence joy to the children – the wooly covering of the lamb. This poem is from the *Songs of Innocence*, and so, such a point-of-view is given, obviously as this is how the innocence would look at it.

[486] *tender...rejoice* – This forms an anti-thesis, for the tender voice is able to fill up the entire valley. However, this also brings in the allusion to the Bible, where the angels come to the shepherds watching their flocks by night, telling them to "Rejoice", for the Saviour has been born. It must be noted that Christ is often symbolized as a lamb in the Bible.

[487] *He* – i.e., Jesus.

[488] *He...child* – i.e., Baby Jesus. Christianity states that Jesus, the Son, the Lord, came as flesh and blood to take away the sins of the people, as per the promise made by God to Moses and the other prophets.

> I a child,[489] and thou a lamb,
> We are called by His name.[490]
>> Little Lamb, God bless thee.
>> Little Lamb, God bless thee.

Background of Composition

This poem belongs to the anthology *Songs of Innocence*, which Blake published in the year 1789. This is a very renowned piece from that collection. For a better understanding of the general motif of the *Songs of Innocence*, readers should look into the introductory poem of this anthology. The theme that runs through all these poems is that they bring out aspects of the human world from the point of view of someone who is in the state of innocence.

Themes and Symbols in the Poem

As told in the Background of Composition, the poem deals with points of view which reveal a state of innocence. In this poem, the speaker, who is a little boy piper (as would be clear when one reads the introductory poem in the anthology), is delighted in the figure of the lamb, as a child would be delighted. In his excitement,

---

[489] *I...child* – Notice the transformation from "He became a little child" to "I a child". The poet now talks about himself as a child. In other words, he refers to the persona of the innocent child who is telling the songs of innocence.

[490] *we...name* – i.e., All the people who believe in Him are called to be those who belong to Christ. Christ talks about having the Father, that is, God, in Him, and that whoever believes in Him will therefore have God as well. In other words, if a man believes in Christ, through Him, he will also let God enter inside him. The fusion of man, Lord and God is brought out through these lines, where the identity of the lamb is with the Christ, man, as well as the animal lamb.

he asks the lamb if it is aware who made him, and looks after him, and then provides the answer, that it is the Lord, who has also chosen the lamb as his symbol.

> Little Lamb, who made thee
> Dost thou know who made thee
> ...
>
> He is called by thy name,
> For He calls Himself a Lamb:
> He is meek and He is mild,
> He became a little child:

The poem tells about the glory of God, and how beautiful things are in His creation:

> Gave thee such a tender voice,
> Making all the vales rejoice:

and how humble the Lord is, and the poem brings out an atmosphere of peace and serenity. The theme that is found in the poem is, therefore, that of revealing the majesty of God, as per the Christian doctrine, that he is majestic as well as humble. The readers, in reading the poem, would be reminded of several passages from the Bible, and feel a reverential ambience to hover in the poem.

There are several symbols which are found in this poem, and all of them have got Biblical allusions. Right at the start, we see the symbol of the lamb. The lamb stands not just for the animal as understood, but also for Christ. In the Bible, Jesus is often referred as "the Lamb of God". The poem states as much some lines later:

> For He calls Himself a Lamb:

The lamb symbolizes the meekness of Christ, and brings out the peace-loving nature of the Son of God. The poem, through this allusion, attaints a tone of serenity.

If we take the symbol of lamb as an animal, (then it would not be a symbol) it would bring out aspects of pastoralist mode of life, and bring out the simple life as it were in times past.

Other than the symbolism of the lamb, we also get the symbol of the child. Here, child assumes various dimensions. On the one hand, it stands for the speaker, who is the boy piper. On the other hand, it stands for the Baby Christ. In other words, in the second representation, it reminds the readers of the fact how the Son of God became a human being to save the lives of the people on earth.

>He became a little child:

The symbolism of the child would bring out the state of innocence, at least, in this instance.[491]

It will be observed here that just as the lamb stands for the animal as well as Christ, so does the child stand for a child in the literal sense and Christ. Therefore, both the symbols have the same figure in common. That is why, after this, the speaker states,

>I a child, and thou a lamb,
>We are called by His name.

The symbols, therefore, help to enrich the mood of the poem.

---

[491] I am stating "in this instance" because in the *Songs of Experience*, the children are by no means in their state of innocence.

Fig. 4: Blake's painting of *The Tyger*.[492]

---

[492] This work is in the public domain and does not require permission for reproduction.

THE TYGER[493]

Tyger, Tyger, burning bright,[494]
In the forests of the night:[495]

---

[493] The variation in spelling is not thematic. This was the spelling of tiger for a long time. It took a long time for the "y" to change to "I". Moreover, as Blake painted his poems, and the title appears in the painting, the name has become a part of the painting and is therefore used as Blake spelled it, although some editors prefer to modernise the spelling to "tiger". Some editions also give an exclamation mark after each "tyger", but as can be seen from the plate, that is not how Blake punctuated it. There appears one stop after "tyger tyger". It is expected that the readers will utter the "tyger" twice before giving a pause, and the fast utterance of "tyger" twice lends a springing tone to the line, which does justice to the animal, which is known to spring out of the darkness.

[494] *burning bright* – i.e., the eyes which are burning bright.
The trochaic tetrameter serves to justify the trepidation of one's beating heart in fear when one beholds the tiger in the darkness of the night.

[495] *In...night* – Here, "the forests of the night" are not just the literal forests, but the forests of obstacles, that grow in the world of experience, making living difficult. "Night" similarly does not refer to the literal night, but all that is negative. In this world where things seem to be full of fear and negative, the eyes of the tiger burns through the darkness. Is this therefore, good, or bad? As the eyes of the tiger seems to dispel the darkness that is all around, it is definitely good. But it can also be seen as a ruler of the dark powers. As ruler of dark powers, it can be equated with Satan, and as someone who controls the darkness, the tiger can be equated with God. Blake keeps both the possibilities open, as for him, God the Father was tyrannical in His rule, ruling by might and fear (As the tiger seems to suggest here), as opposed to the figure of Jesus, the Son, Who, according to Blake, is the Champion of liberty and the true Ruler. Readers must remember that in the association with

> What immortal hand or eye,
> Could frame thy fearful symmetry?[496]
>
> In what distant deeps or skies
> Burnt the fire of thine eyes![497]

Lamb, he mentions Christ, while here, the association is with God, the Father, or even Satan.

John E. Grant, in *The Art and Argument of 'The Tyger'* makes a brilliant observation, that "The contrast between fire and night, of course, corresponds to the contrast of yellow and black stripes ringing the Tyger itself (Grant, 1961).

[496] *What…symmetry* – The hand or eye that made the tiger is truly to be admired, for making such a strong beast, which is feared by all. This obviously refers to God. But here, the image is not that of the benevolent God, as found in *The Lamb*. Here, the image is more malevolent.

[497] *In…eyes* – Here, the poet presents his own notion as to how the tiger was first made. The "distant deeps or skies" refers to the depths of earth, where Hell was supposed to be (hell was supposed to be under the earth and be filled with fire) or the skies of Heaven, and the second line refers to the making of the tiger and giving it life. The poet keeps an open question as to where the tiger was made – in the fires of hell or in the skies of heaven?

The "distant deeps or skies" which seem to be burning is also an allusion to the dark times due to the hostility between England and France, and to the ever-worsening situation of France, leading ultimately to the French revolution.

On what wings dare he aspire?[498]
What the hand, dare sieze the fire?[499]

And what shoulder, & what art,
Could twist the sinews of thy heart?[500]
And when thy heart began to beat,
What dread hand? & what dread feet?[501]

What the hammer? what the chain,
In what furnace was thy brain?[502]

---

[498] *On...aspire* – This talks about the person who might have dared (even on wings) to dream of ("aspire") getting close to the tiger. It appears to be an extremely ambitious undertaking, even if a person has wings. The idea of a person flying high on wings – daring to aspire on wings – also suggests the Greek myth of Icarus, who came too close to the sun and his wings got burned up and he fell and died.

[499] *What...fire* – i.e., no human being dares to harm the tiger (at least, not by hand). We are left with only one option – the Creator, who has made the tiger, if the One who is capable of killing the tiger.

[500] *And...heart* – i.e., It was a great shoulder and art by which the muscles of the tiger were made, and the tiger was given courage. In other words, God, who made the tiger, is exceptionally skilled.

[501] *And...feet* – i.e., When the tiger got life, all became afraid of it. Therefore, the poet remarks on the Creator, who is stronger, and is not afraid of it, but rather, has made it.

[502] *What...brain* – The poet suggests a mythological creation of the tiger. The tiger, being so ferocious, must have been made in a furnace. The allusion to hammering and "furnace" and the other tools in the lines that follow suggests a similarity with the classical god, Vulcan, who was the blacksmith god.

> What the anvil? what dread grasp,
> Dare its deadly terrors clasp?[503]
>
> When the stars threw down their spears
> And water'd heaven with their tears:[504]
> Did he smile his work to see?[505]
> Did he who made the Lamb make thee?[506]

---

[503] *what...clasp* – i.e., It was an extremely fearless grasp which clasped the tiger to make it.

[504] *When...tears* – This continues the allusion to the tiger being made in a furnace in the heavens. After a metal is forged, it is dipped in water to be cooled. Here, the poet says that the stars threw down their spears (spears is to be understood as tools which were used in the making of the tiger) and with their tears, watered heavens, so that the tiger, which was just forged, could be cooled.

This can also be seen as a reference to the wars fought between the good angels and the bad angels, as the Bible tells, and as Milton expounds in *Paradise Lost*. The stars throwing their spears can be seen as an end of the battle, and watering heaven with their tears can be seen as the grief over the fallen angels. However, this image suggests war in the heavens, and that not everything is as beautiful in heaven as is imagined, this is what might be the intended message.

This can also be seen as a reference to the wars that were being fought between England and France at that time, and also, the gradually worsening situation of France, which ultimately lead to the French Revolution.

Harold Bloom makes the following interpretation:
> The raw power of the tiger appears to be too much for the heavens to take. Blake describes the denial of dominance over the animal. The stars give up rather than fight for mastery of the tiger (Bloom, 2003).

[505] *Did...see* – It is here that the poet truly brings out the feelings that are to be generally found in the Songs of Experience. The poet raises doubt on God's happiness in seeing His work filled with strife (this would be the meaning, if the second or third explanation is taken for the previous lines). If the first meaning of the previous

> Tyger. Tyger, burning bright,
> In the forests of the night:

---

lines is to be taken, the line would mean that after making the tiger, and seeing what kind of a ferocious creature it is, was God happy? The explanation is not given, but readers can frame the possible answers. If the answer is positive, it would raise questions as to how God can love a ferocious creature as that, and would call into question God's mercy and love. If the answer is negative, it would raise question as to why God kept it. Both the answers, whether positive or negative, would lead to the next line of the poem.

[506] *Did...thee* – It is here that the poet presents the conflicting image of the Creator; so far, it was not explicitly stated. Now, he asks if it is the same Creator who made the timid lamb and the ferocious tiger. If the same Creator has created them both, what can be said about the nature of the Creator – that is something which the poet tries to explore. Should man take the first image that comes up, that is, the one about the lamb, or should man take the second image, that is, the one formed about the tiger? It does seem possible that man can look at the same Creator to have made the tiger and the lamb. However, that is where the readers would go wrong. The purpose of the *Songs of Experience* is not to debunk whatever has been stated in the *Songs of Innocence*, but rather, to show that opposites exist parallel. Blake once stated, "Without contraries is no progression". Here, it is not the fact that the poet wants to state that the same God could not have made the two different creatures, or that the nature of God is not that good, for He has made such a creature, but rather, to state that the Creator must make both. Here, the tiger is not to be conceived as a force of evil. Rather, it is a force which checks evil. It is a force which is filled with an aura that stuns others. The tiger has to be seen as a force which is there to control the harsh things that are there.

What immortal hand or eye,
Dare[507] frame thy fearful symmetry?

Background of the Poem

This is one of the very important poems of the *Songs of Experience*, and was printed in 1789. Five years later, Blake combined the two anthologies into one volume: *The Songs of Innocence and of Experience: Shewing the Two Contrary States of the Human Soul*. This subtitle is very important, for it makes clear to the reader that the two states are not one after the other; they are simply opposites. It is not that innocence is the first stage and experience comes after that. That has been the idea among many readers of Blake. It must be understood that Blake wanted the readers to take them as two parallel states, existing together. In the same age, one person might be in the state of innocence, and another in the state of experience. Therefore, readers must avoid statements that Blake subverts what he has previously been stated in the *Songs of Innocence*, and in the *Songs of Experience*, the real picture is got, for such statements are not scholarly, at least, not in Blake. The state of experience is simply a different perspective from that which is got in the state of innocence, and in combining the two, Blake has tried to show how different these two parallel states are.

The introductory poem that is found in the *Songs of Experience* is that of a speaker, who asks the world to "hear the voice of the bard/ Who present, past and future sees". This prophet-like human, the bard, asks the earth to return from its state of misery and sin. The earth that is presented in the *Songs of Experience* is therefore, an earth filled with sin and corruption and all sorts of evil. That is what will be found in the poems in this group.

---

[507] *Dare* – The readers should notice the change from "Could" in the first stanza to "Dare" in this stanza, thereby telling about the power of the Creator to have made this creature.

Themes and Symbols in the Poem

The Tyger, falling under the *Songs of Experience*, presents the issue of conflict. However, in the other poems of *Experience*, the conflict is very open – there is explicit protest against the unjust things which are there in the world. In *The Tyger*, the conflict is of a different kind. It is the conflict of darkness (literally and figuratively), and the conflict in the conscience of man. This is the most dominant theme that is present in the poem, and is brought out right from the opening lines:

> "Tyger, Tyger, burning bright,
> In the forests of the night:"

The alliteration that is found in the opening line brings out the deep passion in the utterance of the /b/ sound.

The tiger seems to be a brightly burning creature when all the rest is dark. This energy that is there in the tiger is something which is fearful. The atmosphere that is created through the opening lines is an atmosphere of mysterious darkness, where the heart of man is filled with fear, and one creature seems to dominate over the darkness by its light, but instead of casting a ray of relief, it rather adds to the fear. In fact, it seems fiercer than the darkness which surrounds the place.

Another theme which is found in the poem, and which is linked to the first theme, is that of passion. This is brought out in all the lines which describe the tiger. The tiger is filled with passion, and the poet says that the Maker of the tiger also had to do it with passion, to make so energetic a creature.

> "In what distant deeps or skies
> Burnt the fire of thine eyes!
> On what wings dare he aspire?
> What the hand, dare sieze the fire?

And what shoulder, & what art,
Could twist the sinews of thy heart?"

This energy which is there in the tiger is something which we also get to see in the poems of Shelley. Shelley's poems also present energy inside the things, and he is concerned about focusing on that energy.[508]

In this poem, there is doubt about the nature of the energy – whether it is for good or evil. The poet even asks,

"Did he who make the lamb make thee?"[509]

With this, we come to the major symbol in the poem – that of the tiger. Is it a symbol of evil or good? It has been remarked earlier that the tiger seems to evoke fear; it seems to be brightly burning in the surrounding darkness. There is no doubt about the fact that the tiger is not a symbol of meekness like the lamb. But does it represent tyranny? Some would be of the opinion that it stands for all that is tyrannical – all the authorities which seek to impose. Viewed from that light, the darkness would be the darkness of their tyrannical rule, that is, there is evil all around because of their misrule or dictatorship, and men are prevented from seeing light, and beholding and feeling warmth. So, all they feel is darkness around them (that is the bad situation of the tyrannical rule) and the ruler makes them feel fear. The ruler, in other words, is the controller of this darkness, and rules in it.

Another view can be made, and that is, the tiger is the controlling power over the darkness of evil, and so, it needs to be fiercer so as to control, that is, check, it. In this view, the tiger does not come out as a symbol of dictatorial and tyrannical power, but rather, as a power which guarantees that evil does not reign supreme.

---

[508] This will be better understood when the readers have read the poems of Shelley which are there in this book.

[509] Please see the annotation to this line to come to a better understanding.

Therefore, where all is dark, it burns brightly, and is stronger than darkness.

Be it good or bad, there is no doubt that the tiger stands for authority. The same Creator who made the meek lamb also made the tiger; just as the lamb is for salvation, the tiger is for punishment – both are needed. Blake states himself,

> "Without binaries there is no progression."

and this poem, taken along with *The Lamb*, reveal the contrary states which are there.

12. Introduction to Romantic Poetry

It is widely acknowledged that what is called the "Romantic Age of English Poetry" began with the publication of the *Lyrical Ballads* in 1798, under the joint venture of Wordsworth and Coleridge. But stating it in this way would create a false impression, that there was no poetry written by them before, and that this started it all. No age in literature can come on a day and end on a day, though there might be specific events to mark them off. Wordsworth and Coleridge were both writing years before the publication of the *Lyrical Ballads*, and this venture was begun with no thought of the honour that is now placed on it. In fact, readers would be quite surprised to learn that Wordsworth had, before writing the *Lyrical Ballads*, written poems which were not at all characteristic of the Romantic poems, but rather, which were more akin to the Neo-classical poetry. This is been discussed briefly under *Tintern Abbey*, in "About the Poet".

Let us come to the characteristic features of Romantic poetry. It must be told here that poetry of this age must always be written with "R" in the upper case, that is, "Romantic", and never "romantic". The latter would refer to the romances that were popular during the medieval ages. So, this brings us to the first aspect about Romanticism: it is not being romantic in the sense of indulging in romance. Some would like to state that Romanticism is about Nature. Well, they are not wrong, but they are not right, either. Romanticism is about Nature, but more than that. Romanticism is excitement – it is excitement and passion for and about everything that is in nature, and is natural. It is about emotions – passionate display of emotions. Romanticism has to be understood in contrast to the age that came before it. The Neo-Classical age advocated restraint in all fields. The poetry that was there was characterized by restraint of emotions. It was controlled, shaped and produced by the mind, but lacked spirit. The bitter satire is one outcome of this age, at which Pope mastered. Romanticism, coming after it, advocated all that Neo-Classical age did not advocate. Chiefly, it advocated profound display of emotions. So, it can be said that even the medieval romances were filled with emotions. True, they were. But they were for human beings at a personal level, that is, they talked of personal love, and consummation of love. Romanticism is not about love-making; it is about excitement and passion for all that is natural in nature.

The word "natural" is very important. The pioneers of the Romantic Age, Wordsworth and Coleridge, were highly and negatively influenced by the French Revolution and its atrocities. The "Reign of Terror" that followed horrified Wordsworth, and he was shocked at the brutality. He condemned war highly in his poems by advocating a return to nature, and abandoning all that is artificial in mankind. Therefore, Romantic poetry is essentially about everything that is natural.

The other important aspect about Romanticism is that it is poetry of imagination. A question might arise in the minds of the readers, that were the poems of other ages not poems of imagination? Was there no imagination involved? Of course, there was. But the imagination of Romantic poetry is not just thinking in the mind: it is thinking fancifully. Coleridge said that the poet must be endowed with a secondary imagination, which is the imagination found in the creative genius. It is this imagination which is the shaping spirit of poetry, according to Coleridge. He also made a distinction between fancy and imagination. Fancy is to imagine what is not there. It is not negative, but positive. Secondary imagination and fancy combine in the poet to result into poetry, as per Coleridge's view.

Romantic poetry has often been called poetry of the "I", that is, poetry of individual assertion. The poets do not separate themselves from the poem; they form an emotional attachment with the matter of the poems. Therefore, it would be wrong to apply post-structuralism and deconstruction to state that the "I" does not exist as the identity of the poet. One must understand the historical perspective of an age, and the historical background of an age, and not blindly go by the dazzling propositions put forward by theorists to neglect all historical matter.

These are the basic and essential aspects of Romantic poetry. However, if the readers assume that all Romantic poetry is of the same type, they would be highly wrong. Each poet of this age has presented these aspects in his own unique way. Wordsworth's poetry is about Nature, Creation and God, the Creator. According to him, Nature is a manifestation of the Creation of God, and everything in Nature is linked. Man, a part of Nature, is also part of this link. His poetry seeks to bring out this link running through creation, and wishes to bring out the place of man as a happy creature, when he understands the link and seeks to maintain it. Coleridge, his contemporary, talks about the Supernatural. His poetry is about the uncanny. However, this Supernatural has got aspects of Divinity in it, he sees God as The One whose presence is felt everywhere, and who draws all Creation towards Himself.

Shelley and Keats come in the next group of Romantics, along with Byron. Chronologically, Byron comes before them. However, the scope of this book does not permit me to talk about him, or give his poetry in the anthology. Shelley's poetry is filled with energy in everything. This energy is either positive or negative. He sees the world filled with energy, and often, the rulers as beings with tyrannical power and energy. There is also a personal touch in many of his poems. Keats, junior to Shelley by only a few years, writes about Classical influence in things. His poetry is about Greek and Roman (more Greek than Roman) standards, and even in the English climate, he would love to talk about Greek aspects. His poetry is filled with Classical mythological allusions, and he was often labelled as a heathen, for the pagan content of his poems. Though this anthology does not talk about Yeats, a few words must be said about him. He is often hailed as one of the last Romantic poets. His poetry shows two aspects: his initial poems show an inclination towards escapism, and they are more towards nature; his later poetry is filled with symbolism. Like Blake, he too, created his own mythological figures.

After Yeats, the Romantic poetry gave way to Victorian poetry, and Tennyson became the prominent figure in that age. So, in analyzing the types of Poetry that is written by he major Romantic poets, we see that their matter vary from one to the other, and if one looks at the matter of Wordsworth and Yeats, there would be a great amount of difference. This is perhaps one of the reasons why some now use the term "Romanticisms". However, though the matter is different for these poets, they are all predominant with the aspects of Romantic poetry that have been discussed above.

13. William Wordsworth
(1770-1850)

About the Poet

William Wordsworth was born in 1770, in Cockermouth, Cumberland. The next year, his sister, Dorothy, was born. Together, they were five siblings, Wordsworth and Dorothy being the second and third, respectively. He lost his mother in 1778 and his father in 1783. He received his schooling at Hawkshead Grammar School, where he went from 1779 to 1787. After that, he went to St John's College, Cambridge, from 1787 to 1791. In 1791, he went to France to learn French. In 1792, he falls in love with Annette Vallon from Blois. In December that year, a child was born from that relationship, in Orleans. Wordsworth had left France about two months before that. He returns to London, and in July 1793, goes by Tintern Abbey on his way to North Wales. In 1795, he begins staying at Lake District, and the surrounding left heavy impact on his poetry. However, the financial condition of Wordsworth was not very good at that time. At the end of the year, however, he got £900 from a relation named Raisley Calvert, whom he had nursed till death. In 1795, he met William Godwin, and was heavily influenced by his ideas. Godwin influenced him to practice restraint of the natural feelings, and believe in the civilization and culture to shape human personality in the true way. Following his ideology, Wordsworth was about to suffer a nervous breakdown, and was saved by the philosophy of Rousseau, who talked of the role of nature in bringing up a human being. Wordsworth found it better to follow him, and subsequently, began to write poems which expressed his natural desires for nature. *The Tables Turned* and *Expostulation and Reply* are poems which speak about his return to nature, while *Guilt and Sorrow*, written during his belief in Godwin's theory, shows a very different kind of poetry, very artificial. In the year that he met Godwin, he also met Coleridge, and developed friendship with him. Together, they published *The Lyrical Ballads*, which first came out in 1798. In 1802, Wordsworth married Mary Hutchinson, and later begot five children. He met Keats in 1817, and was appointed as a Justice of Peace in 1819. He was also given the honour of Poet Laureate in 1843. His *Poetical Works* was published in 1827 in five volumes, and its final edition came out in 1849. He died in 1850 at Rydal Mount, and *The Prelude* was published three months after his death. His sister Dorothy had mentally deteriorated from 1835 onwards, and she died in 1855. His wife, Mary, died in 1859.

Wordsworth's Views on Poetry and the Poet

Wordsworth presents his views regarding poetry in his *Preface* to the *Lyrical Ballads*. The first edition of the *Lyrical Ballads* had no preface; instead, there was an advertisement. The *Preface* was added by Wordsworth in the second edition of the *Lyrical Ballads*. He added some lines to the *Preface* in the third edition of the *Lyrical Ballads*. In the *Preface*, he states his famous thought on what poetry is. He says that poetry is the "spontaneous overflow of powerful feelings". These feelings are achieved when the emotions are "recollected in tranquillity". Poetry must aim to be natural, and so, he chooses nature as his subject matter. A little bit has already been said about the nature of poetry that Wordsworth writes.[510] Wordsworth's presentation is in the language of the common people, which is what he claimed. However, several scholars have pointed out that many of Wordsworth's poems are not at all written in the language of the common people.

To return to Wordsworth's views, he said that rhetoric should not be used just to decorate the lines, but when they are necessary.[511] The question arises as to what the difference is between prose and poetry, if the language of poetry is in the way in which the common people speak, if the subject matter is the most ordinary, and if rhetoric is to be used only when necessary. The answer is diction. It is diction that separates poetry from prose. The rhythm that is there in poetry is not to be found in prose. So, it is metre that separates poetry from prose.

---

[510] See Introduction to Romantic Poetry.
[511] This too, is highly contradictory, for he does not really follow it in practice.

A good poet is someone who is able to keep out all the unnecessary words, and keep the theme such that it is ordinary, and keep the language such that it is easily understood by all. There should be flow of emotions in the lines of the poems.

LINES WRITTEN A FEW MILES ABOVE TINTERN ABBEY, ON REVISITING THE BANKS OF THE WYE DURING A TOUR, JULY 13 1798

> Five years have passed; five summers, with the length
> Of five long winters![512] and again I hear
> These waters rolling from their mountain-springs
> With a sweet inland murmur.[513]--Once again
> Do I behold these steep and lofty cliffs,
> Which on a wild secluded scene impress
> Thoughts of more deep seclusion;[514] and connect

---

[512] *Five...winters* – The epanaphora serves to bring out the poet's deep feelings upon his remembrance of the visit five years' back, and placing it with what he is seeing before him. The feeling is that of the meeting of past and present. Summer and winter represent the pleasurable time and the time of hostility. Here, they mean both types of feelings, i.e., Wordsworth recollects all things of the visit – the good and the bad – and places them with what he is seeing in front of him.

[513] *These...murmur* – Wordsworth's note states the following:

> "The river is not affected by the tides a few miles above Tintern."

[514] *Once...seclusion* – It is to be noted how the lofty cliffs are in total contrast to the image of the sky, for one is filled with projections; the other, plain. The two meet in Wordsworth, for he sees not the physical difference between them, but connects them together with the same thread that runs through them – the thread

The landscape with the quiet of the sky.
The day is come when I again repose
Here, under this dark sycamore, and view
These plots of cottage-ground, these orchard-tufts,
Which, at this season, with their unripe fruits,
Among the woods and copses lose themselves,
Nor, with their green and simple hue,[515] disturb
The wild green landscape. Once again I see
These hedge-rows, hardly hedge-rows, little lines
Of sportive wood[516] run wild: these pastoral farms
Green to the very door;[517] and wreaths of smoke[518]
Sent up, in silence, from among the trees,

---

of quietness. Moreover, both the images of the lofty cliffs and the sky present heights, not depths; the purpose they serve to the poet is to create a "more deep" sense of seclusion. The heights and their quietness make Wordsworth think and feel deeply the aesthetic atmosphere.

[515] The readers must not fail to recollect the expression "making the green one red" (*Mac.*) Wordsworth and the other Romantics held Shakespeare in high esteem, and this expression might be a conscious or unconscious refraction of Shakespeare.

[516] *sportive wood* – The woods grow in a playful manner, without restrictions. In other words, they are not lined, but are found here and there, as if they are playing, and so, are running all over the place.

[517] *These…door* – the farms stand on ground which is filled with grass, and the grass extends right up to the doors of the farms.

[518] *wreathes…smoke* – Readers must not miss the metaphor, for such expressions characterize Romantic Imagination. The circles of smoke are, in Wordsworth's Romantic imagination, like wreathes. His Romantic imagination makes him look upon something which is nothing but vapour as something which is beautiful like flowers made to form wreathes.

With some uncertain notice,[519] as might seem
Of vagrant dwellers[520] in the houseless woods,
Or of some hermit's cave, where by his fire
The hermit sits alone.[521]
                      Though absent long,[522]
These forms of beauty have not been to me,
As is a landscape to a blind man's eye:[523]
But oft, in lonely rooms,[524] and mid the din[525]

---

[519] *With...notice* – Without giving a definite signal beforehand, that is, the trees are sending the 'wreathes of smoke' to the heavens just as a florist would send wreathes to some person, and has not informed the person that he is sending them. The literal thing that is happening is that the smoke is not very dense, and is so light that it can be faintly seen. The faint visibility of the smoke makes the poet say that they are 'uncertain' as their movements do not display determination, being very light.

[520] *vagrant dwellers* – homeless people

[521] *The...alone* – The solitary Hermit is not a pitiable figure, rather, it is pleasant to Wordsworth that the Hermit sits alone. Compare with the solitude of *The Solitary Reaper* and the Hermit of Coleridge's *The Rime of the Ancient Mariner*.

[522] *Though...long* – While the rest might be beautiful, the houseless dwellers are certainly in a poor condition. Gilpin states their wretchedness as "The poverty and wretchedness of the inhabitants were remarkable...and seem to have no employment, but begging". It cannot be expected of Wordsworth to talk of poverty and bring out the pitiful condition of human beings when he is in such a contemplative mood. Blake, in his place, would have done this, but Wordsworth, being different, chooses to differ.

[523] *These...eye* – i.e., Wordsworth has not forgotten them in the gap of five years. A blind man will not be able to have any real image of a scene, being deprived of vision; Wordsworth, if he had forgotten the scene, would have been like a blind man who is unable to describe the scene.

[524] *But...rooms* – Readers must not fail to notice the similarity with the opening of the last stanza of *Daffodils*.

Of towns and cities, I have owed to them
In hours of weariness, sensations sweet,
Felt in the blood,[526] and felt along the heart,[527]
And passing even into my purer mind[528]
With tranquil restoration:--feelings too
Of unremembered pleasure;[529] such, perhaps,
As may have had no trivial influence
On that best portion of a good man's life;[530]

---

[525] *din* – Noise.

[526] *blood* – Spirit.

[527] *heart* – Emotions. *Blood* represents the spirit, while *heart* represents the seat of this spirit.

[528] *purer mind* – The sublime mind, as opposed to the mind in general. The sublime mind is the mind of tranquillity, where emotions are recollected, which is necessary for the writing of poetry, as Wordsworth states in his *Preface* to the *Lyrical Ballads*.

[529] *Feelings...pleasures* – It is the feelings which are more important than the memories; memories, where they come in, serve only to rouse up the feelings associated with the memories. It might be hard to think how feelings can be brought up if the incidents are not remembered, and this can be said as a criticism. But Wordsworth means over here that the incidents are too many to be remembered distinctly, and so, he gets a feeling which is a mixture of all these collected pleasurable memories, which are not prominent enough to feature distinctly, but are important enough to form good feelings. Moreover, as Wordsworth states in the next line, *unremembered* is used in the sense of that which is not remembered by others. If we are to apply that sense here, the meaning that we would get is that Wordsworth gets delight from the little things which are not remembered by others.

[530] *As...life* – These feelings have a great influence in a person's life. *No slight or trivial influence* is a litotes. It means a lot of influence.

PRE-ROMANTIC AND ROMANTIC POETRY

> His little, nameless, unremembered acts
> Of kindness and of love.[531] Nor less, I trust,
> To them I may have owed another gift,
> Of aspect more sublime; that blessed mood,
> In which the burthen[532] of the mystery,[533]
> In which the heavy and the weary weight
> Of all this unintelligible world,[534]
> Is lighten'd: -- that serene and blessed mood,
> In which the affections[535] gently lead us on,--
> Until, the breath of this corporeal frame,[536]
> And even the motion of our human blood
> Almost suspended,[537] we are laid asleep

On...life – Here, two words are to be noticed: *best* and *good*. The great influence is not just upon any man, but on a *good* man, and not on all his years, but his *best* years. Wordsworth, thus, states that the ungrateful man will have no such feelings, and it is only the good man who will get such feelings, and that too, at his best times, so that the effect of the feelings is maximum.

[531] *His...love* – These bring out the simplicity that Wordsworth intended the poems of the *Lyrical Ballads* to be.

[532] *burthen* – Burden.

[533] *mystery* – The mystery of creation.

[534] *unintelligible world* – World whose actions are unfathomable = irrational = headless. The reference to the French Revolution and its atrocities, which left a deep mark upon Wordsworth, and was crucial in turning him again towards nature, is unmistakable.

[535] *affections* – Emotions.

[536] *corporeal frame* – The physical body; the life.

[537] *And...suspended* – So sublime is the state that even the flow of blood seems to stop, and all the body and soul seems to be still. Readers would do well to read *Upon Westminster Bridge*, where

In body, and become a living soul:[538]
While with an eye made quiet by the power
Of harmony,[539] and the deep power of joy,
We see into the life of things.[540]
                If this
Be but a vain belief, yet, oh! how oft,
In darkness, and amid the many shapes
Of joyless daylight; when the fretful stir
Unprofitable, and the fever of the world,

Wordsworth speaks of such a state where everything is absolutely still.

[538] *we...soul* – The person, in such a state, goes into a trance. So, he is absolutely still in his body, and it is only through the soul that he sees – the soul becomes the eyes, the ears, and all the other senses, to give the person a divine insight. The image of the thought is similar to that of *The Rime of the Ancient Mariner*, where the Mariner goes into a trance when the ship moves at a tremendous speed, and hears two supernatural beings talking about the ship and about his state.

[539] *With...harmony* – The eye is the spiritual eye, which is open in this trance-like state, as has been noted in the previous annotation. The harmony is the link that is there in nature. As told in the introduction, Wordsworth believed in God, Creation (as the manifested work of God), Nature (as the manifestation of Creation on Earth) and Man (as a part of Nature). In Wordsworth's views, all things are linked with each other. Man is linked with God through Nature, which is part of Creation. But it is a pity that Man decides to break that bond with Nature, something which Wordsworth expresses in *Lines Written in early Spring*. In this sublime state, man is capable of feeling the binding harmony once more.

[540] *We...things* – Are able to see that there is a Grand Plan in Creation, and feel the link that is there in everything.[540]

Have hung upon the beatings of my heart,[541]
How oft, in spirit, have I turned to thee,
O sylvan Wye![542] Thou wanderer through the woods,
How often has my spirit turned to thee![543]

And now, with gleams of half-extinguish'd thought,[544]
With many recognitions dim and faint,[545]
And somewhat of a sad perplexity,
The picture of the mind revives again:[546]
While here I stand, not only with the sense
Of present pleasure,[547] but with pleasing thoughts
That in this moment there is life and food
For future years.[548] And so I dare to hope

---

[541] *How…heart* – There have been times when Wordsworth has felt depressed by the wrongs that go on in the world.

[542] *How…Wye* – The poet apostrophises the Wye land, and states that in his depressing times, he has turned to it.

sylvan – Connected with forests and trees.

[543] *Thou…thee* – The poet assumes a spirit to be there in the woods, and addresses it. By spirit, no ghostly being is meant; Wordsworth merely writes about the ambience of the woods.

[544] *And…thought* – This is the first line in the poem where we get a glimpse of the fact that Wordsworth's memories are old, and he does not remember all of them. His present self is a shadow of the former young self – he is not so young and vigorous now, as he himself will say a few lines afterwards.

[545] *dim…faint* – These words emphasise the old age coming on the poet, as has been previously noted.

[546] *The…again* – This reviving of the picture of the mind means that the poet, in seeing the Wye land once more, is recollecting his previous images.

[547] *present pleasures* – The present pleasures are the pleasures which the poet gets in seeing the Wye land.

[548] *That…years* – Just as the previous visits had given lots of pleasurable memories to Wordsworth, this visit too, will give him lots of memories, which he will remember long in the future.

Though changed, no doubt, from what I was when first
I came among these hills;[549] when like a roe[550]
I bounded o'er the mountains, by the sides
Of the deep rivers, and the lonely streams,
Wherever nature led;[551] more like a man
Flying from something that he dreads,[552] than one
Who sought the thing he loved. For nature then
(The coarser pleasures of my boyish days,
And their glad animal movements[553] all gone by,)
To me was all in all.--I cannot paint
What then I was.[554] The sounding cataract[555]

Compare this with the last two lines of *The Solitary Reaper*, "The music in my heart I bore/Long after it was heard no more".

[549] *Though...hills* – Look at note 529.

[550] *roe* – i.e., Roe Deer, a small deer found in Asia and Europe.

[551] *Wherever nature led* – This should be kept in mind, for, as told, Wordsworth at first, loved nature, then, following Godwin, went after education as being cut off from nature, and finally, turned back to nature once again. Here, he is talking about those times when he loved nature before going in for Godwinian philosophy.

[552] *more...dreads* – Readers must not fail to notice the similarity between these lines and *The Rime of the Ancient Mariner*.

[553] *coarser...movements* – The phrases, *coarser pleasures* and *animal movements* is to be noted. The previous enjoyments in his youth were only enjoyments – it is later that he reflects and feels the emotional value of the pleasures. While he was enjoying in his youth, he was simply in the effect of the enjoyments – he did not observe them. This becomes clear when one reads *Daffodils*, where Wordsworth states, "I gazed – and gazed – but little thought/What wealth the show to me had brought".

[554] *I...was* – Wordsworth cannot write in his poems what he exactly was in his youth – for he is not grown, and is not the same youthful person. However, this seems to be a contradiction to his

PRE-ROMANTIC AND ROMANTIC POETRY

> Haunted me like a passion: the tall rock,
> The mountain, and the deep and gloomy wood,[556]
> Their colours and their forms, were then to me
> An appetite:[557] a feeling and a love,
> That had no need of a remoter charm,
> By thought supplied, or any interest
> Unborrowed from the eye.-That time is past,
> And all its aching joys[558] are now no more,
> And all its dizzy raptures. Not for this
> Faint I, nor mourn nor murmur: other gifts
> Have followed, for such loss, I would believe,
> Abundant recompence.[559] For I have learned
> To look on nature, not as in the hour
> Of thoughtless youth,[560] but hearing oftentimes

---

own statement in *Preface* to the *Lyrical Ballads*, a poet needs to work himself to an emotional state, so that he is able to get those very feelings which he felt at the time of the incidents, and then, poetry would flow. This is how it becomes emotions recollected in tranquillity.

[555] *sounding cataract* – A large, steep waterfall.

[556] *gloomy wood* – This gloom is not a gloom of sadness, but a cold and soothing gloom.

[557] *were...appetite* – The sense of sight satisfies the stomach – he seems to be eating the sights. This is an example of *synaesthesia*, where senses are fused with each other.

[558] *aching joys* – This is an oxymoron. The joy is not an ache to the poet, as he cannot enjoy them any more.

[559] *Not...recompense* – For the loss of the joys (loss as Wordsworth cannot enjoy them any more), the poet has got other things in life.

[560] *thoughtless youth* – As remarked above, while a youth, the enjoyments were not observed; they were experienced in the body without reflecting upon them.

The still, sad music of humanity,[561]
Nor harsh nor grating, though of ample power
To chasten and subdue.[562] And I have felt
A presence that disturbs me[563] with the joy
Of elevated thoughts;[564] a sense sublime
Of something far more deeply interfused,
Whose dwelling is the light of setting suns,[565]
And the round ocean, and the living air,[566]
And the blue sky, and in the mind of man,
A motion and a spirit, that impels
All thinking things, all objects of all thought,
And rolls through all things.[567] Therefore am I still
A lover of the meadows and the woods,
And mountains; and of all that we behold
From this green earth; of all the mighty world
Of eye and ear, both what they half-create,
And what perceive; well pleased to recognize
In nature and the language of the sense,

---

[561] *still...humanity* – This is an allusion to the French Revolution and the atrocities that followed after it.

[562] *Nor...subdue* – Nature, though it is not harsh, is capable of correcting mankind. Readers can compare these lines with *Ode to Duty*.

[563] *disturbs me* – Moves me; makes me restless.

[564] *elevated thoughts* – Thoughts which are high (over here, making the poet high in spirit and in mind).

[565] *Whose...suns* – The effect of the light that is there in the sky when the sun sets is the effect which the poet describes. The readers should not literally try to locate an actual dwelling place.

[566] *living air* – Air which gives life.

[567] *A motion...all things* – Compare Coleridge's *Frost at Midnight*, where Coleridge says about God: "Himself in all; all things in Himself".

The anchor of my purest thoughts, the nurse,
The guide, the guardian of my heart, and soul
Of all my moral being.

                Nor, perchance,
If I were not thus taught, should I the more
Suffer my genial spirits to decay:
For thou[568] art with me,[569] here, upon the banks
Of this fair river; thou, my dearest Friend,
My dear, dear Friend, and in thy voice I catch
The language of my former heart, and read
My former pleasures in the shooting lights
Of thy wild eyes. Oh! yet a little while
May I behold in thee what I was once,[570]
My dear, dear Sister! And this prayer I make,
Knowing that Nature never did betray
The heart that loved her;[571] 'tis her privilege,
Through all the years of this our life, to lead
From joy to joy: for she can so inform
The mind that is within us, so impress
With quietness and beauty, and so feed
With lofty thoughts, that neither evil tongues,
Rash judgments, nor the sneers of selfish men,

---

[568] *thou* – Wordsworth's sister, Dorothy.

[569] *For…me* – This might be an allusion to Ps. 23, "Even though I walk through the valley of the shadow of death, I will fear no evil, for You are with me, Your rod and Your staff, they comfort me".

[570] *what…was* – i.e., Wordsworth's youthful self. Wordsworth's sister is still youthful, and Wordsworth finds a reflection of his former jovial spirit in her.

[571] *Nature…her* – Those who love nature (including Wordsworth himself) are rewarded by her. Nature, unlike humans, is not ungrateful.

Nor greetings where no kindness is,[572] nor all
The dreary intercourse of daily life,
Shall e'er prevail against us, or disturb
Our cheerful faith that all which we behold
Is full of blessings.[573] Therefore let the moon
Shine on thee in thy solitary walk;
And let the misty mountain winds[574] be free
To blow against thee: and in after years,[575]
When these wild ecstasies shall be matured
Into a sober pleasure,[576] when thy mind
Shall be a mansion for all lovely forms,[577]
Thy memory be as a dwelling-place
For all sweet sounds and harmonies; Oh! then,
If solitude, or fear, or pain, or grief,
Should be thy portion, with what healing thoughts
Of tender joy wilt thou remember me,
And these my exhortations![578] Nor, perchance,

---

[572] *greetings...is* – fake greeting.

[573] *Shall...blessings* – No evil thing shall prevail against those who love Nature, and all evil shall fall short of the blessings that will be got by a person who loves Nature. Compare this with the epistle of St. Paul to the Romans, where he states that no earthly power or tribulations will be able to shake their faith.

[574] *misty-mountain winds* – Mountain winds which are full of mists, because there is mist in the mountains.

[575] *after years* – later on in life.

[576] *When...pleasure* – When Dorothy's youthful spirit will be like Wordsworth's present spirit, which is now not physically active, but gets a sense of calmness in remembering his former self.

[577] *when...forms* – When her mind will have all lovely thoughts, just as a mansion will have all lovely shapes of furniture.

[578] *then...exhortations* – If at that point of life, Dorothy Wordsworth suffers from any cause of pain, these joyful memories

If I should be, where I no more can hear
Thy voice,[579] nor catch from thy wild eyes these gleams
Of past existence, wilt thou then forget
That on the banks of this delightful stream
We stood together; and that I, so long
A worshipper of Nature, hither came,
Unwearied in that service: rather say
With warmer love, oh! with far deeper zeal
Of holier love.[580] Nor wilt thou then forget,
That after many wanderings, many years
Of absence, these steep woods and lofty cliffs,
And this green pastoral landscape, were to me
More dear, both for themselves, and for thy sake.[581]

1798.

Background Information

Wordsworth had first visited Tintern Abbey in 1793, while going to North Wales from the Isle of Wight. That was in the month of July. In 1798, again in the month of July, he undertook a walking tour in Wye Valley, and visited Tintern Abbey once more. It is this walking tour which occasioned the cause of the *Lyrical Ballads*,

---

will comfort her, and she will remember that Wordsworth had told her of them.

[579] *If...voice* – i.e., if he is dead.

[580] *Rather...love* – i.e., rather than coming back with an untiring spirit, Wordsworth came back with a wormer feeling for the place, a feeling which was "holier" than the feeling he had for the place before.

[581] *both...sake* – These features were lovely to Wordsworth because these features were lovely in the first place, and more so, because of the presence of the loving sister, Dorothy.

for Wordsworth and Coleridge decided to come up with some poems which they wished to publish in order to meet the expenses of the tour. Dorothy was also on that trip. Though she did not write any poems in the *Lyrical Ballads*, she did help the two men in their compositions.

Regarding the poem, Wordsworth himself wrote:

> No poem of mine was composed under circumstances more pleasant for me to remember than this. I began it upon leaving Tintern, after crossing the Wye, and concluded it just as I was entering Bristol in the evening, after a ramble of four or five days, with my Sister. Not a line of it was altered, and not any part of it written down till I reached Bristol. It was published almost immediately after in the little volume of which so much has been said in these Notes. — (The Lyrical Ballads, as first published at Bristol by Cottle.)

Form of the Poem

The poem is written in blank verse. This makes it suitable to be read like prose, that is, as a person would speak. The divided lines indicate stanza breaks, as in:

> The guide, the guardian of my heart, and soul
> Of all my moral being.
>   Nor perchance,
> If I were not thus taught, should I the more

The poem is presented as the recollection of a person who is observing the differences between a past visit and the present visit.

Critical Summary of the Text

The poem is about reminiscence. It is reminiscence of the past, seeing the present before the person. Wordsworth recollects his previous visit to the Wye Valley in 1793, as he comes back to it in 1798, five years later. Memory plays a very crucial role in the poem, like any other poem of Wordsworth. His poetry is about the recollected feelings which he gets out of memory. Memory here must not be understood only as something which makes him recollect the facts; he recollects the emotions also. In fact, the stress is more on the emotions than the facts.

The poem opens with the poet stating that "Five years have passed" since he last visited the place. The summers and the winters that he mentions are to create the effect of contrast. In other words, the poet tells that lots of happy things (summers) and lots of unpleasant things (winters) have happened in this span of five years. He lists the things he sees once more, and describes their effect upon him, both in the previous time, and this present time. The "steep and lofty cliffs" bring in him "thoughts of more deep seclusion"; he rests under the dark sycamore tree and views the cottage-grounds and the orchard trees, whose fruit is yet to ripe. He sees the "wreaths of smoke" going up from cottage chimneys between the trees, and in his Romantic imagination, feels that there are "vagrant dwellers in the houseless woods," who are producing the smoke, or they are coming from the cave of a hermit who resides in the forest.

The poet then tells how the memory of these "beauteous forms" has been with him in these five years. When he was by himself, or in crowded areas, they were to him "sensations sweet, / Felt in the blood, and felt along the heart." The memory of the woods and cottages offered "tranquil restoration" to his mind, and even affected him subconsciously, leading him to actions of kindness and love. He goes on to state that the memory of the scene gave him access to that mental and spiritual state in which he feels relaxed, so that the stress of the world does not affect him, and in this relaxed state, he becomes a "living soul" with a view into "the life of things". He then states that he might be wrong in overestimating the helpful powers of the charming memory of the Wye Valley, but even if his belief has been in "vain", he has got help from the memory at times when he was troubled.

Even as the poet sees the landscape at present, the memory of the previous visit comes before him, and he feels the difference between the two visits in a bittersweet way. However, he is happy in thinking that this present visit will be in his memory for many years, and help him in his times of sorrow, just as the previous memory had helped him. He accepts that he is different now from how he was in those long-ago times, when, as a boy, he "bounded o'er the mountains" and through the streams. At that time, he loved Nature and its forms with innocent happiness; the features of the land gave shape to his passions, his tastes, and his love. This obviously refers to the time before he was influenced by Godwin. In fact, he met Godwin the year after that. That time is now past, he says, but he does not grief for it endlessly, because he sees before him the things he has got now: he can now "look on nature, not as in the hour/Of thoughtless youth; but hearing oftentimes/The still, sad music of humanity"; he can now sense the presence of something far more sublime in the things that he sees, like the light of the setting sun, the ocean, the air itself, and even in the mind of man. This power seems to him "a motion and a spirit that impels/All thinking thoughts.... /And rolls through all things." Previously, he just got immature joy in seeing the natural landscape; now, he feels their impact upon him. So, he still loves the natural landscape – mountains and pastures and woods, for they hold his purest thoughts and guard the heart and soul of his "moral being."

The speaker then says that everything that he sees assume bigger proportions of happiness for him because of the presence of his "Sister," who is also his "dear, dear Friend," and in whose voice and manner he observes his former self, and beholds "what I was once." He prays that he might continue to do so for a little while, knowing, as he says, that "Nature never did betray/The heart that loved her," but leads rather "from joy to joy." Someone who loves nature is, according to Wordsworth, not susceptible to "evil tongues," "rash judgments," and "the sneers of selfish men". Instead, such a person is filled with "cheerful faith" that the world is full of blessings. The poet then assures the sister the comforting light of the moon will shine upon her, and the wind will happily blow upon her face, and he says to her that in later years, when she is sad or fearful, the memory of this experience will help to heal her, in the same manner that it has helped him. If he himself is dead, she can remember the love with which he viewed nature. Thereby, she will remember the joy he got from the woods, not just because the woods were lovely, but also because she was with him at that time. The poet thus, moves out from a general description of nature and ends the poem by stating the bond that is there between himself and his sister.

Tintern Abbey as Growth of a Poet's Mind

As told before, Romantic poetry is personal. The mind of the poet is present in the poem, and his shaping thoughts can be seen, even if he creates other characters, like in *The Rime of the Ancient Mariner*. *Tintern Abbey* came out first as a poem in the *Lyrical Ballads*. The poem is composed of the poet's re-visiting the Wye Valley in 1798, five years after his first visit of 1793. The poet explores the differences that are there between that visit and this visit. But these differences are not about the changes that have taken in the features of the land, but in the poet's body and mind. He has become older, and grown in spirit also.

Tintern Abbey must be studied with another poem of Wordsworth's, *Immortality Ode*, for it is there that Wordsworth fully develops his idea about the role of nature in building up a human personality, and how man can reach God. Wordsworth talks about the stages in the development of the individual from infancy to adulthood; he does not talk about the physical growth, but the spiritual growth. He states,

> But trailing clouds of Glory do we come
> From God, who is our home;
> Heaven lies about us in our infancy!

According to Wordsworth, in infancy, we are spiritually nearest to God; as we grow up, "shades of the prison-house", that is, the world, begin to cloud over this blessed state, and the growing child starts separating from God, as he enters more and more into the worldly things. Finally, when he is grown up, and totally into the material world, he loses all of spirituality. He compares this loss (quite ironically, it would appear) with the east and the rising sun. The east, from where the sun rises, is the time of infancy, when one can view the splendorous glory of the new day (new day is like an infant). As the sun rises higher and higher in the sky, or rather, as the earth progresses through the day, it goes further and further away from the sun, and when it is proper day, that is, when the child has grown up, he "fades into the light of common day". In other words, at day, light is commonly displayed over the face of the earth, and there is no distinction; the splendour of dawn is not longer to be found during the day. So, the spiritual glory is lost. But the journey does not end there; the soul sets in the west, that is, when day ends, the earth is furthest from the sun, being in the west. At the time of death, man has totally lost God, that is what Wordsworth seems to be saying. This is the general picture; Wordsworth himself believes to retain this naivety within him. This is where we shall explore *Tintern Abbey* as a poem which shows the growth of the poet's mind not as a growth of decay, but of retention.

Wordsworth's initial inclination was towards nature, and he expresses the same in the lines:

> what I was when first
> I came among these hills; when like a roe
> I bounded o'er the mountains, by the sides
> Of the deep rivers, and the lonely streams,
> Wherever nature led: more like a man
> Flying from something that he dreads, than one
> Who sought the thing he loved. For nature then
> (The coarser pleasures of my boyish days,
> And their glad animal movements all gone by)
> To me was all in all.

He loved nature as an infant would: without understanding the impact, but simply feeling a joy about it all. Now that he has grown, he understands the impact that nature has on him, and understands its importance in the Creation. So, he says, "I cannot paint what then I was". But he has not lost what he previously was. Though he would no longer be able to leap through the hilly landscape, he would still enjoy it, and this time, it would be better, for he has with him the understanding which he had previously lacked. So, for him, the journey from east to the "common day" has not been a journey of degeneration of spiritual decay, but an increase of it. His statement about the spiritual decay, expressed in *Immortality Ode* is for the general human race; for him and others who follow nature, there is no decay of spirituality, but an increase in understanding. Wordsworth's mind has grown so as to understand that, and he wishes his sister to have the same kind of blessing, as he has had, in viewing nature.

Tintern Abbey as a Philosophic Poem

It has been told in the beginning that all Romantic poetry is personal to some extent. Wordsworth's personal views are much reflected in this poem, like any other poem written by him. He was, in his youth, devoted to nature, and later, was influenced by the philosophy of Godwin, who led him to believe that refined culture is the only way to bring about the true human personality. Being influenced by such a philosophy, Wordsworth composed poems which were highly artificial, but as a result of the repressed emotions, he was about to suffer a nervous breakdown, when he found the saving medicine in the philosophy of Rousseau, who propounded natural learning over superficial codes of conduct. Following him, Wordsworth returned to nature, after having followed the philosophy of Godwin for four years. *Tintern Abbey* brings out the philosophical musings of Wordsworth when he was a youth, and now, at his present self.

Rousseau talked about leaving a child to learn from nature. There should not be anything coming in the natural learning of the child. Such a philosophy is found in *Tintern Abbey*, when Wordsworth says,

> The sounding cataract
> Haunted me like a passion: the tall rock,
> The mountain, and the deep and gloomy wood,
> Their colours and their forms, were then to me
> An appetite; a feeling and a love,
> That had no need of a remoter charm,
> By thought supplied, nor any interest
> Unborrowed from the eye.

Nature was his food at such a time. Four years later, he realizes that just "animal movements" is not enough; in fact, it is after the "animal movements" have receded that the maturer thought comes in, and in that, Wordsworth hears, "the sad music of humanity". This "sad music of humanity" does not however, prevent the poet from expressing his good feelings. Just has "pleasant thoughts bring sad thoughts to the mind" (*"I Heard A Thousand Blended Notes"*), the sad tune brings in Wordsworth a transcendental feeling, through which Wordsworth sees "into the life of things".

Nature, according to Wordsworth, has never-failing powers to restore a person who is low in the spirits. Wordsworth, in saying so, obviously refers to the fact that nature has restored him from his attachment to Godwinian philosophy. Wordsworth views Nature as a restoring agent.

In Introduction to Romantic Poetry, it has been told that Wordsworth feels that Nature is the manifestation of the Creation of God, and everything in Creation is linked with each other in perfect harmony. Man is a part of this link, but it is sad that Man has decided to break the link, and destroy Creation. This is the "sad music of humanity", the French Revolution and the Napoleonic wars, and England's war with France. Wordsworth states that man can really have peace when Man begins to love Nature. It is then that man will be free from "evil tongues," "rash judgments," and "the sneers of selfish men", and maintain the harmony that God wants Man to maintain.

Wordsworth, in *Tintern Abbey*, does not preach like Dante does in *The Divine Comedy*. As he said, his subject is of the common and simple things in life. By simply observing Nature, and loving Nature, Wordsworth gets a great loving feeling, which brings him immense happiness in his soul when he later thinks about it. He writes,

> And I have felt
> A presence that disturbs me with the joy
> Of elevated thoughts; a sense sublime
> Of something far more deeply interfused,
> Whose dwelling is the light of setting suns,
> And the round ocean and the living air,
> And the blue sky, and in the mind of man;
> A motion and a spirit, that impels
> All thinking things, all objects of all thought,
> And rolls through all things.

In these lines, there is the sense of something unified running through all that is there in Creation. It would be wrong to bring in claims of pantheism in such lines, where the intention is nothing but mono-theistic. Wordsworth talks about One Spirit which is running through all that exists, holding them to Itself. This is not pagan, but Christian, which preaches God as one, and all nature manifesting the glory of God. Coleridge writes similar lines in *Frost At Midnight*,

>   So shalt thou see and hear
> The lovely shapes and sounds intelligible
> Of that eternal language, which thy God
> Utters, who from eternity doth teach
> Himself in all, and all things in Himself.
> Great universal Teacher! He shall mould
> Thy spirit, and by giving make it ask.

This good feeling in the poet makes him wish good for his son; Wordsworth, too, feeling good, wishes good things for his sister. So, it can be said that the harmony that Wordsworth believes to be running through Creation has been found by him, and he wishes to pass it on to his sister.

Thus, is can be said that good feelings coming from Nature will make a person wish good for the others around him, that is the philosophy that *Tintern Abbey* brings out, and that is what we get to know about the belief of the poet.

The Role of Memory in *Tintern Abbey*

It has been said in Wordsworth's Views on Poetry and the Poet that he feels true poetry is that which flows spontaneously.[582] The emotions are aroused when the poet sits and reflects over an incident, till he feels what he had felt at that time. In other words, true poetry is that which comes from the memory of the poet. He can recollect these emotions only when he is in a tranquil state, otherwise, the feelings will not come.

In *Tintern Abbey*, Wordsworth recollects the previous visit from his memory. However, here, the difference is that he does not write the poem when he is distant from that place, as we find in

---

[582] See the section to refer to the words of Wordsworth in this regard.

Daffodils and *The Solitary Reaper*, but is at present, in sight of the place. He recollects his previous visit while he visits it at present, this is what makes it different from most of the other poems of Wordsworth.[583] In recollecting, he lights upon the thought that he is no longer the same youthful person as he previously was. He says, "I cannot paint when then then I was". However, he is not sad at this; the realisation that the previous memory would only be a memory, and would not be something that he would be able to do – like leaping from place to place, in "animal movements" – does not deter him from loving nature, for he says that this time, he has got other things which were not there previously. In the previous visit, there was only joy, without understanding the impact of nature. Now, there is joy (though the joy is subdued, because there will not be physical action in it) along with understanding. Just as the previous visit had made him feel happy every time he had thought about it in his mind (again, resorting to memory), this visit too, would continue to make him feel happy each time he thinks about it, and the memory of this visit will be there with a philosophic understanding, which was lacking in the previous visit. He says, regarding the pervious visit:

> These forms of beauty have not been to me
> As is a landscape to a blind man's eye:
> But oft, in lonely rooms, and 'mid the din
> Of towns and cities, I have owed to them
> In hours of weariness, sensations sweet,
> Felt in the blood, and felt along the heart;
> And passing even into my purer mind,
> With tranquil restoration

Regarding his present visit, he says,

> And now, with gleams of half-extinguished thought,
> With many recognitions dim and faint,
> And somewhat of a sad perplexity,
> The picture of the mind revives again:
> While here I stand, not only with the sense
> Of present pleasure, but with pleasing thoughts

---

[583] Another set of exceptions are the *Yarrow* poems.

> That in this moment there is life and food
> For future years.

It is in this visit that he has got a better understanding of the impact of Nature upon him, and upon all those who love Nature. He says,

> Not for this
> Faint I, nor mourn nor murmur, other gifts
> Have followed; for such loss, I would believe,
> Abundant recompence. For I have learned
> To look on nature, not as in the hour
> Of thoughtless youth; but hearing oftentimes
> The still, sad music of humanity,
> Nor harsh nor grating, though of ample power
> To chasten and subdue.

So, it can be said that the memory that was there previously is not lost for Wordsworth; rather, wisdom has been added to it, which will help him better when later, he recollects this visit.

14. Samuel Taylor Coleridge (1772-1834)

About the Poet

Samuel Taylor Coleridge and Wordsworth were very close friends, though they did have a lot of disputes. He, along with Wordsworth, published the first edition of the *Lyrical Ballads*, but due to dissent, withdrew his name from the anthology, and the second edition of the *Lyrical Ballads* was published without his name in it, though he did write poems for it, and they were there, even in the second edition, with some modifications.

Coleridge was the youngest of nine siblings, born to Reverend John Coleridge, in Devon. Right from the start, he was interested in nature, and more so, the mysteries of it. In 1780, he ran away after a quarrel with his brother Frank. His father died in 1781. His mother sent him as a "charity boy" to Christ's Hospital School, London, and Coleridge came home only during holiday visits, for the next ten years. He called himself as an 'orphan".[584] In 1789, he begins writing some of his early poems. It is in this year that he meets Charles Lamb. Two years later, his sister, Anne, died.[585]

Coleridge was a very good scholar in Greek. The year he collaborated with Wordsworth, he also went to Germany, and gathered a lot of knowledge about the German philosophy that was popular then. However, his health was not good, and he had to resort to sedative drugs frequently. In 1817, he published his famous *Biographia Literaria*. In 1834, the third edition of his

---

[584] Readers should note the line in *The Rime of the Ancient Mariner*: "An orphan's curse can drag to hell/A spirit from on high".

[585] Coleridge commemorates her in two sonnets.

Poetical Works came out in March. Four months later, he died in Hampstead.

KUBLA KHAN

Or

A VISION IN A DREAM. A FRAGMENT

In Xanadu[586] did Kubla Khan[587]
A stately pleasure-dome decree:[588]
Where Alph,[589] the sacred river, ran

---

[586] *Xanadu* – Xandu, or, Shangdu, as described by Marco Polo in his book *Il Milone*. Purchas included it in his *Pilgrimage, Vol XI, 231*. Coleridge notes that while he fell asleep over Purchas' *Pligrimage*, most of the ideas of the poem came to him.

[587] *Kubla Khan* – Kublai Khan, grandson of Ghengis (or Chengis) Khan, emperor of Mongolia and China, and belonging to the Yuan Dynasty.

[588] *A...decree* – Passed a law that a grand palace should be constructed. It must be told over here that Kubla Khan used to spend his summers in Xanadu, and had actually made his subjects build him a grand palace for that purpose.

[589] *Alph* – Alph is a river in Western Greece. This might seem to be a mis-location for Xanadu, but Coleridge is over here, fusing real rivers and imaginary rivers. A common mistake would be to state the Alph river to be a river in Antartica. The setting that Coleridge creates over here has got ice in it, but he is not referring to the icy-river Alph, for it was named by Griffith Taylor on his Terra Nova Expedition, in 1911-1913.

> Through caverns[590] measureless to man
>   Down to a sunless sea.[591]
> So twice five miles[592] of fertile[593] ground
> With walls and towers were girdled round:
> And there were gardens bright with sinuous[594] rills,[595]
> Where blossomed many an incense-bearing tree;[596]
> And here were forests ancient as the hills,
> Enfolding sunny spots of greenery.[597]

There is also the belief that Alph is an underground river in Europe – its underground flow symbolizing the flow of hidden knowledge. This is something that comes near the theme of the poem – secrecy and mystery.

[590] *caverns* – Large caves.

[591] *sunless sea* – Dark sea. However, the image of the sun never shining on it is a horrid one, and there is the idea of a devoid-from-grace state in which Kubla Khan lives – i.e., devoid from the grace of God, making all features seem monstrously mysterious, and not divinely charming.

[592] *So...miles* – Ten miles.

[593] *fertile* – The readers should keep in mind that the ground is fertile. It is productive.

[594] *sinuous* – Turning while moving.

[595] *rills* – Meandering streams.

[596] *Incense-bearing tree* – The trees no not bear flowers or fruits, but incense, that is, lovely fragrance. Even if they bear flowers or fruits, that is overshadowed by the fact that they bear incense. It is their bearing of incense which has been empahsised. Coleridge wants to state that there is a lovely fragrance in that place.

[597] *Enfolding...greenery* – The sun is shining in through the patches of the woods of the forest. It must be noted here that previously, it was stated that the sun does not shine on the sea. However, it shines through the forest. So, the effect which is

PRE-ROMANTIC AND ROMANTIC POETRY

> But oh! that deep romantic chasm[598] which slanted
> Down the green hill[599] athwart a cedarn cover![600]
> A savage place![601] as holy and enchanted
> As e'er beneath a waning moon[602] was haunted

---

created is that the sun's rays are not found on all parts of this territory – the sea is sunless, but the forests receive sunlight. There is the contrast of light and darkness.

[598] *chasm* – A deep crack or opening in the ground.

[599] *green hill* – The readers should note the colour of the hill. A green hill is an unusual sight. Given the situation in the poem, this might also be called unnatural. The only natural explanation would be that the forests on it make it appear green. However, even if it is so naturally explained, a study of Coleridge's poetry would reveal that he wishes to present unnatural things in a natural way, and so, it would not be wrong to say that he states *green hill* to bring in this supernatural feeling.

[600] *cedarn cover* – The foliage of the cedarn trees.

[601] *A...place* – The monsterous image has already been noted. There is a sense of devilishness in the ambience. This savagery is in contrast with Christianity, and also with civilization in general. Post-colonial critics might criticise this on the grounds that just because it is about the east, it is savage to the eyes of the English Coleridge. This criticism is all right, as long as it remains on the surface level, that is, as long as it just states that the east is presented as savage from the point of view of a western poet. However, it would not be advisable to lay accusations of such sort on the Romantic poets. Though Coleridge calls it savage, he does not denounce it. The savagery has got its charm, and he is bringing that out, and not just condemning it, for in the next few words, he states, "as holy and enchanted".

[602] *waning moon* – The moon has always been associated with lunacy, and in legends and myths, with supernatural creatures, e.g.,

By woman wailing for her demon-lover![603]
And from this chasm, with ceaseless turmoil[604] seething,[605]
As if this earth in fast thick pants were breathing,[606]
A mighty fountain momently[607] was forced:
Amid whose swift half-intermitted burst
Huge fragments vaulted like rebounding hail,[608]
Or chaffy grain[609] beneath the thresher's flail:[610]
And 'mid these dancing rocks at once and ever
It flung up momently the sacred river.

---

a full-moon brings out a were-wolf. The waning moon brings out a fading image of the mysterious powers.

[603] *By...lover* – There is no reference about this. This might mean that a woman, who fell in love with a were-wolf, or such a beast-man, whose shape changes with that of the moon, cries in the absence of the lover under the waning-moon. The demon-lover is not there, as it is a waning-moon. In Shelley's *The Moon*, the moon is looked upon as a dying old lady at first, then as a lady who is searching fruitlessly to find a lover, but finds no one.

[604] *ceaseless turmoil* – Continual chaos and noise.

[605] *seething* – To move about quickly or violently.

[606] *As...breathing* – The image of the panting earth in such a state is similar to that of a mother in labour pain. As a mother gives birth to a child, the earth gives birth to this fountain.

[607] *momently* – In a moment.

[608] *Huge...hail* – Huge chunks of rocks burst from it.

[609] *chaffy grain* – Grain mixed with chaff. The chaff is the part which is thrown out; the grain is stored. Here, the idea of the grain still filled with chaff after the threshing seems to be unusual. What Coleridge means is that the fountain is filled with fragments of rocks, and that makes it appear like fine grain mixed with chaff.

[610] *flail* – A tool with a long handle, and a stick swinging from it, to separate the grain from the chaff.

> Five miles meandering with a mazy motion[611]
> Through wood and dale[612] the sacred river ran,
> Then reached the caverns measureless to man,
> And sank in tumult to a lifeless ocean:[613]
> And 'mid this tumult Kubla heard from far
> Ancestral voices prophesying war!
>   The shadow of the dome of pleasure
>   Floated midway on the waves;[614]
>   Where was heard the mingled measure[615]
>   From the fountain and the caves.[616]

---

[611] *Five...motion* – The readers should not miss the alliteration.

[612] *dale* – Valley.

[613] *And...ocean* – The readers should notice the plethora of contrasting images that are brought out in this line. First of all, the river is said to be sinking – as if its life is going away; as if it's drowning. The next word *tumult* envisages life and activity, and is therefore, in contrast with the image of life gradually sinking. However, the next word *lifeless* again brings back the idea of death, but this epithet is placed with *ocean*, which cannot be conceived as lifeless, but always teeming with life. This mixture of opposites creates a harmony over here, and these opposites are a characteristic feature of the poem.

The only way in which tumult can go with death is in war, and that is what Coleridge states in the next two lines.

[614] *The...waves* – The image, even if conceived, is not possible. The readers can simply imagine it and wonder – that is what the poem demands.

[615] *measure* – Tone.

[616] *From...caves* – If one goes by the analogy of the earth giving birth to the fountain, then the fountain, at its origin, represents birth, the fountain itself represents life, and the caves "measureless

> It was a miracle of rare device,
> A sunny pleasure-dome with caves of ice![617]

> A damsel[618] with a dulcimer[619]
> In a vision once I saw:[620]
> It was an Abyssinian maid,
> And on her dulcimer she played,
> Singing of Mount Abora.[621]
> Could I revive within me
> Her symphony and song,
> To such a deep delight 'twould win me,
> That with music loud and long,

---

to man" represent death. However, there are also other symbolic associations. The fountain represents the sacred, while the caves represent the dark savagery.

[617] *A...ice* – Once again, the readers can simply read and wonder, but never relate to an actual geographical feature.

[618] *damsel* – A beautiful girl, who dances at a court.

[619] *dulcimer* – A musical instrument with strings.

[620] *A...saw* – This is the beginning of the third part of the poem, and Coleridge states that we wrote it after coming back. This part seems to have abruptly begun, and does not show connection with the previous parts, and so, might be one of the reasons why Coleridge calls it "A Fragment".

[621] *Singing...Abora* – In *Paradise Lost*, Minton mentions Mount Amara. He calls it to be one of the supposed places which men have thought to be the location of Paradise. Purchas describes the "hill of Amara". Coleridge might have fused both the readings. The damsel sings of the "supposed" paradise, on Mount Abora (Amara becomes Abora), and this idea of paradise is retained till the end of the poem.

> I would build that dome in air,[622]
> That sunny dome! those caves of ice![623]
> And all who heard should see them there,
> And all should cry, Beware! Beware![624]
> His flashing eyes, his floating hair![625]

---

[622] *That...air* – Coleridge is no longer the passive dreamer over here – from these lines onward, he becomes an active dreamer. He wants to build such a "dome of pleasure" in the air out of music. The song, thus, would act as a song of inspiration for him, like the song of the muses, inspiring the poet to work.

[623] *That...ice* – The exclamations bring out the ecstasy that has been created in the poet.

[624] *Beware! Beware* – This might seem surprising, as to why people should say, "Beware! Beware!" This means that the poet, being in a state of inspired frenzy, arouses fearful awe in the minds of the others.

[625] *His...hair* – There might be a Biblical allusion here, to the book of Revelations, where Christ appears with eyes like a flame of fire, and hair as white as snow. This might seem odd, for everything about the poem is, so far, heathen. However, any reader who is familiar with Coleridge would know that at the end of his poems, he draws in Christian religious statements, like that in *The Rime of the Ancient Mariner*, "He prayeth well, who loveth well,/Both man and bird and beast./He prayeth best, who loveth best,/All things both great and small/For the dear God, who loveth us/He made and loveth all." or in *Frost at Midnight*, "Himself in all, all things in Himself". So, it might just be that he is talking about that state when Christ will come to restore things, at which time, the people would be fearful, and would ask the rocks to fall on them and to the mountains to hide them. The reaction of the people over here is similar to that.

Other than the Biblical allusion, the interpretation is that the poet, being inspired, looks very wild, as would anyone who is inspired with divine spark.

Weave a circle round him thrice,⁶²⁶
And close your eyes with holy dread,⁶²⁷
For he on honey-dew hath fed,
And drunk the milk of Paradise.⁶²⁸

---

⁶²⁶ *Weave...thrice* – The numbers three, seven and nine are important in numerology as numbers which are connected with divinity or supernatural things. In fact, three and seven are numbers which are important in all religious occasions. The weaving of a circle around someone is to mark him off from the rest; weaving it three times is simply to give it a charm. The people wish to mark him off, as he is the inspired poet, and has become different from the others, being possessed of divine knowledge.

⁶²⁷ *And...dread* – The people would be so fearful that they would wish to close their eyes in fear of seeing the sight of the inspired poet. This brings out the un-holiness of the people, who are beneath the level to welcome divinity, for they are so low, that they are afraid of it. This closing of eyes out of fear for the person who has got divine insight might again be a Biblical allusion, where the people could not look upon Moses after he would come from the mountain, so full of glory his face would be. The Bible also states that no man can look at the face of God and be alive, and Christ tells that only the angels of Children are able to see "the face of My Father always", and that the "pure in heart" shall "see God". The Ultimate Sacred is thus, not for being seen by everyone, and everyone would also not be able to bear the sight.

⁶²⁸ *For...paradise* – This is the result of muddled borrowing from Purchas, where he mentions words like "milk" and "paradise" a lot of times. Purchas describes the palace to be a place where damsels dance, and there is drinking with it. This palace becomes paradise to the subjects of the kingdom. Other than this material explanation, which does nothing but ruin the imagery created in the poem, we must look at other explanations. Kubla Khan had lots of horses ready at his palace, and those who did something worth a reward were given permission to drink the milk of the horses, and so, the "milk of paradise" image. Coleridge, however, does not merely wish to state so. He has already made himself the inspired poet, and drinking the milk of paradise is to be taken at a figurative

PRE-ROMANTIC AND ROMANTIC POETRY

Background of the Poem

Coleridge records in notes about the poem:

> The following fragment is here published at the request of a poet of great and deserved celebrity [Lord Byron], and, as far as the Author's own opinions are concerned, rather as a psychological curiosity, than on the ground of any supposed poetic merits.
>
> In the summer of the year 1797, the Author, then in ill health, had retired to a lonely farm-house between Porlock and Linton, on the Exmoor confines of Somerset and Devonshire. In consequence of a slight indisposition, an anodyne had been prescribed, from the effects of which he fell asleep in his chair at the moment that he was reading the following sentence, or words of the same substance, in Purchas's Pilgrimage: ``Here the Khan Kubla commanded a palace to be built, and a stately garden thereunto. And thus ten miles of fertile ground were inclosed with a wall." The Author continued for about three hours in a profound sleep, at least of the external senses, during which time he has the most vivid confidence, that he could not have composed less than from two to three hundred lines; if that indeed can be called composition in which all the images rose up before him as things, with a parallel production of the correspondent expressions, without any sensation or consciousness of effort. On awakening he appeared to himself to have a distinct recollection of the whole, and taking his pen, ink, and paper, instantly and eagerly wrote down the lines that are here preserved. At this moment he was unfortunately called out by a person on business from Porlock, and detained by him above an hour, and on his

---

level – it is divine nourishment that he has got (milk as a drink of nourishment); he has got a taste of divinity, which is figuratively stated to be "milk of paradise".

return to his room, found, to his no small surprise and mortification, that though he still retained some vague and dim recollection of the general purport of the vision, yet, with the exception of some eight or ten scattered lines and images, all the rest had passed away like the images on the surface of a stream into which a stone has been cast, but, alas! without the after restoration of the latter!

Then all the charm

Is broken--all that phantom-world so fair
Vanishes, and a thousand circlets spread,
And each mis-shape the other. Stay awile,
Poor youth! who scarcely dar'st lift up thine eyes--
The stream will soon renew its smoothness, soon
The visions will return! And lo, he stays,
And soon the fragments dim of lovely forms
Come trembling back, unite, and now once more
The pool becomes a mirror.
Yet from the still surviving recollections in his mind, the Author has frequently purposed to finish for himself what had been originally, as it were, given to him. : but the to-morrow is yet to come.
As a contrast to this vision, I have annexed a fragment of a very different character, describing with equal fidelity the dream of pain and disease.

In another note on a manuscript, Coleridge states:

This fragment with a good deal more, not recoverable, composed, in a sort of Reverie brought on by two grains of Opium taken to check a dysentery, at a Farm House between Porlock & Linton, a quarter of a mile from Culbone Church, in the fall of the year, 1797.

Imagination in the Poem: The Supernatural Element

As told in the Introduction to Romantic Poetry, imagination is the prime force to be found in the poetry of this age. For Coleridge, it was something even more special. By imagination, he meant two types: primary and secondary. The primary imagination is the basic faculty to think, and that is there in all the individuals. It is the secondary imagination that is the special gift of the artiste. The secondary imagination is the special faculty by which a person can think creatively, and weave things together. Such a person is not an everyday individual, but an artiste.

Coleridge also distinguished between imagination and fancy. The secondary imagination shapes the poetry and it builds from thee things that are there; fancy is simply imagining what is not there. In *Biographia Literaria*, Coleridge states that in the *Lyrical Ballads*, he and Wordsworth divided the tasks of writing poetry – Wordsworth was to write on natural things in a way that is unusual, so as to excite the senses about them, while Coleridge was to write about the supernatural things in a natural manner. As such, a strong flow of unusual elements is to be found in his poetry, and the poet would present them in such a manner so that the reader feels that this is the normal thing, after all! In order to make this happen, the reader must stop doubting the poet, and practice what he phrases as, "willing suspension of disbelief". In other words, the reader must put out all ideas of disbelief regarding the things presented in the peom.

Kubla Khan is no exception. The first two lines take up the reader's imagination to towering heights with the image of the "pleasure dome". The image of the "sunless sea" three lines after that would stretch his fancy.

The imagination evoked in the poem plays on the effects of light and darkness. And the traditional associations of light and darkness come into play with these images: light represents good; darkness represents evil. But here, the unusual part is that the two do not contrast – they combine. While the gardens are bright, the sea is sunless; the cave is dark and light at the same time.[629] The finest example of imagination is perhaps in these lines:

> The shadow of the dome of pleasure
>
> Floated midway through the air

for the readers would be at a loss to even visualise a floating shadow on air. The place becomes magical through such lines. Coleridge remarks about such magic:

> A savage place, as holy and enchanted

and in stating the place to be savage, he uses an epigram, for the place which is savage is "holy and enchanted".[630]

The last part of the "fragment" is perhaps the most alluring of all the parts, with a dancing damsel. Sources state that Coleridge wrote this part later on, and so, this part does not seem to flow with the rest of the poem. However, the savagery that is found in the other parts of the poem is found here, too, and it is mixed with sacredness, just like the sacredness that is there in the place that is described by Coleridge in the previous lines of the poem. Coleridge fuses Greek mythology (that of the muses), and the habit of the damsels to dance around a group of drinking men (the men had special ranks)[631], and threads them with his imagination to produce a very charming part. Finally, the image of the inspired poet completes the circle, for a poem where the poet can write on such levels of imagination is surely written by a poet who is inspired.[632]

---

[629] The symbolism that is found in the cave has already been discussed in the footnote to that.
[630] I have commented on this in the footnote.
[631] See footnote to this part.
[632] There is a very important topic in the poem – that of symbolism, but all of that has been discussed in the critical annotations. The reader should read the annotations carefully to get an idea of that topic.

Kubla Khan as a Fragment

As per the note added by Coleridge after the title of the poem, it is a fragment. However, scholars have never been satisfied to draw a satisfying line, and so, despite the claims of the poet, the arguement goes on as to the poem being fragmented.

The final part of the poem, that which beings with "A damsel…", is the apple of discord. Critics feel this part to be out of place, and quite sudden. It cannot be denied that the images that are brought in this part change the focus suddenly. The pleasure-dome and the fountain and the cave are suddenly gone, and are replaced by the damsel and the drinks, and that image again shifts to the image of the inspired poet. Such sudden changes certainly create the impression of fragments coming together. It can also be said that perhaps the poet himself felt it to be so, and therefore the note on the poem being a fragment.

Now let us look at the other aspect of it. It is obviously a look by the independent reader; by the independent critic. That is the look of wholeness in the poem. Perhaps Coleridge wanted to just give the images, and create such a powerful impression on the readers that the images would connect? This is not a poem like *The Rime of the Ancient Mariner*, where there is a clear flow of narration to link up the events.[633] This is a poem whose central focus is that of imagery. And that is done excellently by the poet. In this regard, the last part is simply a presentation of another image after one has been viewed – this is like a kaleidoscope.

In this sense, the poem does not become a fragment in the sense incomplete, if it was meant to present only a collection of images, and not stich them up. Nevertheless, the sudden beginning of "A damsel…" does bring about fragmentary elements in the poem,

---

[633] However, Coleridge plays with the narrative style there too, by resorting to flash-backs, and exchanges of dialogues between the wedding guest and the ancient mariner.

and it can be clearly understood that the poet composed this part at a later time. The poet himself says as much:

> Could I revive within me

and presents an image of himself as an inspired poet, which seems to have nothing to do with either Zanadu or Kubla Khan. The poem becomes personal, and that is one of the characteristic features of Romantic poetry.

15. PERCY BYSSHE SHELLEY (1792 – 1822)

About the Poet

Percy Bysshe Shelley was born August 4, 1792. He was the eldest of seven siblings born to Timothy Shelley, a squire who later became a baronet. From 1802-1804, Percy attended Sion House Academy, after which he went to Eton. He did not like the atmosphere there. He enrolled in University College, Oxford, in 1810, but was expelled within a few months along with his friend Thomas Jefferson Hogg for charges related to a pamphlet named *The Necessity of Atheism*.

His father insisted that he break links with Hogg, which Percy refused to do. Shelley later eloped with Harriet Westbrook, the 16-year-old daughter of a coffee-house keeper, thereby breaking ties with his father. He went to Ireland for political reforms and published his poem "Queen Mab" in 1813. In 1814, he met William Godwin, the author of *Political Justice*, who was also to influence Wordsworth briefly. Shelley fell in love with his daughter Mary. Mary's mother was Mary Wollstonecraft, who is famous for having written *A Vindication of the Rights of Women*. Mary and Percy eloped to Switzerland in July 1814, taking Mary's step-sister Jane Clairmont along with them.

Shelley's financial condition was made stable to some extent upon receiving some fortune from his grandfather. However, Shelley already had a daughter named Ianthe, and Harriet now bore him a son, Charles, after Shelley had been living with Mary for several months. Claire fell in love with Lord Byron, and they spent some time in Geneva, when Mary wrote *Frankenstein*. Shortly after returning to England, Harriet drowned herself after getting pregnant by another man, and Shelley took on Mary as his wife.

In 1818 the family moved to Italy, where they lost their infant daughter Clara and their son William. However, Percy Florence was born there. Shelley had a close circle of friends around him, and while returning on a yacht from a peacemaking mission on behalf of Byron to Claire Clairmont, Shelley drowned at sea during a fierce storm. Mary Shelley edited his poems and advanced his fame after his death.

ODE TO THE WEST WIND

I

O wild West Wind,[634] thou breath of Autumn's being,[635]
Thou, from whose unseen presence the leaves dead
Are driven, like ghosts from an enchanter fleeing,[636]

Yellow, and black, and pale, and hectic red,[637]

---

[634] *O…Wind* – Notice the alliteration, and the apostrophe.

[635] *Thou…being* – West Wind blows in Autumn, and so, Shelley tells that it is the "breath" (the blowing of the wind is like breath) to Autumn. From the blowing of the West Wind, it can be understood that Autumn has come, therefore, the West Wind gives life to Autumn.

[636] *Thou…fleeing* – With the blowing of the West Wind, the dead leaves on the ground start blowing about. Shelley makes this appear as if the dead leaves, being afraid of the West Wind, are fleeing the place. West Wind is metaphorically looked upon as an enchanter – a person who works with spirits, and controls them, and can make them go out of a place, like an exorcist, and the dead leaves as ghosts who are residing at a place, whom the West Wind is driving out.

PRE-ROMANTIC AND ROMANTIC POETRY

Pestilence-stricken multitudes:[638] O Thou,
Who chariotest to their dark wintry bed

The wingèd seeds,[639] where they lie cold and low,
Each like a corpse within its grave, until
Thine azure[640] sister of the Spring[641] shall blow

Her clarion o'er the dreaming[642] earth,[643] and fill

---

[637] *Yellow...red* – These are the various colours of the Autumnal leaves. In Winter, the leaves fall, but the process starts in autumn, when they become yellow (and sometimes red), after which they fall to the ground. When they fall to the ground, they are dead; so, Shelley states that the process of these leaves turning yellow or red is their sickness.

[638] *Pestilence...multitudes* – Shelley compares the leaves with human beings who are pestilence-stricken, that is, are affected by some plague, and so, are sick, and hence, those colours of sickness.

[639] *O...seeds* – The West Wind seems to be on a chariot, and drives the leaves to their death-bed – that is, the cover of snow that will come in winter. West Wind is therefore, on a chariot, driving them to that which is to come, that is, winter. It is leading them to their destiny, or rather, to their proper resting place.

dark...bed – The cover of snow in winter, under which these leaves would be buried.

[640] *azure* – Bright blue in colour.

[641] *Thine...Spring* – The East Wind, which blows in Spring.

[642] *dreaming* – Sleeping.

[643] *blow...earth* – In Spring, the East Wind shall blow her trumpet over the sleeping earth, and wake it up. In winter, things were dead under the cover of snow; spring would bring them back to life. The image of someone blowing a trumpet over the graves and bringing

(Driving sweet buds like flocks to feed in air)
With living hues[644] and odours plain and hill:[645]

Wild Spirit, which art moving everywhere;
Destroyer and Preserver;[646] hear, O hear![647]

II

Thou on whose stream, 'mid the steep sky's commotion,[648]
Loose clouds like earth's decaying leaves are shed,[649]

---

to life all that is dead is an allusion to the Bible, where, in the Second Coming, an angel shall sound the trumpet to announce His coming, "and all who are in the graves will rise", for everlasting life, or for judgement.

[644] *living hues* – Living colours. The fresh leaves will be green, and not yellow, pale or hectic red.

[645] *plain...hill* – The plains and the hills shall be filled with greenery and the fragrance that proceed from that greenery.

[646] *Destroyer...preserver* – The West Wind is both the destroyer (for it destroys the leaves) and preserver (it keeps them in store, till spring comes and rescues them). However, the preserver needs to be understood in other sense. It is being looked upon as a Spirit which contains force. This force both creates and destroys. Therefore, as the West Wind is an embodiment of this force, it is both destroyer and preserver.

[647] *hear...hear* – What will it hear? The answer is found in the last stanza. The first four stanzas simply invoke the West Wind to do something, which the poet reveals only in the last stanza.

[648] *'mid...commotion* – The sky appears as it would during a storm.

[649] *Thou...shed* – The West Wind is here looked upon as a stream. Just as there are decaying leaves on the ground, there are clouds in the way of the blowing West Wind. The clouds are scattered in the

Shook from the tangled boughs of heaven and ocean,

Angels of rain and lightning: there are spread
On the blue surface[650] of thine aery surge,[651]
Like the bright hair uplifted from the head

Of some fierce Mænad,[652] even from the dim verge[653]
Of the horizon to the zenith's[654] height,
The locks of the approaching storm.[655] Thou Dirge[656]

Of the dying year, to which this closing night
Will be the dome of a vast sepulchre,[657]

---

sky as the leaves are on the ground, and they shed themselves on the West Wind, forming a stream. The first meaning of stream is *path*, and the second meaning of stream, the literal stream, is what comes up after the two lines are read.

[650] *blue surface* – Sky. The sky is by itself blue, but there are clouds on the surface of the sky.

[651] *surge* – A quick rise. The West Wind is rising (that is, its intensity is increasing) like a wave surging in the ocean.

[652] *Maenad* – They were mythological women, who used to worship Dionysius. They are also known as the bacchanals. They used to drink and let loose their hair in their ecstasy. The clouds which are scattered in the sky appear as the loose hair of a maenad.

[653] *verge* – Corner.

[654] *zenith* – The highest point in the sky, that is, the point which appears right on top of the earth.

[655] *The…storm* – The clouds in the sky are compared with the locks of the Maenad's hair.

[656] *dirge* – A funeral song or music.

Vaulted with all thy congregated might[658]

Of vapours, from whose solid atmosphere[659]
Black rain and fire and hail will burst: O hear![660]

III

Thou who didst waken from his summer dreams
The blue Mediterranean,[661] where he lay,
Lulled by the coil of his chrystàlline streams,[662]

Beside a pumice isle in Baiæ's bay,

---

[657] *to...sepulchre* – The West Wind tells of the approaching winter, and the end of the year. So, that makes it appear as if the year is dying. The night is like the dark vault of a sepulchre, where the year will lie buried.

[658] *Vaulted...might* – The West Wind will seal it will all its might.

[659] *solid atmosphere* – How exactly is the sky, or even the cloud, solid, is not clear.

[660] *O hear* – As told above, what the poet wants the West Wind to hear is to be found in the final stanza.

[661] *Thou...Mediterranean* – Shelley here personifies the Mediterranean Sea, and tells it to have been asleep in dreams. The West Wind awakes it. What actually happens is that the Mediterranean Sea was calm and quiet, and the blowing of the Wind over it caused disturbance over its surface.

[662] *Lull'd...streams* – In his Romantic imagination, Shelley states that it's as if the Mediterranean Sea has been bound by its own streams, which run and form it. These streams, which run down to the Mediterranean, are like coils, because of their meandering shapes. The water of these streams is clear, so Shelley calls it "crystalline".

And saw in sleep[663] old palaces and towers
Quivering within the wave's intenser day,[664]

All overgrown with azure moss, and flowers
So sweet, the sense faints picturing them![665] Thou
For whose path the Atlantic's level powers[666]

Cleave themselves into chasms,[667] while far below[668]
The sea-blooms[669] and the oozy[670] woods[671] which wear

---

[663] *And...sleep* –i.e., the Mediterranean has seen in his sleep.

[664] *Quivering...day* – The palaces and towers seem to quiver because of the intense heat of the sandy area.

[665] *So...them* – It should be noticed here that Shelley moves aside from West Wind to the description of the palaces and towers by themselves. He comes back to the effects of the West Wind right after this, but here, he digresses a bit.

[666] *the...powers* – The various currents of water in the AtlanticOcean.

[667] *Cleave...chasms* – It seems as if to create path for the West Wind, the waters of the Atlantic Ocean are moving aside. What actually happens is that the blowing of the West Wind over the surface of the Atlantic Ocean disturbs the water currents. However, the moving aside of the waters to create a path for somebody is an allusion to the Bible, about Moses' and the Israelites, when God divided the Red Sea for them to pass.

[668] *far below* – Under the ocean surface.

[669] *sea-blooms* – Flowers and such vegetations under the sea.

[670] *oozy* – Very soft mud, especially at the bottom of a lake or river. (OED)

[671] *woods* – Forest-like growth found under the sea.

The sapless[672] foliage of the ocean,[673] know

Thy voice, and suddenly grow gray with fear,[674]
And tremble and despoil themselves:[675] O hear![676]

IV

If I were a dead leaf thou mightest bear;[677]
If I were a swift cloud to fly with thee;
A wave to pant beneath thy power, and share

The impulse of thy strength,[678] only less free

---

[672] *sapless* – Sap is the juice that is found inside plants and trees. It is the life-giving fluid of the plants and trees. Inside the ocean, the woody growth is sapless, for it is surrounded by water.

[673] *foliage...ocean* – Just as the trees would be the foliage on earth, these tree-like growths form foliage of the ocean.

[674] *know...fear* – Shelley states that even under the surface of the ocean, the marine land features are aware of the mighty West Wind. The West Wind has got its sway even deep down under the earth.

[675] *And...themselves* – They seem to shake with fear, and move from their original place in their hurry to get out of their places.

[676] *O...hear* – Once more, the answer is found in the last stanza.

[677] *If...bear* – From this time onwards, the poem becomes personal. Shelley attaches himself with the poem. The characteristic Romantic "I" of the Romantic poem makes its first appearance from this line.

[678] *and...strength* – In the first three statements, Shelley compares himself with a leaf, a cloud and a wave. In all these comparisons, he would be carried about by the Wind. However, in these words, he states that he does not wish to be hopelessly carried about by the

Than thou, O Uncontroulable![679] If even
I were as in my boyhood,[680] and could be

The comrade[681] of thy wanderings over Heaven,
As then,[682] when to outstrip thy skiey speed

West Wind – he is comparing himself with these things only because he wants to share the strength of the Wind as it blows. He wants to feel the grand feeling of being with something so mighty.

[679] *only...uncontrollable* – Shelley wants to be free, and so, he wishes the West Wind to lift him up as a leaf, a wave or a cloud. It has been noted above that Shelley does not present the hopelessness of being carried about by the West Wind, but wishes to experience the thrill of being lifted and flown about. So, if that is done, he will experience the sense of being free from bondage. However, the poet would still be under the control of the West Wind, so he states these lines. The West Wind, on the other hand, is uncontrollable.

[680] *if...boyhood* – Shelley longs for his boyhood days, when he was young and restless. Compare this with *Tintern Abbey*, where the poet pleasantly describes his boyhood days, when he would leap about from hill to hill, but now has grown old, and cannot do that. For Wordsworth, however, there is acceptance of this fact that he has grown old, and wishes to see his youthful self in his sister, and states that even if he is no longer that youthful, he will still have the recollections of it. He states, "I cannot paint what then I was". For Shelley, there is no acceptance – there is only revolt. And where the revolt is not possible, he laments for what he has lost. He wishes to get back his youthful vigour once more. Nevertheless, it is an irony that Shelley, even while writing this poem, was still in his youthful days, and he died young. Therefore, this tendency to feel that he has lost his vigour is perhaps more psychological than physical.

[681] *comrade* – A friend, a companion, who undertakes the same thing with someone.

Scarce seemed a vision;[683] I would ne'er have striven

As thus with thee in prayer in my sore need.[684]
Oh! lift me as a wave, a leaf, a cloud!
I fall upon the thorns of life! I bleed![685]

A heavy weight of hours[686] has chained and bowed
One too like thee: [687]tameless, and swift, and proud.

V

---

[682] *then* – i.e., In the poet's boyhood days.

[683] *As...vision* – In his boyhood days, Shelley was so youthful that to beat the Wind at a race would have hardly bothered him. This is obviously a hyperbole.

[684] *I...need* – If the poet had retained his youthful self, he would now not have asked the West Wind to help him in his sore need. Thus, it will be noticed that in Shelley's poem, there is the dominance of the ego of the poet, something not found in the other Romantic poems, even though they have the characteristic Romantic 'I' in them.

[685] *I...bleed* – This excessive metaphor gives the poem both beauty and a feeling of repulsion. While the reader admires the beauty of the lines, the reader (the neutral reader) does feel that the image of bleeding takes it too far, and might feel repulsed at that image. There have been critics who have linked this to political references in Shelley's life.

[686] *A...hours* – The metaphor is that hours are like heavy weights, which are linked with chains, and these chains have been tied around Shelley, and he cannot get out because the chains are held on by the heavy weights. What he actually means is that time has tamed his youthful spirit, and that he is going through hard times.

[687] *One...thee* – Shelley refers to himself as someone who is (or rather, was) similar in nature to the West Wind.

Make me thy lyre,⁶⁸⁸ even as the forest is:⁶⁸⁹
What if my leaves⁶⁹⁰ are falling like its own!⁶⁹¹
The tumult of thy mighty harmonies

Will take from both⁶⁹² a deep, autumnal tone,⁶⁹³
Sweet though in sadness.⁶⁹⁴ Be thou, Spirit fierce,

---

⁶⁸⁸ *Make...lyre* – A lyre is a harp-like instrument. When the Wind blows through it, it produces sound. Shelly wants the West Wind to make an instrument of him, that is, let the West Wind blow through him (inspire him) and produce sounds in him (make him write poetry or other creative works).

⁶⁸⁹ *even...is* – The forest is already like a lyre to the West Wind. The Wind blows through the forests, and that makes sounds in the trees. So, the forest is like a lyre.

⁶⁹⁰ *my leaves* – Shelley's youthful parts (figuratively).

⁶⁹¹ *What...own* – Shelley's youthful nature is falling of its own accord, and not out of the action of the West Wind. But Shelley states that that is no reason for the West Wind to make him its instrument.

⁶⁹² *take from both* – Create in both, that is, the forests and Shelley.

⁶⁹³ *a...tone* – A falling tune of music.

⁶⁹⁴ *Sweet...sadness* – It will be sad in tone, but sweet (pleasant, not harsh) to hear. Compare this with *To a Skylark*, where Shelley states, "Our sweetest thoughts are those that tell of saddest thought". Compare also the song of the Solitary Reaper, which Wordsworth states was "melancholic strain" but was far thriller than that of the cuckoo bird and more refreshing than the nightingale. Compare also the ending line of *The Rime of the Ancient Mariner*, "A sadder and a wiser man he rose the morrow morn".

My spirit!⁶⁹⁵ Be thou me, impetuous⁶⁹⁶ one!

Drive my dead thoughts over the universe
Like withered leaves, to quicken a new birth!⁶⁹⁷
And, by the incantation of this verse,⁶⁹⁸

Scatter, as from an unextinguished hearth⁶⁹⁹

---

⁶⁹⁵ *Be...spirit* – Shelley asks the spirit of the West Wind to come inside himself. In the manner of invoking the Holy Spirit to come and reside within a person, Shelley asks the West Wind to reside within him. There is a little inclination towards heathenism in such an invocation to a spirit of nature, but for Shelley, religion lay in engery and power, and the right means to channelise it. It is from here that Shelley begins to state what he wants the West Wind to hear.

⁶⁹⁶ *Impetuous* – Moving on impulses, acting without thinking about it, or of the consequences.

⁶⁹⁷ *Drive...birth* – As the West Wind drives the dead leaves over the ground, to bury them for winter, to be rejuvenated in spring, the poet wants the West Wind to spread his dull works ("dead thoughts") all over the earth. These writings, which are now dead (that is, not cared for, are forgotten) would, in travelling over the world, rouse up the interest of the people in them, and the people would begin to read them all over the world, and thus, there would be rejuvenation for his works.

⁶⁹⁸ *the...verse* – This poem would be like a mantra (a charm, an enchantment).

⁶⁹⁹ *hearth* – Floor under a fireplace; the area in front of the fireplace. Here, this is synecdoche for the fireplace itself, which is not extinguished. However, it is not fully lighted up also, and the sense is that it is about to be extinguished, and is still not extinguished. It is not a burning hearth; it is an unextinguished hearth. The hearth here symbolically refers to Shelley himself, whose youthful self is gone, but he is still writing, though they are

Ashes and sparks, my words among mankind![700]
Be through my lips[701] to unawakened Earth[702]

The trumpet of a prophecy![703] O Wind,
If Winter comes, can Spring be far behind?[704]

Background to the Poem

not properly recognised. So, the hearth is not extinguished – there is still life in it.

[700] *Scatter…mankind* – While in this state of being unextinguished, the West Wind should scatter (like scattering of ashes and sparks if the Wind were to blow over an actual hearth) his works to the people all over the earth, that they may be read. The West Wind should bear his message to all the people of the world. Thus, it can be noticed that the poem has moved away from being an Ode to the West Wind, and has become totally personal.

[701] *Be…lips* – This is continuation of the lyre image. The West Wind should inspire the poet to write new verses. These will be uttered through the poet's mouth. The idea of the inspired poet is also found at the end of *Kubla Khan*.

[702] *unawaken''d earth* – Earth which is still sleeping. Earth which has not yet been disturbed.

[703] *The…prophesy* – His words will be like a prophesy to the whole earth, and it shall be as sharp as the blast of a trumpet. Once more, the image of the earth sleeping, and a trumpet sound waking it up, and the word "prophesy" is a Biblical allusion to the Second Coming of Christ. See note 10 for an explanation of this Biblical allusion.

[704] *O…behind* – The poem ends with this rhetoric question, whose answer is "No". Spring cannot be far behind if Winter comes. The poem ends in a note of hopeful expectations. It ends in a positive note.

Shelley notes:
> This poem was conceived and chiefly written in a wood that skirts the Arno, near Florence, on a day when that tempestuous wind, whose temperature is at once mild and animating, was collecting the vapors which pour down the autumnal rains. They begin, as I foresaw, at sunset, with a violent tempest of hail and rain, attended by that magnificent thunder and lightning peculiar to the Cisalpine regions. (Shelley 239)

This poem was composed in November 1819. The note which has been given above tells that the atmosphere had a certain impact on him, as is bound to be in Romantic poetry. The poem, though it begins as an ode to the west wind, ends up being a personal address. Some critics have also detected political implications in the poem. Shelley himself equated poets with politics in a way. In *A Defence of Poetry*, he writes, "Poets are the unacknowledged legislators of the World".

Style of Composition – Metre and Imagery

Ode to the West Wind is written in iambic pentameter. Shelley uses the metre with variations to being out the mood of the poem very well. This is how it goes:

O wíld |Wést Wínd, |thou bréath| of Áut|umn's béing,

The readers should note that each of the stressed syllables (wild, West, Wind, breath, Aut-, being), would create an effect that is very similar to that of a rolling thunder, which grows louder and shorter, and rumbles quite a few times. After that, the rain falls, and the second and third lines bring out that effect, too.

Thóu, from| whóse ún|seen pré|sence the| léaves dead
Are drí|ven, like| ghosts from| an en|chánter| fléeing,

The iambic pentameter has got lots of variations here, and the lines run very fast because of the pyrrhics, and the trochees give it a falling note, and the effect is that of the rain, which is falling very fast.

Shelley uses a lot of imagery in his poem, as in any other of his poems, to bring out the mood, and create a diversity of moods. The poem is more about the effects of the West Wind than about the West Wind. At first, the poet talks about the West Wind to be driving the fallen autumnal leaves to their "dark wintry bed", and at the end, he gives hope of rejuvenation. The West Wind is, in the beginning, conceived as a charioteer, and then moves on to the picture of the shy which is beset by the stormy West Wind. The clouds are compared with the hair of "some fierce Maenad", and so, the West Wind can be called Bacchius, for the clouds are dancing in his power.

The West Wind is always active – it is always a force which seems to be "uncontrollable". It rouses up the sleepy Mediterranean and makes the waters afraid of it. This force is by no means to be conceived as a threat – for Shelley, forceful energy lies in creation, and he always seeks that out. The Mediterranean which is previously lulled to sleep, and is under the "coils" of the stream, is in a negative state of being; the West Wind frees it. The imagery of the Mediterranean, therefore, helps to bring out the West Wind as a redeemer. Therefore, we see two associations of the West Wind – on the one hand, it is charioting the leaves to their death, and on the other hand, it is redeeming the Mediterranean. This duality makes Shelley state: "Destroyer and preserver, hear, O hear!"

The West Wind is a positive force in the universe, and Shelley calls to that power. The poem ceases to be an ode in the last two parts, where Shelley makes it a personal poem; the ode becomes a prayer, where Shelley asks the West Wind to restore him to his former energy, and at the end, tells it to spread his thoughts among mankind, so that is unhonoured verses would get honour later, which would be the coming of spring, giving new life to his verses. Here, he uses the images of fire and hearth, and the Wind blowing on them and scattering them. These images are very apt to bring out the energy that is there in the poet, which he speaks about, which is burning low, and which he wants to burn with all its might. As it would light up again, there would be hope; there would be new life, and the poet brings the image of the coming spring, and ends the poem on that happy image.

The Journey in the Poem: From Negative to Positive

The poet begins the poem with a description of the West Wind which drives the leaves to their death. However, at the end of the poem, he ascribes to it positive values. It can, therefore, be said that the poem moves from a state of negative force to that of positive force.

The poem presents the forces through the images. At the beginning, there are images of "pestilence-stricken multitudes", "pale", "hectic red" leaves, which are falling from the tress, and are being driven by the West Wind to be buried under the under, and laid under the cover of "snow". These are images of sickness and death.

In the next stanzas, the images are fierce. They are of a stormy sky; of clouds flying in the sky. Here, the simile that is used to compare the clouds stands out. The clouds have been compared with the hair of some "fierce Maenad". Though the images here are not of sickness and death, they are certainly not restorative.

It is from the images of the Mediterranean that the images keep getting stronger towards being more hopeful. The West Winds rouses the Mediterranean from the "coils" which bind it, and in this way, acts as a redemptive agency. The images of the towers and the sands and the waters are not at all fierce, but soothing. This marks the transition. In the next lines, where he talks about the waters parting to make way for the West Wind, the poet strengthens the positive force that is ascribed to the West Wind.

Parts four and five are totally positive. Shelley asks the West Wind to redeem him from his state of decaying inactivity (as he supposes), and the West Wind is seen as a mighty, but certainly good force. He asks the West Wind to spread his words among mankind. The important imagery here is that of the hearth, from which ashes and sparks are flying. This image is not one of destruction, but one which speaks of a new creation. So, in the end, he states "can spring be far behind?" and this rhetorical question makes the poem on a totally hopeful note, that there will be new life and re-freshening of things.

To a Sky-Lark

> Hail to thee, blithe[705] Spirit!
>   Bird thou never wert —[706]
> That from Heaven, or near it,[707]
>   Pourest thy full heart
> In profuse strains of unpremeditated art.[708]
>
> Higher still and higher
>   From the earth thou springest[709]
> Like a cloud of fire;[710]
>   The blue deep thou wingest,[711]

---

[705] *blithe* – Happy, carefree. Note the recurrence of the carefree (unchained) image right at the start of the poem.

[706] *Bird…wert* – This is obviously a hyperbole.

[707] *from…it* – The bird is so far into the sky that it seems to have almost reached the heavens, or has neared it.

[708] *That…art* – The bird seems to be singing from its height in the heavens. The singing is profuse, and is instinctive ("unpremeditated" = not thought out or practised before) in its content.

[709] *Higher…springest* – This is an example of an inversion. The correct syntax would be: "Thou springest higher and higher from the earth". Note the use of the word "springest". Shelley is constantly accociating it with energy; here, as springing (jumping in spirit) with energy.

[710] *Like…fire* – Like a cloud of fire, which will spring higher and higher from the earth, the Skylark flies higher and higher.

[711] *Like…wingest* – "Like…wingest" is carried on in the next line also. The image changes. Now, it is like a cloud of fire spreading in the sky. In other words, just as a cloud of fire would spread in the sky, the bird spreads its wings over the entire heavens.

And singing still dost soar, and soaring ever singest.[712]

In the golden light'ning[713]
  Of the sunken Sun,[714]
O'er which clouds are brightning,[715]
  Thou dost float and run;
Like an unbodied joy[716] whose race is just begun.[717]

---

[712] *And...singest* – This is a very noted example of chiasmus. For more explanation on this, please refer to my work, *Compact English Prosody and Figures of Speech* (Macmillan India).

[713] *light'ning* – Note that it is not "light" but light'ning. The apostrophe has been placed on "lightening" to make a pun on the word. On the one hand, it means lighten – lo light up; on the other hand, it means lightning. The second use brings out the energy – the power – that Shelley has been ascribing to the bird right from the start of the poem.

[714] *In...sun* – These two lines create an epigram – the image contains a contradiction within it, and rouses the reader's attention for a second reading. The sun is sinking – but the light that it is spreading is golden. Of course, this is how it would be at sunset, for which we have the phrase, "golden sunset", but the way in which Shelley presents it does pose a contradiction within it – the setting life displays life force.

[715] *O'er...bright'ning* – In the golden sunlight, the clouds seem to be becoming bright with the golden colour. Note that here, too, Shelley presents something that is connected with energy. Here, it is the life-force of nature. Shelley, however, in these few lines, moves away from skylark and seems to be totally immersed in giving a description of the sunset. It is only at the end of the stanza that he draws the connection by stating that the bird is flying over these clouds. But such a connection fails to be a strong one, and it is felt that Shelley merely connects it at the end of the stanza.

[716] *unbodied joy* – Joy which cannot be contained in the body, hence the active nature of the bird.

> The pale purple even[718]
> Melts around thy flight,[719]
> Like a star of Heaven
> In the broad day-light
> Thou art unseen, - but yet I hear thy shrill delight,
>
> Keen as are the arrows
> Of that silver sphere,[720]

---

[717] *Like...begun* – As a racer, who is racing new, and so, is eager, and can hardly contain himself and his energy.

[718] *even* – Evening. Notice the alliteration of "pale, purple". This heightens the colourlessness of the evening – like a dying person, devoid of energy. Readers should read, *The Moon* in this regard, where Shelley looks upon the moon at first as a dying old lady, and tells that it is pale. Moreover, in *Ode to the West Wind*, Shelley looks upon the autumn leaves as "pale" leaves, which are dying out of "pestilence". However, the use of the word "purple", the colour of royalty, tells us that Shelley does not talk about the evening sky as powerless, but as someone who has lost the power, has faded from glory.

[719] *The...flight* – The evening sky seems to melt before the flight of the bird. This can only be read, and tried to be imagined, but I dare say readers will never really be able to successfully imagine this, for to speak neutrally, the image, though lofty, does not really connect to make any sensible image.

[720] *Of...sphere* – The sphere of the Moon. Shelley here refers to the teleological belief during the time of the Renaissance. Till then, it was thought that the universe is made up of nine spheres. Beyond these spheres lay the *prima mobile*, which moves first, and the other spheres move, and the universe moves (rotates) because of that. With the movement of these spheres, a music is produced, which cannot be heard by human ears, and this music maintains the

> Whose intense lamp narrows
>   In the white dawn clear[721]
> Until we hardly see — we feel that it is there.[722]
>
> All the earth[723] and air
>   With thy voice is loud,
> As when Night is bare
>   From one lonely cloud
> The moon rains out her beams — and Heaven is overflowed.[724]

---

harmony in the universe. This music is named, "Music of the spheres".

Shelley combines the Renaissance belief with the classical myth. Phoebe/Diana was the moon-goddess, and was also associated with hunting. The arrows are of that. Here, the rays of the moon are like the arrows of Diana.

[721] *Whose...clear* – The light of the moon ("intense lamp") fades ("narrows") with the coming of dawn.

[722] *Until...there* – At dawn, the light of the moon fades, and it can be hardly seen, only felt that the moon is still there in the sky. The bird's presence is also like that. It cannot be seen, but only felt. Shelley is not only talking about the physical sight of the bird in this way, but also about the music of the bird. The music of the bird can be heard in this way – the source cannot be seen; only the bird can be heard, and so, felt by its singing. This creates a sublime effect. To talk about the sense of hearing by talking about the sense of sight is an example of synaesthasia.

[723] *earth* – i.e. Ground.

[724] *As...overflow'd* – The voice of the bird fills up the entire land and air, and its effect is like that when the night is all clear, and the moon peeps from just one cloud, and shines all its beams from that place. The land and air is silent; from one place, the voice of the skylark is coming and filling up the entire place. The readers must notice the use of synaesthesia.

> What thou art we know not;[725]
>   What is most like thee?
> From rainbow clouds[726] there flow not
>   Drops so bright to see
> As from thy presence showers a rain of melody.
>
> Like a Poet hidden
>   In the light of thought,[727]
> Singing hymns unbidden,[728]
>   Till the world is wrought
> To sympathy with hopes and fears[729] it heeded not:[730]

---

[725] *What...not* – Readers must not take this literally. Shelley is here deliberately mystifying the bird. At the beginning, he had said, "Bird thou never wert". Continuing that line of thought, he says that what the skylark is, one can never know. In other words, man can never fully appreciate the gifted skylark.

[726] *rainbow clouds* – Rainbow and clouds. The fusion creates a very good Romantic vision.

[727] *light...thought* – The thoughts are compared with light. This is a metaphor. The source of the metaphor might be the Bible, where the Word of God is looked upon as Light. Moreover, one of the Psalms state that "The entrance of Thy word giveth light". As thought brings knowledge, it enlightens, and therefore, the comparison with light.

[728] *unbidden* – Without being requested for.

[729] *To...not* – The feeling that the singing of the skylark arouses among the readers is that of both hopes and fears. However, it must be noted that these feelings are both harmonious.

[730] *it...not* – The world had previously not paid attention to these things; the singing of the skylark makes them turn their attention in that direction.

Like a high-born maiden
  In a palace-tower,
Soothing her love-laden
  Soul in secret hour,
With music sweet as love — which overflows her bower:

Like a glow-worm golden
  In a dell[731] of dew,
Scattering unbeholden
  Its aërial hue[732]
Among the flowers and grass which screen it[733] from the view:

Like a rose embowered
  In its own green leaves —
By warm winds deflowered —
  Till the scent it gives
Makes faint with too much sweet those heavy-wingèd thieves:[734]

Sound of vernal showers[735]
  On the twinkling grass,
Rain-awakened flowers,
  All that ever was

---

[731] *dell* – A small valley with trees.

[732] *aerial hue* – The colours are spread in the air, and are not seen, but felt. The feeling of colours is again an example of synaesthesia.

[733] *screen it* – Prevent it; hide it.

[734] *those…thieves* – The bees and other insects, like butterflies, which come to nest on the flowers and take honey. This "Makes faint with too much sweet" is similar to the lines in *Ode to the West Wind*, "So sweet, the sense faints picturing them".

[735] *spring showers* – Showers in spring.

Joyous, and clear and fresh, thy music doth surpass.[736]

   Teach us, Sprite[737] or Bird,
     What sweet thoughts are thine;
   I have never heard
     Praise of love or wine
That panted forth a flood of rapture so divine:[738]

   Chorus hymeneal[739]
     Or triumphal chant,[740]
   Matched with thine would be all
     But an empty vaunt,
A thin wherein we feel there is some hidden want.[741]

---

[736] *thy...surpass* – The singing of the skylark surpasses the beautiful effect produced by the spring showers, when the grass is sparkling with rain-drops and the flowers are freshened by the rain. This is similar to *The Solitary Reaper*, where Wordsworth compares the singing of the solitary reaper with that of the nightingale and the cuckoo bird, and says her singing surpasses them.

[737] *sprite* – Spirit.

[738] *I...divine* – The poet asserts that all those who have spoken in favour of love and wine have spoken mightily for it, but none of them has been able to reach the state which the skylark has reached. Their statements have not been so filled with rapture, as the singing of the skylark is.

[739] *Chorous hymeneal* – A chorus singing a hymn.

[740] *triumphal chant* – Song or slogan celebrating victory.

[741] *Match'd...want* – When compared with the singing of the skylark, the hymn sung by the chorus and the song or slogan of victory would fall short, it would seem as if there is something missing from them – as if they lack something.

What objects are the fountains
 Of thy happy strain?
What fields or waves or mountains?
 What shapes of sky or plain?
What love of thine own kind? what ignorance of pain?[742]

With thy clear keen joyance
 Languor[743] cannot be —
Shadow of annoyance
 Never came near thee;
Thou lovest — but ne'er knew love's sad satiety.[744]

Waking or asleep,
 Thou of death must deem[745]
Things more true and deep
 Than we mortals dream,
Or how could thy notes flow in such a chrystal stream?[746]

---

[742] *What...pain* – The answer to all these rhetorical questions is "Nothing". To the skylark, these things are nothing, and matter not.

[743] *Langour* – A state of feeling lazy, and enjoying the same.

[744] *Thou...satiety* – This is perhaps one of the most moving lines of the poem. The skylark sings sweetly, and so, the poet says that it must have loved. But the skylark's singing is purely joyous; there is no strain of sadness in it. So, the poet says that the bird has never felt the sadness of love, not felt its pain, but has known only happiness. Here, this is not a limitation of the skylark's singing. The poet just praises it. After two stanzas, however, the poet speaks in favour of sadness.

[745] *deem* – To have an opinion about something.

[746] *Or...stream* – The music of the skylark is being compared with a flowing stream, whose water is crystal-clear. Compare this with *The Solitary Reaper*, where Wordsworth writes, "O listen! For the vale profound,/Is overflowing with the sound". For Shelley, the skylark must be aware of higher things than what is known by the human beings, that is why it can sing with such perfect happiness.

> We look before and after,
>   And pine[747] for what is not —
> Our sincerest laughter
>   With some pain is fraught[748] -
> Our sweetest songs are those that tell of saddest thought.[749]
>
> Yet if we could scorn
>   Hate and pride and fear;
> If we were things born
>   Not to shed a tear,
> I know not how thy joy we ever should come near.
>
> Better than all measures
>   Of delightful sound —
> Better than all treasures
>   That in books are found —
> Thy skill to poet were,[750] thou Scorner of the ground![751]

---

[747] *pine* – Long.

[748] *Our…fraught* – There is pain behind some happy thing which is achieved. Compare this with *A Musical Instrument*, written later by Elizabeth Barrett Browning.

[749] *Our…thought* – This is a famous line. For the human beings, what gives real pleasure is that in which there is some sort of pain. The pain attunes us to the real world, where there is pain, and we feel closer to the things that tell of sad things. This does not go, however, to state that sadness should be encouraged, or only sad things should be listened to. What the poet tells is that in our world, the appeal of sadness is greater than the appeal of joy. But for the skylark, it has achieved divine bliss, where there is no sadness. Its sweet song is of sweetness only.

[750] *Better…were* – This is an inversion. The correct syntax would be: "Thy skill to poet were better than all the measures of delightful sound, better than all the treasures that in books are found".

> Teach me half the gladness
> That thy brain must know,
> Such harmonious madness
> From my lips would flow,
> The world should listen then — as I am listening now.[752]

Background of Composition

In the *Manuscripts of the Younger Romantics*, the following entry is found:

> This poem was composed near Leghorn (Livorno) in late June 1820 and published with *Prometheus Unbound*. Lines 1-4, 31-35, and 76-77 were drafted in Bodleian MS Shelley adds. e.6, pp 97 rev. – 96^A rev. (*BSM*, V). Shelley's holograph fair copy, with his own corrections, is in Harvard MS Eng.258.2, pp 100-105 (*MYR: Shelley*, V).

Thematic Division

The poem can be broadly divided into three parts: the first presents the flying away of the skylark (lines 1-30); an attempt to compare the song of the bird with something else (lines 31-60); the plea to the bird to tell its secret to the human world, so that there is total joy (61-105).

---

[751] *thou...ground* – The skylark does not seem to touch the ground and all that is earthly. It remains in the air. This is the basic difference between the skylark of Shelley and the skylark of Wordsworth. Wordsworth's skylark flies up, and comes back to the ground.

[752] *Teach...now* – As in *Ode to the West Wind*, where the poet gets personal and asks the West Wind to spread his words in all parts of the world, so that he is read, he asks the skylark to teach him how it has been able to get half of its gladness, so that the poet can compose better lines so that all the world would listen to him, mesmerized, as he is now listening to the skylark.

Form

The poem is written in trochaic trimeter, and the last line of each stanza is an iambic hexameter. The last line of each stanza being long tries to run like a stream over all that has been said in the other lines of the stanza, and creates a levelling effect upon the poem, just like the song of the skylark has got a levelling effect upon the mind and heart of the poet.

Shelley's Image of the Skylark

It has often been claimed that the Romantics did not really present what they were writing on, and Shelley's *To A Sky-Lark* stands among the accused poems. Critics have often said that nowhere in the poem do we find the skylark; in fact, the poem is about anything but a skylark.

Such an accusation is not totally wrong, for we do not really get any description of the actual bird. In fact, Shelley states right at the beginning, "Bird thou never wert". His skylark is more of a spirit; it is the energy of the skylark that Shelley is concerned with than the physical form of the bird.

The skylark is not just an actual bird; it is a symbol. It is a symbol of pure joy, "whose rase is just begun". The skylark stands for all that is to be aspired for; all that is free from corruption. It inspires men to rise upwards, while no one seems to come near it. In this respect, it can be viewed as the Platonic ideal, which remains beyond the reach of men, but improves the standard of the men when they try to get it. The bird is that ideal – it can be heard, hardly seen, but never caught.

The joy that is among men is not without sorrow; all that is successful has got in it elements of sorrow. Shelley comments on the vanity of man to be seeking fruitlessly what is futile. He quotes from *Hamlet*:

> "We look before and after,
> And pine for what is not —"

and thereby, states that perfect happiness is really not filled with total happiness:

> "Our sincerest laughter
> With some pain is fraught -
> Our sweetest songs are those that tell of saddest thought."

The skylark, on the other hand, is filled with total purity in its songs. There is not the shadow of sorrow in it; it does not know it. The poet wants men to aspire to such levels by being influenced by the bird. So, the bird becomes a symbol of a teacher, one who can lead men to where they want to go, to get heavenly happiness.

> "Teach me half the gladness
>   That thy brain must know,
> Such harmonious madness
>   From my lips would flow,
> The world should listen then — as I am listening now."

Therefore, the skylark ceases to be only a bird; it assumes the personified shape of the Platonic ideal, set to take men to new heights.

Theme of Joy and Sorrow

The poem presents joy and sorrow to be fused together in the life of human beings. Joy is never by itself – there is always a mixture of sorrow in it. But this sorrow that the poet talks about is not really totally negative – it is a sorrow that seems to make men experienced.

The outlook towards sorrow is very Romantic, for it hails the sorrowful feelings as feelings which are sweetest. Shelley states,

> "Our sweetest songs are those that tell of saddest thought"

While it is true that if taken in context with the previous lines, it would mean that human joy is not pure, for there are tons of sorrow in it, it is also true that this line also presents an issue by itself. Shelley makes it clear that the "sweetest songs" are not just fused with sorrow, but deal with sorrow – in fact, they are totally sad in nature. Readers must not forget the charming quality of the melancholic song of the Solitary Reaper that Wordsworth writes. Even though the starin is melancholic, he is mesmerised, and feels that the song is more refreshing than that of the nightingale or the cuckoo bird. Readers must also not forget the association of sorrow with wisdom at the end of *The Rime of the Ancient Mariner*, where Coleridge writes,

"A sadder and a wiser man, he rose the morrow morn"

Therefore, this sorrow that the poet talks about is a sorrow which is there in the heart of man, because of which man finds a universal kinship with it, despite the pain and suffering it causes.[753] The seriousness of sadness would make men come together, and then would they set to achieve what the poet wants – divine joy, which is better than earthly joy.

This divine joy can be sought only when men set about it seriously, and that can be achieved only when men are connected through the universally serious feeling of sorrow. Once this joy is achieved, man would really overcome sorrow and learn to stay in harmony.

---

[753] If we observe actual songs, we will not fail to miss the inference that the songs which are sad are more popular than the songs which are of happy themes, but this does not mean that we do not like the happy songs; what I am trying to state is that if we compare the songs which we like – both happy and sad, we will see that we like the sad songs better. Psychologically, it can be interpreted that humans find the sad songs to be closer, for everyone has experienced sadness, and can relate to the events, or at least, feel them, whereas, the joyful incidents would depend as per the tastes of the person. Moreover, men seek to release their pent up emotions, and by connecting with the sad songs, men can do that.

So, it can be said that this poem presents sadness and joyfulness as emotions which are both needed, and places the ultimate value on divine joy as the vanquisher of all that is negative in the human world.

16. JOHN KEATS

(1795 – 1821)

About the Poet

John Keats belongs to the second group of the Romantic poets along with Shelley. He was born in 1795 in Moorfields, London. He lost his father at the age of eight and his mother at the age of fourteen. He was very close to his two brothers, George and Tom, and his sister Fanny. Keats received his education at Clark school in Enfield. In 1810, he was apprenticed to an apothecary-surgeon. His first attempts at writing poetry date from about 1814, and he imitated the style of Spenser at that time. In 1815, he left his apprenticeship and became a student at Guy's Hospital, London. This lasted only one year, for he left medicine for poetry. Keats's first volume of poems was published in 1817. It attracted some good reviews, but Blackwood's magazine made some critical comments on his poems, and other such negative reviews followed. However, he kept on pursuing his interest in this field, and came up with *Endymion*, which was published next year. Keats toured the north of England and Scotland in the summer of 1818, returning home to nurse his brother Tom, who was ill with tuberculosis. After Tom's death in December, he moved into a friend's house in Hampstead. There he met and fell deeply in love with a young neighbour, Fanny Brawne. During the following year, despite ill health (he suspected he also had tuberculosis) and financial problems, he wrote a good amount of poetry. His second volume of poems appeared in July 1820. Soon afterwards, he set off with a friend to Rome, where he died the next year, in February. As noted in the Introduction to Romantic Poetry, his poetry is filled with references to classical literature and art.

ODE TO AUTUMN

Season of mists[754] and mellow[755] fruitfulness,
Close bosom-friend of the maturing sun;[756]
Conspiring[757] with him how to load[758] and bless
With fruit the vines that round the thatch-eves run;
To bend with apples the moss'd[759] cottage-trees,
And fill all fruit with ripeness to the core;
To swell the gourd,[760] and plump[761] the hazel shells[762]

---

[754] *mists* – Fog.

[755] *mellow* – Soft, calm and gentle.

[756] *Close…sun* – Keats tells Autumn to be a close friend of the Sun. the word 'maturing' brings in the association of a ripening fruit, continuing the analogy from the previous line. Here, Keats personifies Autumn and the Sun, and if "maturing sun" is considered, it becomes a metaphor, for it compares the sun to a fruit which is maturing.

[757] *Conspiring* – Here, the word has not been used in a negative sense. It does not mean plotting, but planning. Keats is using the etymological meaning of the word: *con*. (Lat. For *with*) and *spirare* (Lat. for breathe). To breathe also means to give life, and that is the sense in which Keats is using it – the Sun and Autumn are planning how to bless the trees with fruits.

[758] *Load* – The word "load" has also not been used in a negative way. It does not mean burden, but to pile = fill.

[759] *mossed* – Filled with moss.

[760] *gourd* – A type of large fruit, not normally eaten, with hard skin and soft flesh. Gourds are often dried and used as containers. (OED)

> With a sweet kernel;[763] to set budding more,
> And still more, later flowers for the bees,
> Until they think warm days will never cease,
> For Summer has o'er-brimm'd[764] their clammy[765] cells.
>
> Who hath not seen thee oft amid[766] thy store?
> Sometimes whoever seeks abroad may find
> Thee sitting careless on a granary floor,[767]
> Thy hair soft-lifted by the winnowing wind;[768]
> Or on a half-reap'd furrow[769] sound asleep,
> Drows'd with the fume of poppies,[770] while thy hook[771]

---

[761] *and plump* – i.e., to make plump.

[762] *hazel shells* – Shells of hazel nuts.

[763] *kernel* – The inner portion of a nut or sweet.

[764] *o'erbrimmed* – Filled so much that it overflows.

[765] *clammy* – Damp in an unpleasant way.

[766] *amid* – In the middle of.

[767] *Who...floor* – Autumn is over here, personified. Autumn is the time for harvest, for after that, Winter comes, and so, all the crops need to be cut and stored before the coming of winter. Keats personifies Autumn as a lady who is sitting inside the room where the grains are stored, and her hair is getting lifted in the wind.

[768] *winnowing wind* – Wind which is blowing through the gains to make the chaff open up, so that the actual grain can be got.

[769] *furrow* – A long cut which is usually made by the plough, in which seeds are planted. Here, Keats refers not just to the line, but to the entire field. So, this is a synecdoche.

[770] *poppies* – Wild garden plant. Opium is obtained from one of the varieties of poppies. It is commonly told that while passing through poppy fields, one feels drowsy.

Spares the next swath[772] and all its twined flowers:
And sometimes like a gleaner[773] thou dost keep
Steady thy laden head across a brook;
Or by a cyder-press[774], with patient look,
Thou watchest the last oozings[775] hours by hours.

Where are the songs of Spring?[776] Ay, where are they?
Think not of them, thou hast thy music too, --[777]
While barred clouds[778] bloom[779] the soft-dying day,[780]

---

[771] *hook* – i.e., the sickle.

[772] *swath* – A long strip of land, especially one in which crops have been cut. (OED)

[773] *gleaner* – Someone who obtains information with a lot of difficulty from different places.

[774] *cider-press* – The place where cider is made. It is a drink that is made from the juice of apples, which does not contain alcohol.

[775] *oozings* – The alcohol coming out is referred to as "oozings".

[776] *songs of spring* – Happy songs ,as Spring is the time of rejuvenation of nature.

[777] *thou...too* – Autumn has also got things to be sung about. Keats over here states that Spring has always been glorified, and Autumn has been neglected. The poet wants to praise Autumn.

[778] *barred clouds* – Clouds which act as obstacles. These act as bars to the sky.

[779] *bloom* – As the clouds are puffed up, they seem to be blooming, just like flowers on the earth.

[780] *soft-dying day* – As the day is dying, the clouds seem to fill the sky, and bloom. So, the dying day is replaced by blooming clouds. Autumn is, in this sense, not the harbinger of deathly winter, but a bloomer of life.

And touch the stubble-plains with rosy hue:[781]
Then in a wailful choir the small gnats mourn
Among the river sallows, borne aloft
Or sinking as the light wind lives or dies;
And full-grown lambs loud bleat from hilly bourn;[782]
Hedge-crickets sing, and now with treble soft[783]
The red-breast[784] whistles from a garden-croft;
And gathering swallows twitter in the skies.

Background of Composition

Ode to Autumn was composed on 19 Spetember, 1819, and published the next year in a volume of Keat's poems. This is the last of the 1819 odes. It was composed after a walk near Winchester in an evening. In a letter to John Hamilton Raynolds, Keats writes,

> "How beautiful the season is now – How fine the air. A temperate sharpness about it [...] I never lik'd stubble fields so much as now [...] Somehow a stubble plain looks warm – in the same way that some pictures look warm – this struck me so much in my sunday's walk that I composed upon it." (Houghton 2008)

---

[781] *And...hue* – During sunset, the colour of the sky is red. That colour seems to be spreading to the ground also. The "rosy hue" does not only refer to the red colour, but also metaphorically states the plains to be blooming, just like roses.

[782] *And...bourne* – As the night approaches, the lambs make some noises.

[783] *treble soft* – This is an oxymoron, as "treble" means high pitched. So, it is high pitched, but not loud. It is shrill, but soft.

[784] *The redbreast* – The Robin, with redbreast.

Themes in *Ode to Autumn* or The Central Ideas Found in the Poem

Ode to Autumn might appear as a poem which just describes a season, but it is filled with themes, and they are presented in a very complex way. In fact, if the poem appears simple, it is only because the themes do not appear on a surface reading.

The poet describes three aspects of the season in the three stanzas of the poem. In the first stanza, he describes its fruitfulness; in the second, he describes the work involved; in the third stanza, he describes the fall that is associated with it. A parallel imagery that runs along this is that of day progessing and fading into dusk. So, it can be stated that there is the theme of progression and decline in this poem.

> "Where are the songs of Spring? Ay, where are they?
> Think not of them, thou hast thy music too, --
> While barred clouds bloom the soft-dying day,
> And touch the stubble-plains with rosy hue:
> Then in a wailful choir the small gnats mourn
> Among the river sallows, borne aloft
> Or sinking as the light wind lives or dies;"

Here, this decline is not something that is to be feared, but something to accept. Metaphorically, the poem also connects a man's life to maturity and then decline to meet death. It is something that the poem welcomes here. There is no contradiction of this image, as there is contradiction in the odes of Keats.[785] Harold Bloom states that this poem presents the theme that growth is no longer necessary when maturity is reached. Life and death seem to be in harmony at this stage.[786]

---

[785] See *Ode to a Nightingale*.

[786] Bloom 1968 pp. 95–97

Walter Jackson Bates, in his book, *The Stylistic Development of Keats*, states that there is a mutual agreement between the real and the ideal in this poem, and that leads to satisfaction. The poet seems to have gained bliss by describing the archetypal images that are associated with autumn.[787]

At the end of the poem, after having talked of the decline, he mentions the singing of the little insects like crickets, which makes us come back to the reality of the world, and tells us that after all the glory has faded away, songs and noises which are despised or kept back are heard. This would also refer to a man's life, which after his days of glory are past, his days of sadness begins. Here, the poet wants us to accept it. So, the singing of the cricket is also a feature of Autumn as is the harvest time a feature of autumn. Both are to be accepted.

ODE TO A NIGHTINGALE

My heart aches, and a drowsy numbness pains
My sense, as though of hemlock[788] I had drunk,
Or emptied some dull opiate[789] to the drains[790]
One minute past, and Lethe-wards[791] had sunk:

---

[787] While many other poets seem to describe bliss in a surrounding, the descriptions are not real; they are mostly exaggerated. Here, the descriptions pertain to autumn.

[788] *hemlock* – The flower hemlock, from which poison is made. Here, Keats refers to both the flower and the poison made from it.

[789] *dull opiate* – Drug made from opium. Opium induces sleep. 'Dull' over here has been used in the sense of not properly responsive to the senses.

[790] *to...drains* – To have drained it all out, that is had it all.

[791] *Lethe-wards* – i.e., Towards Lethe. Lethe was one of the rivers of Classical mythology which bordered Hades. It was the river of

'Tis not through envy of thy happy lot,[792]
But being too happy in thine happiness,--[793]
That thou, light-winged Dryad[794] of the trees,
In some melodious plot
Of beechen green,[795] and shadows numberless,[796]
Singest of summer[797] in full-throated ease.[798]

O, for a draught[799] of vintage![800] that hath been
Cool'd a long age in the deep-delved earth,

---

forgetfulness. The dead would have to bathe in it, and forget their lives on earth.

[792] *'Tis...lot* – This feeling that the poet has is not a feeling which he has got by being envious (and thereby, frustrated and disappointed) of the good conditions of others.

[793] *But...happiness* – The poet is delighted by the nightingale, so delighted that his senses become drowsy.

[794] *Dryad* – A female spirit who lives in the trees, as per classical mythology. The nightingale is like a dryad to the poet.

[795] *beechen green* – Greenery of the beech trees. Beech trees are tall, whose barks are grey, and leaves are shiny, and they bear small nuts.

[796] *shadows numberless* – The shadows made by the leaves.

[797] *Singest...summer* – Summer is the time for glory of nature. The nightingale's song is glorious to hear.

[798] *Full-throated ease* – The nightingale sings with full force, yet it is not with strain. It is with "ease" that she sings.

[799] *draught* – A draught is one continuous action of drinking liquid. Here, it means medicine in a liquid form.

[800] *vintage* – Wine that was produced in a particular year or place.

> Tasting of Flora[801] and the country green,
> Dance, and Provençal[802] song, and sunburnt mirth!
> O for a beaker full of the warm South,[803]
> Full of the true, the blushful Hippocrene,[804]
> With beaded bubbles[805] winking at the brim,
> And purple-stained mouth;[806]

---

[801] *Flora* – Plants. If the wine is cooled by being long inside the earth, it would taste of the grass and the other vegetation that covers it.

In a letter to Fanny Keats c.May 1, 1819, Keats writes: "O there is nothing like fine weather ... and, please heaven, a little claret-wine cool out of a cellar a mile deep -- with a few or a good many ratafia cakes -- a rocky basin to bathe in, a strawberry bed to say your prayers to Flora in" (*Letters*, II, 56).

[802] *Provençal* – Of Provence, France. In the Middle Ages, the poets of Provence were famous for their love lyrics.

[803] *O...South* – A beaker full of freshness. The summer breeze blows from south.

[804] *Hippocrene* – Hippocrene was a fountain on Mt. Helicon, and sacred to the nine muses of inspiration, as per classical mythology. It was supposed to have been formed by the hooves of the flying horse, Pegasus. Etymologically, the word means 'Horse's hooves'. These two lines by keats might have been inspired by Hesiod's lines,

> And after they have washed their tender skin in Permessus or Hippocrene or holy Olmeidus, they perform choral dances on highest Helicon, beautiful, lovely ones, and move nimbly with their feet. (Theogony)

[805] *beaded bubbles* – Bubbles which are like beads, that is, strung together like beads.

[806] *And...mouth* – Keats refers to the lips of the nightingale.

That I might drink, and leave the world unseen,
And with thee fade away into the forest dim:

Fade far away, dissolve, and quite forget
What thou among the leaves hast never known,
The weariness, the fever, and the fret
Here, where men sit and hear each other groan;[807]
Where palsy[808] shakes a few, sad, last gray hairs,[809]
Where youth grows pale, and spectre-thin, and dies;[810]
Where but to think is to be full of sorrow
And leaden-eyed despairs,[811]
Where Beauty cannot keep her lustrous eyes,[812]

---

[807] *Fade...groan* – The poet wishes to fade far away with the nightingale, and forget the human sorrows, which the nightingale has never felt in this bliss amidst the trees.

[808] *palsy* – Shaking of arms and legs without control. Here, this palsy is not a palsy that comes because of some disease, but because of excitement. In other others, this palsy means activity, youthfulness, the ability to stir, to vibrate with feelings.

[809] *Where...hairs* – This means that there is hardly anyone who vibrates with life; most are old people, who hardly have got hairs left, which can shake when the body is in motion. And the hairs which are there are grey hairs. So, there is no youthfulness in them.

[810] *Where...dies* – A youthful man progresses to an old man, who becomes pale, and loses his physique, and dies. Compare this with the seven ages of man, talked of by Jacques in *As You Like It*.

This is also a reference to Tomas Keats, brother of John Keats, who died of consumption on 1 December 1818.

[811] *leaden...despairs* – Despair causes a man to be unable to sleep at night, and so, their eyes become heavy (leaden-eyed).

[812] *Where...eyes* – A beautiful person does not always remain beautiful. Compare this with the theme of fading beauty in Shakespeare's *Sonnets*.

Or new Love pine at them beyond to-morrow.[813]

Away! away! for I will fly to thee,
Not charioted by Bacchus and his pards,[814]
But on the viewless wings of Poesy,[815]
Though the dull brain perplexes and retards:
Already with thee![816] tender is the night,
And haply[817] the Queen-Moon is on her throne,
Cluster'd around by all her starry Fays;
But here[818] there is no light,[819]
Save what from heaven is with the breezes blown
Through verdurous glooms[820] and winding mossy ways.

I cannot see what flowers are at my feet,
Nor what soft incense hangs upon the boughs,
But, in embalmed darkness, guess each sweet
Wherewith the seasonable month endows
The grass, the thicket, and the fruit-tree wild;

---

[813] *new...to-morrow* – As the beauty fades away, the love and the desire also fades away, this is what the poet says. Moreover, as a person loses beauty, she is no longer the centre of wooing.

[814] *Bacchus...pards* – Bacchus was the classical god of wine and agriculture, and fertility. 'Pards' means leopards.

[815] *Poesy* – Poetry.

[816] *Already...thee* – In his imagination, the poet feels that he is already with the nightingale.

[817] *haply* – Happily.

[818] *here* – i.e., on the earth.

[819] *there...light* – There is no light from the earth itself.

[820] *verdurous glooms* – The gloom that is cast by the shade of the think verdure plants.

White hawthorn,[821] and the pastoral eglantine;[822]
Fast fading violets cover'd up in leaves;
And mid-May's eldest child,[823]
The coming musk-rose,[824] full of dewy wine,[825]
The murmurous haunt of flies on summer eves.

Darkling I listen; and, for many a time
I have been half in love with easeful Death,
Call'd him soft names in many a mused rhyme,
To take into the air my quiet breath;
Now more than ever seems it rich to die,
To cease upon the midnight with no pain,
While thou art pouring forth thy soul abroad
In such an ecstasy![826]

---

[821] *hawthorn* – A bush or a tree with thorns, and pink or white flowers, with little dark red berries growing on them.

[822] *eglantine* – A type of wild rose.

[823] *And...child* – i.e., The musk rose. This flower comes out in mid-May, so, Keats calls it to be the first child of mid-May.

[824] *musk rose* – A type of rose with large while flowers. (OED) These lines seem to be an allusion to *A Midsummer Night's Dream*:

> I know a bank where the **wild** thyme blows,
> Where oxlips and the nodding violet grows,
> Quite over-canopied with luscious woodbine,
> With **sweet musk-rose**s and with **eglantine** (*MND* II.i.249-52)

[825] *dewy wine* – The rose is filled with dew drops, and that is like wine to the flies, in the poet's imagination.

[826] *for...ecstasy* – The poet has often thought about death and has desired to die, and feels that if he could die while listening to the enchanting music of the nightingale, it would be fittest. Compare this with Antony's desire to die at the place where Caesar lay dead,

Still wouldst thou sing, and I have ears in vain —
To thy high requiem[827] become a sod.[828]

Thou wast not born for death, immortal Bird!
No hungry generations tread thee down;
The voice I hear this passing night was heard
In ancient days by emperor and clown:
Perhaps the self-same song that found a path
Through the sad heart of Ruth,[829] when, sick for home,
She stood in tears amid the alien corn;
The same that oft-times hath
Charm'd magic casements, opening on the foam
Of perilous seas, in faery lands forlorn.

Forlorn! the very word is like a bell
To toll me back from thee to my sole self!
Adieu! the fancy cannot cheat so well

---

by the instruments which killed him, and by those conspirators who killed him, in *Julius Caesar*.

[827] *requiem* – A Christian ceremony for people who have recently died. It also refers to the music that is made for this ceremony. Here, as Keats deals with the music coming from the nightingale, it would be better to fit "requiem" with the latter meaning.

[828] *sod* – Someone or something, but especially a man, who causes unpleasantness or problems. Here, Keats tells that his presence would be like the presence of an unpleasant man who has come to a requiem.

[829] *Ruth* – The story of Ruth is very important in the Bible, for it tells the story of a loyal daughter-in-law, who refused to abandon her mother-in-law even after the death of the husband, even at the telling of the mother-in-law. She goes with her, and works at a field owned by Boaz, a relative. With the mother-in-law's advice, she ultimately marries him. Obed is born of the marriage, and becomes the grandfather of David.

As she is fam'd to do, deceiving elf.[830]
Adieu! adieu! thy plaintive anthem fades
Past the near meadows, over the still stream,[831]
Up the hill-side; and now 'tis buried deep
In the next valley-glades:[832]
Was it a vision, or a waking dream?
Fled is that music: – Do I wake or sleep?[833]

---

[830] *the...elf* – The nightingale becomes a "deceiving elf" here. As the poet gets out of the enchantment, and then says that as he is able to get out of it, the charm of the nightingale is not that as it is famed to be. Her power is like an elf, which lures people by music at night.

[831] *still stream* – This is an oxymoron. The stream cannot be still. It is always streaming, that is, flowing. The poet means the stream is calm, and the flowing water seems to be making no noise.

[832] *glades* – Small open areas in woods or forests.

[833] *Fled...sleep* – As Keats comes out of the charm of the music of the nightingale, he is unable to decide if the music was in his vision (imagination, dream) or if he had hallucination. The last question brings back the enchanting quality about the nightingale's singing. The poet asks if this present state of not hearing the bird is a dream, or if he is awake. Given the first answer, the poet feels that hearing the bird was the awakened state, and now that he cannot hear the bird anymore, that must be his dream. Given the second answer, the poet feels that hearing the music of the bird was a dream; this does not happen in reality. However, the undecided state of the poet tells us that the singing of the bird had been very enchanting for the poet.

Ode to a Nightingale as a Poem of Escape from Reality into the World of Reflection

A Romantic poet would love to indulge in secondary imagination.[834] As such, he is bound to enter a world which is very different from the real world, even though the thoughts might be stirred from things of the real world. Though he might present things which are common, as per the suggestion of Wordsworth,[835] he would dive into a world which he perceives and fancies with his strong sense of creative imagination. Therefore, the claim that Keats is an escapist poet in the sense that the poems try to enter another world, is a claim that would also be in agreement with the other Romantic poets, and in fact, many other poets also.

So, there should not be any doubt on the fact that the poem tries to escape from the world of reality, for the poet himself says,

> Away! away! for I will fly to thee,
> Not charioted by Bacchus and his pards,
> But on the viewless wings of Poesy,

The question therefore, is not to debate on whether or not it is a poem of escape, but how much of a poem of escapism it is, and if it is only a poem of escapism.

Throughout the poem, the poet indulges in creating beautiful visual descriptions, all of which take the poet and the reader to another world. The very beginning of the poem, in fact, has nothing to do with a nightingale, but presents the poet's drowsiness and confirms right from the start that the poet is tired of this world, and seeks another abode in another world, either physically, or mentally and spiritually. The song of the nightingale is what charms him; it makes him relax and feel that he is in a state of blissful oblivion. He states,

---

[834] See Coleridge – About the Poet.

[835] See Wordsworth – About the Poet.

> My heart aches, and a drowsy numbness pains
> My sense, as though of hemlock I had drunk,
> Or emptied some dull opiate to the drains
> One minute past, and Lethe-wards had sunk:

In these lines, we see the poet's happy surrendering to the world of sense of forgetfulness of all that attaches him with the world in his desire to be with the bird.

The poet not just wishes to be with the bird and forget his sorrows, he also condemns the world and for all that is wrong with it. He writes:

> "The weariness, the fever, and the fret
> Here, where men sit and hear each other groan;
> Where palsy shakes a few, sad, last gray hairs,
> Where youth grows pale, and spectre-thin, and dies;
> Where but to think is to be full of sorrow
> And leaden-eyed despairs,
> Where Beauty cannot keep her lustrous eyes,
> Or new Love pine at them beyond to-morrow."

The poet wants to forget all these negative aspects that fill the human world, and he wants to fly away with the bird, which has never known these grotesqueness of the human beings.

Given all these instances, it can be properly seen that the poem is one where the poet talks about not facing the real world, but escaping to another world, even though imaginary, because he finds it intolerable to stay among the corrupt men and their corruptions. However, it would not be proper to say that the poem is totally an escapist one. The reason for this is that the poet states at the end of the poem that as the song ends, the spell breaks, and he realises that he is in the real world, and even doubts the singing of the bird to have been a dream.[836]

---

[836] See the footnote at the end of the poem.

He calls the bird "deceiving elf", and that tells clearly that he is aware that what he thinks that the bird is capable of giving him cannot actually be done; he is merely charmed by the music of the bird to think that, as a person who is drunk would imagine a lot of things and would like to forget his sorrow. In fact, that is another interesting angle from which the initial drowsiness of the poet can be examined. Is it a drowsiness of being mesmerised, or is it that of the senses being made numb due to some strong liquor, to believe something that is actually not so. The second interpretation cannot be done away with, for the poet does state something similar:

> "Adieu! the fancy cannot cheat so well
> As she is fam'd to do, deceiving elf."

As the poet comes back to his "sole self" at the end of the poem, it cannot be a totally escapist poem. Therefore, it can be said that the poet presents an escapist nature in the poem, and though his choice is clearly in favour of escaping to the world of poetic imagination, he knows that he is walking on the earth, and comes back to solid ground from flying "on the thoughtless wings of poesy".

REFERENCES

BIOGRAPHIES

Evans, G. Blakemore, ed. *The Sonnets*. Cambridge University Press. South Asian Reprint, New Delhi, 2005.

Everett, Glenn. *John Keats: A Brief Biography*. The Victorian Web, July 2000.

-- -- -- *Shelley Biography*. The Victorian Web, July 2000.

Holmes, Richard, ed. 'The Poet's Chronology'. *Samuel Taylor Coleridge: Selected Poems*. Penguin Books: London, 1996.

John Donne: Biography. www.online-literature.com

Logan, Stephen, ed. 'Chronology of Wordsworth's Life'. *William Wordsworth*. Everyman's Poetry: London, 1998.

Merriman, C.D. *William Blake: Biography*. Jalic Inc. 2006. www.online –literature.com

Purkis, John. *A Preface to Wordsworth*. Pearson Education: 1986. First Indian Reprint, 2003.

Texts and Critical Matter

Bate, Walter Jackson. *The Stylistic Development of Keats*. New York: Humanities Press, 1962. (Originally published 1945.)

-- -- -- *John Keats*. Cambridge, Mass.: Belknap Press of Harvard University Press, 1963.

Blunden, Edward, ed. *The Poems of John Keats*. Rupa Classics. Rupa and Co.: New Delhi: 2000.

Brijraj Singh, ed. Five Seventeenth-Century Poets. Oxford University Press: New Delhi, 1992.

Driver, Paul, ed. *Poetry of the Romantics*. Penguin Popular Poetry, Penguin Books: London: 1996.

Dwarakanath, K. *William Blake: Songs of Innocence and Songs of Experience*. Macmillan's Annotated Classics. Macmillan India: New Delhi, 1980.

Evans, G. Blakemore, ed. *The Sonnets*. Cambridge University Press. South Asian Reprint, New Delhi, 2005.

Gupta, Jayati, ed. *Reading Poems: An Annotated Anthology*. Macmillan India: 2002.

Grant, John E., ed. *Discussions of William Blake*. Boston: D.C. Heath and Company, 1961.

Bloom, Harold. "The Ode *To Autumn*" in *Keats's Odes* ed. Jack Stillinger, 44–47. Englewood, NJ: Prentice-Hall, 1968.

-- -- -- ed. *William Blake*. Bloom's Major Poets. New York: Chelsea House, 2003.

Holmes, Richard, ed. *Samuel Taylor Coleridge: Selected Poems*. Penguin Books: London, 1996.

Logan, Stephen, ed. *William Wordsworth*. Everyman's Poetry: London, 1998.

Prince, F.T. ed. *Milton: Paradise Lost. Books I and II*. Oxford: Oxford University Press, 1962.

Reiman, Donald H. and Neil Fraistat, ed. *Shelley's Poetry and Prose: A Norton Critical Edition*. W.W. Norton and Company Inc. New York, 2002. South Asian Reprint 2007.

Rolfe, W.J. ed. *Shakespeare's Sonnets*. New York: Harper and Bros., 1891.

Warner, C.D., et al., comp. The Library of the World's Best Literature. An Anthology in Thirty Volumes. 1917

Websites

http://www.britannica.com/biography/lentini

http://www.britannica.com/biography/petrarch

http://www.britannica.com/biography/Philip-Sidney

http://www.enotes.com/paradise-lost/q-and-a/write-detailed-answer-about-satans-speeches-book-1-282627

https://interestingliterature.com/2016/08/10/a-short-analysis-of-sir-philip-sidneys-loving-in-truth/

http://neoenglishsystem.blogspot.com/2010/11/satans-speeches-in-paradise-lost-book-i.html

https://www.poetryfoundation.org/poems-and-poets/poets/detail/edmund-spenser

http://www.theguardian.com/culture/2015/jan/31/shakespeare-sonnets-mr-wh-dedication-mystery

www.ingramcontent.com/pod-product-compliance
Lightning Source LLC
Chambersburg PA
CBHW071237160426
43196CB00009B/1098